A HARVEST OF INNOCENCE

THE UNTOLD STORY OF THE WEST MEMPHIS THREE MURDER CASE

DAN STIDHAM

TOM MCCARTHY

Copyright © Dan Stidham, 2023

FIRST EDITION

All rights reserved, including the right to reproduce this book or portions thereof in any form whatsoever without express written permission from the author(s).

A detailed timeline of the case is available at www.danstidham.com

DEDICATION

Dedicated to the loving memory of my son,
Christopher Hamilton Stidham
1987-2021

For Daniel, Chris, Kathryn, and Michael

AUTHOR'S NOTE

A Harvest of Innocence springs from my immersion in deeply tragic events, some more than 30 years ago. I have relived them every day, and they remain startlingly fresh. During many of the conversations and events that follow, I was under no small measure of pressure from being front and center in a complicated death-penalty case. We have made every effort to recall events and conversations as precisely as possible. Quotation marks are used for readability, not as an indication that the words appearing in quotes are exact, though they do precisely capture their mood, meaning, and intent.

— *DAN STIDHAM*

QUOTE

"Scout, simply by the nature of the work, every lawyer gets at least one case in his lifetime that affects him personally. This one's mine, I guess."

— ATTICUS FINCH, TO HIS DAUGHTER, SCOUT,
TO KILL A MOCKINGBIRD

INTRODUCTION

A Harvest of Innocence is my story, until now untold, regarding my involvement in the West Memphis 3 murder case. I stepped into its current as a young lawyer unaware of its strength and the immutable, unpredictable eddies that would forever change my life and my view of the law. I tell it now because it must be told. I have spent most of the past 30 years viewed in widely disparate lights. In the beginning, to some I was a pariah, a man so bold as to represent a teenager accused of being a Satanic child killer. Much later, others began to respect my efforts in seeking justice for Jessie Misskelley. In the real world, it is much more complicated than that. I was nothing more than a lawyer committed to doing my job, what was required of me by my moral compass. As a reward for my efforts, I spent a good deal of the past 30 years being pummeled by those hellbent on stopping my quest for justice for the West Memphis 3, young men who spent nearly two decades in prison for heinous crimes they simply did not commit.

Bucking the system has its consequences. There is a hellish experience awaiting you if you find yourself in that unfortunate situation. The day the *Paragould Daily Press* published an article about my writing this book, I received several threats from two continents, and

Introduction

someone blew up my mailbox with a small homemade bomb. This was the second time that this had happened. Publishing this book will no doubt bring me more challenges.

As I look back now, even though I have earned the right to be, I am no longer angry. For years, I have been asked for my side of the story, but I could not do it. I was not ready or able to look back. I can now sum it up in just five words: I don't regret a thing. The longer version that unfolds herein is much more interesting, of course.

Dan Stidham
July 7, 2023

1

The killer is alive today. I am sure of it. He had breakfast today, maybe checked his mail, went to work, watched TV, or took a drive. The killer did whatever most people do most days—whatever he has been doing since May 5, 1993. If there was any remorse it was fleeting and sparked by fear of being caught, not for what he did.

I am certain too, that the person who savaged those young boys is a man. What little evidence left untrampled that day in West Memphis by police, or later ignored by the prosecution and a politically ambitious judge, point to that. The killer has been going about his business for over 30 years, unconcerned about the shattered lives he left in that fetid ditch that day in West Memphis in 1993. Psychopaths are unaffected by consequences and possess no empathy. Guilt, anger, regret—any trace of emotion over the unspeakable things he did to those three young boys would have driven most people mad by now. The case came close to doing that to me.

The prosecution, the police, and the judge were malevolent steamrollers, and I was a young lawyer unable to see that clearly back then. I can now though. While the Alford Plea freed the young men charged and convicted in the case—the West Memphis 3—they are stained for life. Out of prison after almost twenty years, Jessie

Misskelley, Damien Echols, and Jason Baldwin and their appellate lawyers struck a bargain with the State of Arkansas that came at an excruciating price. The West Memphis 3 are free and that is what we all worked hard for so many years. But the Alford Plea means that they will never be compensated for the decades they spent in Arkansas prisons for crimes they did not commit.

And the real killer will never be prosecuted or even pursued by the State of Arkansas, which would like very much for this sad chapter in its history to simply disappear. But I cannot let that happen without a true accounting of what actually transpired. Those young men, now middle aged, are out of prison and moving on with their lives. I am starting to move on with my life as well. And believe me, I am fine with that.

In Arkansas in 2023, the men who put the West Memphis 3 in prison are still highly regarded for their efforts by some. The judge is, in some circles, still praised for the courage it took to put the Devil himself on trial. These men never seemed to be bothered by the fiction they anointed as truth and tried so desperately to preserve. They arrested, prosecuted, and imprisoned three innocent young teenagers for decades as if they were distractedly flicking a stray piece of lint from the cuffs of their freshly pressed suits, concerned only about maintaining appearances. In the face of the real facts of the case—the unassailable truth of what happened—they have yet to ask the one question that has hounded me for over 30 years. Who really did this and why? That someone is out there still.

For years I desperately tried to escape what the case had done to me. On most days it proved to be an impotent and largely useless exercise that produced nothing but anxiety and sleepless nights. As much as I tried, I could not put those gruesome murders and the young men who had been blamed for them behind me. Two things kept me moving-my promise to Jessie Misskelley that I would never let go of it, and my hope that karma has a deadline. Both sustained me, and the wait was worth it.

Jessie Misskelley, Damien Echols, and Jason Baldwin had been identified, arrested, prosecuted, and locked away with a casual indifference to the facts. They were young men from the wrong side of the tracks put in prison by a group of misguided men who wanted nothing more than to burnish their reputations and satisfy a public frenzy that demanded retribution. I was collateral damage, punished for my arrogance in defending an alleged "Devil Worshipper." That does not bother me anymore. It goes with the territory. With each passing year, the detritus from 1993 continues to percolate to the surface.

Whether it is the courageous dying declaration from the only man involved in the case who has ever shown any remorse for his role in the injustice bestowed upon the West Memphis 3, or a guy selling an abandoned storage locker full of Damien Echols' belongings he had found by chance, the story continues to evolve. The point of the sale, or why the storage locker was abandoned, was beyond me, but the interest it sparked in the media is a testament to just how much this case has stayed in the public consciousness after more than a quarter of a century.

Not that long ago, an incident sparked international coverage, with bold headlines replacing the usual small-type police log in the local paper.

JESSIE MISSKELLEY, ONE OF THE WEST MEMPHIS 3, ARRESTED OVER THE WEEKEND

The fact that Jessie Misskelley had been pulled over for driving without a license or insurance did not separate him from the murder charges that will dog him for the rest of his life. Jessie, hapless and well-meaning, was in trouble again. The man cannot avoid it, nor can he escape the inevitable ties to the ghastly murders of three eight-year-old boys. "West Memphis 3" is an indelible mark that will always be appended to his name. Jessie Misskelley was jailed for an entire weekend for minor traffic offenses that no one else would have been subjected to. But he is Jessie Misskelley, always an easy target for law enforcement in Crittenden County, Arkansas, the only home he has ever known other than prison. Nothing had changed since 1993, including his face glaring from newspapers. It appeared much older now, grayer, darker from the wear.

I took great pleasure in the fact that once the word got out that he was in jail, people from all over the world stepped up to pay his fines and secure his release, literally in minutes. The world is still watching to make sure that Jessie Misskelley, is not taken advantage of again.

In April 2020, I received a screenshot of a handwritten note mailed to Jessie from a writer whose limited vocabulary did not include the word "redemption." For a small few of the intellectually lazy, those unwilling to accept the truth, the acid hatred for the three accused has not been diluted by the years or the vindication:

"…Damien is a devil and you just wanted to hang with his dumb ass. You and Baldwin will meet your maker soon and you can come to a sound judgment. Burn in hell bitch cause I'm cuming [sic] to get you and cut off your balls."

In March 2018, watching the Academy Awards from the comfort of my couch, escaping like millions of others in its lightness, I watched Eddie Vedder walk on stage. He was a surprise addition, singing a tribute to the recently departed Tom Petty. Rather than the music, I thought of how I met Eddie for the first time 23 years ago and the great help he was to us in our quest for justice. Seeing him sent me back.

Like all stories, mine has a beginning, a middle, and — I pray fervently — an end. At this point, the jagged edges that intruded on my life for more than 30 years have begun to knit, and things are once again becoming smooth. After all these years, I am beginning to sleep through the night again and I take that as a good sign. Most nights anyway.

The sweep of the story of the brutal murders of those three young boys in West Memphis, Arkansas, and how it affected so many other lives, mine included spreads like a fragile filament that so many times over so many years could easily have snapped. The fate of the West Memphis 3 could easily have been forgotten. Three innocent young men could have remained locked up in a squalid Arkansas prison forever. No one would have given it a second thought.

The arc of my role in the story was hardly graceful or even predictable. It began when I answered a phone call, still dripping wet from the shower, at my home in Paragould, Arkansas. I was a dupe in the beginning, a naïve young lawyer too dumb to just say no. When I picked up that phone, I did not realize I would be taking on a case that would nearly kill me. When I finally told Judge David Goodson that I would represent a young man with a small and troubled mind, I thought of nothing but obligation to my profession. Everyone is entitled to a robust defense no matter what the charge and circumstances. I was a young lawyer, and here was a case and a judge who had thought enough of me to ask me to take it on. It was a compliment, I thought.

Before I accepted the task, I tried to call my law partner, Greg Crow, to get his input. He did not answer the phone. I realized that the twenty minutes Judge Goodson had given me to decide were now almost gone. I was leaning toward accepting the appointment. I guess, more than anything, I was just waiting for someone to tell me not to do it. Instinctively, I turned to what I knew would be an opposing viewpoint. *Surely, she will talk me out of it, I thought to myself.* I asked my wife, Kim, to step into the bedroom. I explained as quickly as I could what Judge Goodson was asking of me. I knew her answer would be a firm "No." To my surprise Kim's response came with no hesitation. "Do it. You love this sort of thing." I was stunned by her answer, but I knew she was right. I called Judge Goodson back and I said yes without a second thought, without even drying off from the shower.

Now, I cannot help but think about a Bob Seger line as I take a deep breath and look back at it all: "I wish I didn't know now what I didn't know then." In my paralyzing darkest hours, and there were many, I would often think of what would have happened had I just said no. Several other attorneys with more caution and more experience had turned down the opportunity. If I had said no and moved on, no one would have given it a second thought. He is, they might have said, smart enough to know better than to get involved in a case involving the brutal murders of three children and the smallness of Arkansas politics.

Kim was right, this was exactly why I went to law school in the first place. In 1993, I was just starting out, and I had the fervor of a newly baptized convert to a religion I had coveted for years. I had always wanted to practice law and immerse myself in its pureness. The phone call provided the chance. Once I said yes, I was in for the long haul. I just did not know how long it would be, or how much it would challenge my unsullied view of the law. It did challenge it, of course. Even then, fresh out of law school and optimistic, I was not inclined to give up after I started something.

Now I can step back and look at my younger self. My view of the law and justice today is firmer and more resolute. It is not any less hopeful, but perhaps less sentimental. My Pollyannaish edges have been eroded by what this case did to me. I am still involved in the law today, and the hard lessons I inhaled representing Jessie Misskelley have been a gift to my endeavors.

It took many years to find perspective. During that time, I sat, unable to tell my story, unwilling to turn over earth that would bring back the frightening revelations that at first shocked my idealistic younger self. They numbed me, those things. I know now it was like keeping a lid on a boiling pot. At some point something had to give. I can now, with some measure of pride, attest it was not me. The West Memphis 3 case sent me on a long journey I had not packed for. Had I just declined the invitation to represent Jessie Misskelley it certainly would have made my life easier. But today two teenagers would be approaching middle age after more than a quarter century in prison. They would be bitter, of course, from thousands of days wondering why they had been sent there in the first place. They were too young to know how to survive that hell and emerge undamaged—if they emerged at all. And a third young man would be dead, courtesy of a cold needle and a lethal cocktail. No one would have lamented his passing. Just desserts for what they had done.

So, in the end, picking up the phone that day and saying "yes" was one of the best things I ever did. But I paid a price for it. The trial was an unwelcome burden, and I was like Sisyphus, condemned to push that heavy rock uphill for the rest of my life. I could have done without it, certainly. It has consumed me for over thirty years. It insinuated itself into everything I did, like the kudzu that creeps, offends, and irritates the Arkansas landscape.

My marriage did not emerge intact from it, my children suffered because of it, and my emotional balance was put to the test. That is an awfully long time to corrode yourself with doubt and feign confidence and strength. Picking up the phone and saying yes brought me later to the very edge, to my knees. By the time I realized how far I had been pulled in, it was too late. At this stage I am contented that I did the right thing, despite the costs.

What I went through was a gentle irritation compared to what the victims' families went through or what Jesse Misskelley, Damien Echols and Jason Baldwin suffered. The darkness that settled benignly on me for so long has pretty much lifted, it intrudes occasionally, though when I think about one lingering, cancerous question, if something so ominous can be said to linger. *Who killed those three young boys so brutally?*

And how can I find him still.

2

I talked to a dead man once. I suspect our talk did him no good, but it changed the way I viewed the law and its inherent power—for good or bad. I thought I could help save Frankie Parker's life. That is how much I believed in the law when I first met him. I suspect Frank Parker knew otherwise. He had seen the way the cards had been dealt and was resigned to the inevitable—not that he had done himself any good to start with. I imagine if I sat with him today in his cold cell, I would agree with him. I would have seen another, darker side of the law, and I would know there was not much a lawyer could do to save him from the lethal injection waiting somewhere down the line.

I met Frank Parker in 1986 when I was still a rosy-cheeked law student working as a law clerk for a young lawyer named W.H. Taylor in Springdale, Arkansas. The prospect of talking to Parker scared the hell out of me. He was a hard ass who had quickly developed a reputation and propensity for violence. That did not deter me, because I was certain I could in a small way help keep him alive. I was blooming with optimism, awed by the gravity—the enormity of working on a death penalty case. I thought there was hope for Frank

Parker and that I would get a front row seat to see how, if properly applied, the law could save a life.

The anxiety was nearly overwhelming that day. It was my first involvement with a case where one wrong move could result in someone's death. I played a minor role, like a walk-on actor in an epic movie that played for years. But it stamped on me several things. There are lives involved and no matter how clear and obvious the evidence or the brutality of the crime, there are almost always mitigating circumstances. A decision in a death penalty case that plays itself to the end—the pulling of a switch and the injection of a needle—cannot be reversed. It is over. No amount of second guessing will ever change that. Posthumous reversals and new evidence can do nothing to bring back someone who has been executed.

Frank Parker's case wound its way through the courts to its inevitable and fatal conclusion while I was being drawn further into my own legal battles trying to save Jessie Misskelley—and along with him, Jason Baldwin, and Damien Echols, who would meet Frank Parker on Death Row years later.

Frank Parker was no saint. He had shot and killed his former wife's parents in 1984. He had tried to kill his former wife's sister. After that, he kidnapped his former wife and drove her to the police station in Rogers, Arkansas, where he shot a police officer. He held off the police for six hours before a police sniper disarmed him, nearly taking off his hand.

When I met him at the Benton County Jail, he had been in the judicial system for nearly two years. I was still wet behind the ears—hopeful, naïve, pretending to be more confident than I was. He was tough, hardened, and unimpressed. Most men awaiting the final verdict on murder charges usually are or pretend to be. I would not have known the difference.

Later, on Death Row, Frank Parker would serendipitously convert to Buddhism after being thrown into the "hole" one evening following one of his periodic fights with a guard. The only item a prisoner in the hole can have with him is a Bible. Parker began beating on the door and demanding a Bible. Thinking he could add to Parker's irritation, the guard gave him something that ended whatever darkness had been driving Frank Parker for years. "Here's your Bible," the guard yelled as he tossed in a worn-out copy of the *Dhammapada*, a Buddhist text.

It was not the Bible, but Parker read the book and it changed his life. Soon, Frank Parker became a model prisoner and adopted the name of Sifu Frankie Parker. Later he would become the only practicing Buddhist on Death Row in Arkansas. His adopted name meant "teacher" or "master," and Sifu Frankie began teaching anyone he could on Death Row about Buddhism, which he described less as a religion and more of a new path of thinking. As he sat on Death Row waiting for his date with the needle, he attracted the attention and support of the Dalai Lama, Nelson Mandela, and actor Richard Gere, also a practicing Buddhist.

I visited Frank Parker in the Benton County Jail long before his Death Row conversion. There was already a seed of hope in him. The guard led me through the maze that was the county jail. We meandered in and around a set of dark hallways. Cinderblock walls painted a dull gray. The scent of the recently stripped and waxed white institutional floor tile mixed with the palpable smell of fear and tension. My pulse was rapid. I was twenty-two years old, a second-year law student, and working for my mentor who had been appointed to represent Frank Parker. Parker had been charged with two counts of capital murder and kidnapping. Guys like Frank Parker do not hire their own lawyers.

This would be good experience for me, I assured myself as we drew nearer to the cell that contained the killer, but I was still nervous as hell. The guard finally deposited me into an exceedingly small and windowless room illuminated by a single light bulb protruding from a wall above the door. A steel cage wrapped around the light bulb offered some protection from anyone who might want to make the room darker still. As the guard left me alone in the cell, I heard the click, and then the buzz of the mechanical door as it shut and sealed me inside.

"Hit the red button when you're done," the guard had said. "I'll come and get you." I surveyed the scene. It did not take long. Inside were only a small table and two plastic chairs. The room seemed to be shrinking, and it sent chills down my spine as I waited for Frank Parker to be escorted to the room. It might have taken only a minute, but it seemed like an eternity. Would he be wild-eyed and ramble on like a crazy man? Was I even going to be safe in here with him?

Suddenly, the door on the opposite side buzzed and clicked, and it opened. A different guard brought him in with no attempt at pleasantries. Then he left. Frankie had none of the restraints I had envisioned and hoped for. No handcuffs, no leg irons, or shackles. Frank Parker moved like a man who already knew his fate as he sat in the chair across from me at the table. I tried not to show how nervous I was, but he seemed to know it, to have sensed it. I had never met a cold-blooded killer before. He seemed to know that as well.

Instinctively, I extended my hand, and he shook it with what remained of his own hand. He was measuring me, just as I was measuring him. He had a warm smile, and his demeanor was nothing like I had expected. I looked down and hit record on the big cassette I had brought with me to record our conversation. I checked to make sure that each of the reels was spinning and I introduced myself. The boss had let him know I was coming.

At first, I stuck to the facts and the script I had prepared. The facts were grim. He had kidnapped his wife, killed both her parents, and shot a police officer. The situation was bad. I knew it, my boss knew it, and so did Frankie.

After about an hour or so of the facts, he looked across the table, and smiled at me. Then his words took me by surprise.

"Go ahead. Ask me."

"Ask you what?"

"You know, why I did it."

I took the bait. *How could I not?*

"Okay, why'd you, do it?"

There were many reasons, most of which I cannot recall today. There were the drugs, alcohol, depression, and the anger. But what I remember more than anything was the remorse. He was so repentant.

Not a "poor pitiful me" kind of remorse, but a sincere matter-of-fact remorse. Thirty-eight years later, this still echoes solidly. It was genuine. "I wish more than anything," he said, "that I could take it all back, just undo it. But I can't and I know I can't, so I am ready to die."

I wondered how I would feel if I were in his shoes. He seemed resigned to the outcome. I wanted to assure him that life in prison was better than dying. I was not sure about that one, so I did not bring it up.

"How are they treating you in here," I said trying to change the subject.

"I shot a cop," he said. "How do you think they treat me?"

"They don't physically mistreat you, do they?"

"No, not that way. They used to do things like spit on my food tray."

"You're kidding."

"No, the guards would spit in my food and then slide the tray right in through the slot into me through the door of my cell."

"No way," I said.

"They did. But that didn't last long," he said.

"How'd you stop it?"

"I just ate the food anyway and then shit on the plate and slid it back to them."

I wanted to laugh, but I was afraid to. First, it probably was not funny to him, and second, I was determined to act professionally despite my tender years.

Then he broke a smile. I did too, and then he started laughing. Then we both erupted into laughter at the same time. It was not casual laughter but deep and guttural—just two mischievous boys having a good chortle. Any remaining nervousness that I had held on to disappeared. I could tell he had not had much to laugh about in a long time. I could also tell he did not have many visitors.

After we talked about his life, he wanted to know about mine. I reached down and turned off the recorder. Now it was time to just be a human being, not a kid who hoped to be a lawyer. I was off the clock. I told him about getting married a few weeks before his arrest. And now, I had a newborn baby son named Daniel. He wanted to know about the rest of my family and my studies. I told him. I had planned to be there for about thirty minutes, but we spent a couple of hours talking. I think the guards had forgotten about us.

"How do you pass the time in here?" I asked him.

"I do a lot of reading. I also teach some of the other inmates how to read."

"That's pretty neat."

"After they figured out that I was a good heat and air man, I started doing a lot of maintenance work now for the county."

"Really," I said.

All my preconceived notions about this man had by then dissipated. My nervousness had been solidly replaced with compassion, basic human compassion. I hoped that he would get a chance to plead guilty and avoid the death penalty. He seemed to have plenty left to offer as a human being even on the inside. I believe that some men should forfeit their right to be on the planet for the crimes they committed. But Frank Parker was not one of these men and it forever changed my thoughts about the death penalty.

Finally, it was time for me to leave. I reached up and hit the red button on the wall. It is a good thing Frankie was not a threat to me because it took the guard twenty-five more minutes to come get me. It was the first of several visits I made with him before his trial, and somehow Frank Parker and I had made a connection. It was a deep bond that I would not understand fully for many years to come.

When I got the phone call in June 1993 asking if I would represent Jessie Misskelley Jr., Frank Parker was sitting on Death Row, awaiting execution. By then I was just five years out of law school, still a young kid really, just building my law practice. I accepted just about any kind of case that made it through my door—divorces, wills and deeds, bankruptcies, whatever it took.

By 1993, I had worked on two other murder cases. One involved a juvenile charged with murder and the other involved the murders of a local doctor and his wife. Those cases would be dramatically different than the journey I was about to embark on with Jessie Misskelley.

There are times when I divide my life between the years before the phone call that drew me to Jessie Misskelley and the murders, and the years following it. It is a clear line now, but it took a while to emerge. Now I have time to indulge in the sort of idle introspection that comes when there are not more pressing things to attend to. That is a luxury I did not have for many years. I think of Frank Parker, then I think of Jessie Misskelley. I take a deep breath and know that I am happy the boys of the West Memphis 3 escaped Frankie's fate.

3

I do not like to go back to the crime scene. I had seen enough of it before, and after, the trial. It had been my responsibility to walk the muddied banks of the drainage ditch. I had needed to see where the boys' naked bodies had been laid by the police. I had wanted to take it in and breathe its ugliness, to imagine the horror and how it unfolded. I needed that knowledge to show my client had never been there and did not have a clue about the murders.

After the trials, I would see that scene in the nightmares that would drop by to announce that my sleep for the evening was over. Now it is my responsibility to lock those memories away, and just let them go. I owe it to myself, my family, and my sanity. But not before revealing the entire truth about this case.

When I first heard about the drainage ditch and the boys' bodies, I was in Little Rock with my father unpacking from a fishing trip. A reporter broke in on a CNN broadcast playing quietly in the background. Searchers had found the bodies of three 8-year-old boys who had been reported missing the day before. The news report was followed quickly with others. The boys had been beaten and at least one had been mutilated. They had been hogtied with their own shoelaces and thrown into the shallow grime of the ditch in the secluded, wooded area off I-40 in West Memphis that the locals called Robin Hood Hills. I turned to my father, Troy, and said "Jesus!"

The three boys were the same age as my oldest son, second graders, Cub Scouts. West Memphis was not Paragould, and my instinctive horror was diluted by the distinction. Whoever had done this was not in Paragould and near my family. I took a breath. The news was shocking. Triple homicides were rare, brutal triple homicides of children almost unheard of. Gang violence in Memphis and Little Rock and big cities everywhere had been skyrocketing in May 1993. Surely the murders of those boys had something to do with that, I surmised. Soon the reports included talk of sexual mutilation. Michael Moore, Chris Byers, and Stevie Branch had all attended school on Wednesday, May 5, 1993, at Weaver Elementary, in West Memphis. They were last seen riding two bicycles on the service road next to the interstate around 6:30 p.m.

Before the alarm about the missing boys went out, Arkansans were still basking in the light of one of their own being elected President of the United States, though that light never seemed to reach West Memphis, a small, tired town of 20,000. Signs were erected on both the Interstate 40 and Interstate 55 bridges so people traveling from parts east of the Mississippi were met with "Welcome to Arkansas: Home of President Bill Clinton."

Those two interstate highways merged in West Memphis, and then separated quickly. Travelers heading for St. Louis and Chicago merged right. Those headed to Little Rock, Dallas or Oklahoma City merged to the left. The broken bodies of the three boys were found in their watery grave in a small patch of woods just south of the service road and directly behind the parking lot of the Blue Beacon truck wash and the huge parking lot of a truck stop.

The water where the boys' bodies were found was nothing more than a dirty, barely moving drainage ditch. The pure unadulterated ugliness of the crime itself far exceeded the fetidness of the water. All three boys had received significant head trauma from a blunt object. All three were found nude and submerged. Each boy had been hogtied with the laces of his own sneakers; their hands bound to their ankles. One victim had significant trauma to his face, neck, and ears; another appeared to be sexually mutilated—his penis and scrotum had been completely removed, apart from the shaft of the penis, which was still intact. One boy had the skin from his face partially ripped from his skull. Police found two hairs and two fibers on the bodies. Investigators took a hair from a tree stump near where one of the bodies was recovered. An Arkansas Crime Lab technician found a hair inside a knot on one of the ligatures that bound victim Michael Moore.

There was a partial handprint and one footprint in the mud along the west bank of the ditch. Police also recovered the victims' clothing submerged in the murk. After searchers found the first body, the entire crime scene was trampled, especially the creek bed. The gruesome details spread immediately on the street and in the increasing number of media reports. Every parent in West Memphis was on high alert. There was a killer, or killers, in their midst. The streets emptied. Everyone stayed inside their homes with their children. There was little sign of normal life anywhere. Parents who typically let their kids walk to school or ride a school bus either guardedly escorted their children to school or drove them directly there and picked them up as soon as the final bell of the day sounded.

The night the young boys were reported missing, May 5, 1993, workers at Bojangles, a restaurant about a mile from the eventual crime scene in Robin Hood Hills, reported seeing a black male who seemed "mentally disoriented" inside the ladies' room. The man was bleeding and had brushed against the walls of the restroom, saturating a roll of toilet tissue with blood, and leaving behind a pair of bloody sunglasses. West Memphis Police Officer Regina Meeks responded to the call—at a moment one would assume police would have been on high alert. There were three young children missing.

Officer Meeks interviewed the restaurant manager via the drive-thru window while she sat in her cruiser, apparently so underwhelmed she could not be bothered to even get out and at least check the bathroom. The restaurant manager told Officer Meeks that he had collected and preserved the bloody toilet paper roll and the sunglasses, but she told him to simply throw them away and that he was free to clean up the mess in the restroom. *Was there a connection between the bloody man and the murdered boys?*

After the discovery of the bodies, West Memphis Police Detective Bryn Ridge returned to the restaurant the next day on May 6 and took blood scrapings from the walls of the ladies' restroom. By then the pair of sunglasses and the bloody roll of toilet paper had been discarded. At least detectives had the energy to leave the comfort of their police car. Later Detective Ridge would testify that he somehow lost the blood scrapings, and they never made it to the State Crime Lab. A hair identified as belonging to a black male was later recovered from a sheet used to wrap one of the young victims by the local coroner at autopsy.

I was never informed of this loss of evidence, and the report of the incident was buried and camouflaged in the discovery provided to us by the prosecution. A Memphis reporter called me and informed me of the significance of this incident. That was just the first inkling of the police lethargy and the concerted efforts of the police and prosecution to arrive quickly at the destination that they had already set their sights on.

In Little Rock on May 6, 1993, talking with my father, the crime was abstract to me. It seemed so far from Paragould and Greene County, Arkansas where I served as a part-time public defender while I built up my new practice. My father, Troy, looked up from the tackle box and rods he was sliding under a workbench in his shop off the garage. "You don't need to get involved in something like that," he said. "I know," I told him, "West Memphis is too far away for that to happen anyway." It was not long before I realized it was not far enough.

4

West Memphis was not a serene and pristine *"Mayberry" as portrayed on the "Andy Griffith Show"* where citizens walked happy paths of bliss. There were many other ghosts about, and the murders of those three boys were not the first evil visited upon the town or the area. West Memphis had an unusual number of high-profile cases of multiple murders involving children. In 1960, fourteen-year-old old Gurvis Basil Nichols shot to death two children with a .410 shotgun, nine-year old Douglas Naylor, and eleven-year-old James Melting, telling police he wanted to die in the electric chair. He was sent to a mental institution and later released. During our investigation he was believed to be living in Germantown, a suburb of Memphis. Police asserted they had tried to locate him, but I doubt they made even the feeblest of attempts.

In 1985, Ronald Ward, aged fifteen, was convicted and sentenced to death for the murders of seventy-six-year-old, Lois Townsend Jarvis, seventy-two-year-old, Audrey Townsend, and twelve-year-old Chris Simmons, in a trial that featured Judge David Burnett and deputy prosecutor John Fogleman, the yeomen I would face in 1993. At the time, Ward became the nation's youngest inmate on death row. Two years later Ward won a retrial on appeal.

An Arkansas Supreme Court Justice, concurring with the motion for a retrial, wrote that some of the photographs of the deceased introduced by the State "tended to arouse prejudice and passion" in the jury, adding that the gruesome photographs "did not illuminate any issue which had not been conclusively proved." The Court suggested to Judge David Burnett and deputy prosecutor John Fogleman that they not engage in this activity at the second trial of Ronald Ward. At the second trial of Ronald Ward, he was convicted again and sentenced to life without parole. He died in prison in 2007 at the age of 37, but not before he became good friends with Jason Baldwin.

Gruesome photographs, hundreds of them, in the West Memphis murder case would arouse "prejudice and passion" in the jury in Jessie Misskelley's trial in 1994. I wish now, almost 30 years later, that I could unsee some of those gruesome photographs, which still haunt me today.

Nor was the West Memphis 3 case the first time the Devil nodded his head in West Memphis, Arkansas. In 1988, Barbara McCoy and Mary Williams killed McCoy's two children, Bianca Tirado, aged seven, and Maximillion McCoy, age two. According to a discussion board devoted to the WM3 case, McCoy and Williams burned the children's "bodies in what friends later characterized as an intense Christian spiritual fixation that went off the deep end. McCoy, an ardent practitioner of the Pentecostal 'gifts of the spirit' doctrine, eventually was diagnosed as having a "bipolar affective disorder" and was found not guilty by reason of insanity." Mary Williams was eventually released as well.

There had also been a spate of other child killings in eastern Arkansas, the connection to which the West Memphis police expended little or no effort to try to link to the West Memphis child murders. In May 1991, in Hickory Ridge, Arkansas, Christina Marie Pipkin, aged nine, disappeared. Her body was found in a ditch five days later. On May 21, 1992, in Wynne, Arkansas, Geneva Smith, aged thirteen, disappeared. Her body was found in the St. Francis River ten days later. And on October 13, 1992, also in Wynne, Gardenia Jones

Cross, sixteen, died of puncture wounds to her temple and cuts to the face and neck.

The Commercial Appeal, the paper of record for Memphis, Tennessee, just across the Mississippi from West Memphis, Arkansas, and for much of the Mid-South, reported that Arkansas officials were seeking to identify a decomposed body found by two farmers in Wynne. "The body is the fourth found in Cross County since May 1991. Foul play was believed to be involved in the other three deaths." Cross County is adjacent to Crittenden County.

People in West Memphis and its environs were not strangers to violence. Given the familiarity of people with brutal and unexplained murders, and one would assume police's own attempts to solve these crimes, it did not take a large leap of faith for me to ask whether perhaps there were others who could have murdered those young boys in West Memphis on May 5, 1993. A month later, the West Memphis Police had their perpetrators neatly and convincingly locked up and ready for Death Row.

5

If the victims had been adults, strangers dumped in the ditch by someone passing through on I-40 and I-55, life in West Memphis would have returned to normal almost immediately. But they were eight years old, they were from West Memphis. Anyone with children at Weaver Elementary School knew those boys. Anyone with children that age would have shuddered, as I did eighty miles away in Paragould. People wanted answers.

News of the murders spread quickly, ignited by the violence and the helplessness of the boys. Whoever had done this had been consumed by evil, driven by something unspeakably vile. Every report recounted the horror of the mutilations and the small naked bodies, hogtied with their own shoelaces and thrown so casually into the ditch. The act was incomprehensible, appalling beyond human understanding. It still is.

Stunned disbelief very quickly turned to anger. No one could wrap their minds around the gruesome wounds and the cruel indifference with which they were committed. There was a deranged killer in West Memphis. Anxiety grew exponentially when there was not an immediate arrest. Every parent in West Memphis was on high alert, edging toward hysteria. When an unspeakable evil descends on any town, everyone will tell you that it is the not knowing what happened, who did it, and why, that paralyzes the community.

In the Mid-South, where most people take their Christianity seriously and the Bible literally, there could only be one answer to the appalling violence that had intruded so starkly into their lives. Panic, superstition, and fear produced a visceral, throbbing anger.

Almost immediately there was talk of the Devil and a Satanic cult. The police, the prosecution, and the community of West Memphis sincerely believed that the three eight-year-olds, Christopher Byers, Stevie Branch, and Michael Moore, were killed as part of a satanic ritual. The murders were so otherworldly in their violence there seemed no other logical explanation. Once they were found, the killer or killers deserved only one thing—to meet Satan in Hell, and as quickly as possible. I would learn soon enough that the same sentiment applied to any lawyer who dared defend one of them.

The concept of Satanic ritualistic homicide has long been discredited. But in the early 1990s it was real—very real. Over the years, I would come to see that one of my most intractable opponents was not a heavy-handed judge, or the obfuscations of facts, or even the manipulation of an intellectually challenged young man. I had to first overcome the rock-solid belief in the long-discredited theory of Satanic ritualistic homicide.

With the boys not yet buried and the killer not yet found, the demands on the unprepared West Memphis Police closed in on them like a vise. The pressure to solve the crime was immediate and unrelenting. No small part of it came with the almost immediate and predictable national attention a small-town Satanic ritualistic slaying would bring. Satellite trucks and swarming reporters from across the country soon took over the town.

The terror and disillusion created scapegoats to deal with the tragedy, and what could not be explained in rational terms was simply blamed on the supernatural. This would ultimately be enough for a town under siege by a supernatural evil. History has shown that human atrocities are often met with more atrocities— "an eye for eye" in a strict Biblical sense. Immediately, it was clear to me that this case would be forever laced and interwoven with mass hysteria— a chancre ready to burst, with real-life lynch mobs overcome with a lust for quick justice. It produced what would soon be known as "Satanic Panic."

Law enforcement served up the perfect patsies to the mob screaming for blood and justice. The West Memphis Police, followed by Prosecutor Brent Davis and Crittenden County Deputy Prosecutor John Fogleman, turned the atrocity into a stage-managed drama that that would consume not just the three victims and their families, but ultimately six families who would lose their sons in its clouded wake.

The people of West Memphis, indeed the entire Mid-South, had wanted a quick arrest and conviction of someone—anyone. The town wanted closure and residents wanted to feel safe again. The confession of Jessie Misskelley provided just that.

During the month it took to make the arrests, a beleaguered police inspector gave daily news conferences, facing the cameras and admitting there were no new leads. The West Memphis police were outgunned and overmatched, their backs against the wall. For the police, the Satanic angle was a beacon guiding them to safety by presenting such an easy and unmoving target. It was devil worshippers who did it. They just had to find some. Damien Echols was their prime suspect.

Detectives would soon both coerce and coach Jessie Misskelley's confession and arrest him. Then they would bring in Damien Echols and Jason Baldwin. West Memphis was suddenly Salem, Massachusetts, revisited 300 years later, and the three young men charged with the crime became modern day witches—convicted without any real evidence by people ready for them to be taken to the stakes and burned. History has a strange way of repeating itself.

6

Back in Paragould before the arrests, I too could only wonder how such a thing could happen. I was thankful my family was safe and praying police would find the killer quickly. Though I told my own father that I would not get involved in the case, I would soon accept Judge David Goodson's request to represent Jessie Misskelley on June 7—a month after the bodies were discovered.

Reporters found me within minutes that day, and it took no time to fully inhale the frenzy. My hair was still wet from the shower when I walked into my office and saw the phone lines lit up. The two office phone lines rang all day and for the two days that followed. My partner Greg Crow and I fielded calls from both local and national media outlets about a case we knew little about and a client we had not yet met. We spoke to producers and correspondents from CNN, ABC, CBS, NBC, 20/20, and *The New York Times*.

In the months and years to come, I would be contacted by virtually every media outlet and talk show in the business. My file today contains phone messages and memos from producers from Oprah, ABC's *20/20*, the *Phil Donahue Show*, *Unsolved Mysteries*, *Inside Edition*, the *Jerry Springer Show*, the *Sally Jessie Rafael Show*, the *Rolanda Show*, *Nightline*, *Current Affair,* and *Dateline NBC*. They all were drawn to the story by injustice, but were afraid of "What if they really did it?" I even found a message from Diane Sawyer's producer at the time. I would have loved to have met her because she is one of my favorite journalists.

Before the arrests, the popular television show *America's Most Wanted* aired a segment on the murders, hoping to receive tips or information. The results were staggering. Many tips suggested a Satanic motive for the crimes and even made unconfirmed connections between the West Memphis murders and similar crimes around the country. None of these crimes could ever be verified, but investigators took them as the gospel. The Satanic Crimes Unit of the New York City Police Department, formed in the wake of the *Son of Sam* murders, faxed their West Memphis colleagues, noting that if the murders involved sexual mutilation and were committed under a full moon, they were Satanic crimes. How could a small department in rural Arkansas question such information?

Psychics offered their assistance, requesting that police use their names on television if their predictions proved to be true. A man in Phoenix became so interested in the case in West Memphis that he went to his local library looking for information about the geography of the region. When he left the library, he inadvertently dropped his folder containing maps and notes about the murders. His folder was turned over to Phoenix police, who contacted the West Memphis Police, who in turn requested that the man be questioned. He was ruled out as a suspect.

But the circle of suspects—a well-defined circle of evil in the eyes of the police—was tightening. The day after the *America's Most Wanted* segment aired, West Memphis Police got a phone tip from three boys, one of whom ironically was Jessie Misskelley. The boys told police that they had become suspicious of a man who tried to lure them into his wooded campsite not far from the crime scene. The man turned out to be the son of a Crittenden County Sheriff's deputy who was known for his mental issues. Police determined the tip was not useful to their investigation. The panic grew, fed by the national spotlight.

On May 19, 1993, Victoria Hutcheson, under suspicion by Marion and West Memphis Police for stealing from her employer, mentioned to police that she had attended an "esbat," a witch's meeting, with Damien Echols and Jessie Misskelley shortly after the murders. Her statements put police further down the trail to the goal they had already determined. She would later become a key witness at the Misskelley trial, used by the prosecution to corroborate the confession of Jessie Misskelley. Years later, long after things had been so neatly wrapped up and the West Memphis 3 in prison, Hutcheson would provide me with startling information about her testimony at trial, which I had known from the beginning was perjurious.

During the murder investigation, police would remove boxes of Metallica and Slayer T-shirts and Stephen King books from the trailers where Damien Echols and Jason Baldwin lived, proof they would submit, of the pair's satanic leanings. Jason Baldwin would later ask why the officers did not take any of his white T-shirts as evidence.

It was thin evidence, to be sure, a desperate clutching of straws to show the three young men arrested were devil worshipers. It would be laughable today. But it was perfect evidence for the hysteria and the lynch mob pounding on the police department's doors for justice. It was a perfect storm. They had their murderers, and they had their motives.

After the arrests, a reporter asked West Memphis Police Inspector Gary Gitchell how strong the case was against Misskelley, Echols, and Baldwin, "on a scale of 1 to 10."

"Eleven," he said, beaming like the Cheshire Cat.

By the time police found Jessie Misskelley in his tired trailer park and brought him in for questioning, they were following an imaginary B-movie horror film script written to meet the public's demand for justice.

In Paragould, I had not given much thought to the consequences of representing the devil worshipping Jessie Misskelley. I was naively unaware of the depth of the fear and the genuine repulsion most people would feel for the accused, and for me. In the beginning days of my representing Jessie Misskelley, my job would be to find an opening that would lead to a plea deal and keep him from a lethal injection. It seemed to be an open and shut case, I thought. My good friend and fellow attorney, Brad Broadaway told me soon after he learned I was involved, that it would be easy, like shooting "a bird on the ground."

I would soon learn that I would be put in the same circle of evil as my client. The community, the entire Mid-South wanted their pound of flesh, and everyone seemed to think that the West Memphis 3, Satanic child killers, deserved to suffer eternally in Hell. This sentiment proved to be an opponent I had little chance of beating.

7

My first major obstacle was muting Jessie Misskelley, Sr., which proved harder than I imagined. I suspect he very suddenly felt betrayed by the West Memphis Police after he had surrendered his son in response to their promise of a $35,000 reward that had been offered to the Misskelleys if "Little Jessie" could provide information about the murders.

Police would craft a short confession from a nearly 12-hour interrogation that began with Jessie Misskelley denying any involvement whatsoever but offering to police that he heard that "Damien Echols did it." This was all the police needed to increase the pressure on Jessie Misskelley.

Jessie Misskelley, Sr. began holding press conferences for a captive and large audience of reporters the night Jessie Jr. was arrested. By the time his son was locked up and settled uncomfortably into the Clay County Detention Center in Piggott, Arkansas, Jessie Sr.'s colorful views had become the center of attention in West Memphis, much to the chagrin of the WMPD.

His stage was a collapsing front porch that clung tenuously to his dilapidated mobile home. "Big Jessie," who had only hours earlier turned his son over to the West Memphis Police, proclaimed his son's innocence to anyone who would listen. No one believed him but it made for great copy.

His nightly proclamations were odd, I thought, given that his son had confessed. Each day at noon, five, six, and ten, he avidly defended Jessie Jr. to a throng of newspaper and television reporters hungry for anything he said. An earthy, oil-stained mechanic with the stage presence of a seasoned trouper and the salty, colorful vocabulary of a backcountry tell-it-like-it-is, no-bullshit orator, Big Jessie made for great sound bites.

Little Jessie was nowhere near West Memphis at the time of the murders, he would repeat emphatically. He was wrestling in Dyess, Arkansas, a small town fifty miles away. The boyhood home of Johnny Cash, Dyess was the site of a "wrestling ring" where Big Jessie stated that Little Jessie, at five feet four and at most 100 pounds, was practicing becoming a professional wrestler. I needed to get the spotlight off Big Jessie, and quickly, while I sorted out what was going on. He had to shut up if I were to have any chance of reaching a plea agreement that would save his son's life.

Two things were working against me. Jessie Misskelley, Sr. liked the attention, and Jessie Misskelley, Sr. was an alcoholic whose nightly media show was fueled by beer brought to his trailer by the illustrious members of the local media. They hauled it in by the case, the more the better. Big Jessie showed no inclination to stop the show despite my urgent requests for him to do so. Through slurred speech, Jessie Sr. fought for his son the only way he knew how. Jessie Sr.'s incessant and well-lubricated conversations with the press were an annoyance for me, to be sure. But they were only a part of the problem.

I have heard that if you place a lobster in a pot of cool seawater then gradually increase the temperature until the water reaches a vigorous boil, the unsuspecting creature feels no pain until it is far too late to do anything about it. It sits comfortably at the bottom of the pot until it is boiled alive. I was in the lobster pot the moment I said I would defend Jessie Misskelley, expecting a quick and easy job of it. I did not realize it until many years later that I had been cooked long before I realized it.

It took one hundred and sixteen days of sitting in that metaphorical lobster pot, absorbing the unrelenting pressure of preparing to defend a totally befuddled and clueless Jessie Misskelley before I had a revelation that would inject new energy into my efforts to plea bargain "Little Jessie" from execution.

I took a lot of heat from everyone in a community that had no second thoughts that Misskelley, Echols, and Baldwin were guilty of the most heinous crimes that had ever taken place in Arkansas. The police never really looked for anyone else, and no one asked them to. Guilt was a foregone conclusion, and my role in preparing to defend Jessie Misskelley was perceived by almost everyone as a shameful act they would not soon forget. While I was trying to figure out a way to stifle Jessie Sr.'s annoying press conferences, I thought back to my first meeting with his son only days before

8

Our car sped through miles of flooded rice fields, from Paragould, toward the Clay County Detention Center in Piggott, a forty-minute drive north. It was hot, ridiculously hot. Arkansas summers do nothing but get hotter. The only thing worse than June in Arkansas, is July. August would make July seem like a distant and cool pleasure. Temperatures during the day exceed 100 degrees Fahrenheit, with humidity hovering around 100 percent—an almost inhumane combination. The heat does not usually break until October. The wells that provided streams of water between the ubiquitous rice levies we passed also offered up an unbroken haze over the fields. The air was so thick it seemed impenetrable, like passing through a sponge.

My law partner Greg Crow was driving. In the car with us was Vicky Krosp, one of our two legal assistants. The other legal assistant, Karen Nobles, strategically placed back at the office to hold down the fort. Both women had been my students at South Central Career College in Jonesboro. I took the job as a professor to help make ends meet by supplementing my income. They had been my two best students, and when they had graduated with their paralegal degrees and as my law practice began to grow, I hired them.

Our plan for the meeting with Jessie Jr. was to have Greg and I conduct the interview, with Vic taking detailed notes. It seemed like a good plan because my handwriting was atrocious, and Greg's was worse. The last thing I wanted to do at our first encounter was to stick another tape recorder in front of the kid. The police's recorder had already done enough damage. I wanted him to be as relaxed as possible.

Jessie Misskelley was about to become a dark part of what would soon ominously and forever be known as *The West Memphis 3*. Later that would be abbreviated to just the *WM3*. He was also about to become a serendipitous responsibility that I would carry without reservation for nearly two decades — and one I still carry without regret today. I would come to know the young mentally challenged Jessie quite well, but it would be a long process. His unambiguous life view would bring a great unanticipated burden to my own life. When I accepted the judge's request to represent Jessie with the vague and hastily formed idea that doing so would be a minor detour from my daily and growing law practice, I had no inkling of the depth of my naiveté.

As ridiculous as it sounds, I had read my client's confession for the first time in a story screaming from the headlines on the front page of the Memphis *Commercial Appeal*. Jessie described how Damien Echols and Jason Baldwin killed the boys as part of a Satanic ritual. Misskelley, the article reported, spoke of a Satanic Cult that he and Damien and Jason belonged to. The group would engage in sex orgies and eat the flesh of dogs they had killed, he said. The newspaper did not report the entire confession, so I called one of the lawyers who had volunteered to represent Damien Echols and asked if he had a copy of the twenty-seven-page transcript so I could read it before I met with my new client. He honored my request, and I stood by the fax machine waiting and reading each curled onionskin page as it slowly emerged.

I was chilled; the gruesome details were far worse than I had imagined. Even so, several glaring inconsistencies leapt out as I read and re-read the statement and a subsequent statement made by

Misskelley to "clarify" the first. Those inconsistencies were further emphasized after I discovered other assertions from Jessie that pushed his confession into the realm of the impossible. Nonetheless, the interrogators had compressed his nearly twelve-hour interrogation into approximately a 30-minute format, none of which was on video. Even so, police proclaimed they had their murderers.

I would discover in the days ahead that police had staged and contaminated Jessie Misskelley's confession. I would in the months before the trial have the great fortune of securing the services of two of the world's leading experts on confessions and interrogation techniques.

The front-page headline of the *Commercial Appeal* after Jessie's arrest was not subtle: TEEN DESCRIBES "CULT" TORTURE OF BOYS. I knew immediately that any potential jury pool had been tainted, no matter where the trial for Damien Echols and Jason Baldwin was held. I wondered in amazement just how the *Commercial Appeal* had managed to get a copy of my client's confession. I also wondered why the *Commercial Appeal*'s story was copyrighted, something quite unusual for a crime news story—or for most newspaper stories for that matter. Soon, I would hear rumors of cops hitting all the news outlets in Memphis trying to sell the Misskelley confession for $5,000. Later, reporters would tell me they had declined to buy "news" of any type from anyone the night of the confession and arrests. *Had the Commercial Appeal bought the confession? And, if so, from whom?*

I still do not know, but not for lack of trying. This was information that should never have gone public. The answer remains a mystery. Protected by the First Amendment, no reporter was required to reveal the source. The closest I ever got was a "non-denial denial" from the former editor of the paper. The once largest newspaper in the Mid-South is now defunct.

A bump on the highway brought me back to the task at hand, meeting my new client. My mind drifted to the small town of Piggott itself. It was the epitome of small-town America.

By 1993, like most of rural Arkansas, and rural America as well, it had seen its more robust and perhaps more famous days. It was once the home of Ernest Hemingway, who wrote parts of *A Farewell to Arms* there, and the shooting location of a major motion picture, *A Face in the Crowd*—which marked the 1957 screen debuts of Andy Griffith, Lee Remick, and Walter Matthau. But at the time of our first visit with Jessie Misskelley, there was nothing left in Piggott that even closely resembled any type of "crowd," and this, even today, remains its absolute charm.

As we covered the last leg of our journey to the Clay County Detention Center, my mind returned to my new client. His police "mug" shot was staggering. The picture had captured the unrepentant scowl of a tough-looking thug with a strong, set jaw and cold dark eyes. The photo fit the part of "Satanic Child Killer" well, though admittedly I had no idea what a Satanic child killer was supposed to look like. He appeared without emotion in his mug shot, and that led me to believe that the young man I was about to meet would be some kind of monster. The strange uneven haircut in the photo did not help matters. I recalled an interview of a wild-eyed and venom-spewing Charles Manson I had seen on television. I thought of other gruesome killers I had read about. I felt I would soon see one of the faces of pure evil, in person, and up close.

Even though I had done it before, the walk down the hall to meet a killer in jail was of no particular comfort to me. At least this time I would have some company and the walk down the hall was not going to be quite as long. There was still an eerie silence among the three of us as we walked in the front door and signed the visitors' log at the Plexiglas window.

A deputy walked us down that hall on the secure side of the facility to a cell that would contain the Satanic child killer, Jessie Lloyd Misskelley. My stomach rolled and the hair on the back of my neck stood up. The deputy used what seemed like a giant's key to open the cell door. I guess the rationale was that no one could leave something that large in their pocket and walk off with it unknowingly. Sitting at a concrete table in the middle of the cell to meet us was a young man incongruous with my preconceptions.

Rather than a snarling devil-worshipping street thug, we looked down at a dwarf of a kid. I did a double take, thinking there must have been a mistake. The deputy had brought us to the wrong cell, I thought. But as he left us, I realized we had to be in the right spot. Jessie Misskelley was the size of a 10-year-old, a featherweight in what was about to become a fifteen-round heavyweight title bout for his life.

"Are you Jessie Misskelley?" I finally managed.

He hesitated, staring intently at the gray concrete floor for what seemed an eternity.

"Uh huh," was all that he said.

I would soon learn that those two syllables were his favorites when it came to anything that resembled conversation. Jessie Misskelley wore an ill-fitting orange jumpsuit with "Clay County Detention Center" stenciled on the back. It was far too big for him. Both the legs and sleeves had been rolled up so you could see his hands and feet. The jailer informed me later that this was the smallest they had, designed for a female inmate. Jessie's shoulders were slumped, and his eyes were fixed on the floor in a dull, blank stare. I was both mesmerized and confused. He did not look like a cold-blooded killer. On his exposed left arm, I could see what appeared to be some shoddily done homemade tattoos. One read simply: F.T.W.

"What is that?" I asked.

"Fuck the World," he replied.

Wonderful, I thought as I made a mental note that this meant long sleeves for Misskelley in the courtroom.

"Got anymore tattoos?" I asked.

He opened his jail jump suit to reveal another on his chest that went nicely with the *Fuck the World* theme. It read: "Bitch." I asked why he would tattoo that on his chest.

"I don't remember," he said.

Greg and I began the interview, and it did not proceed as either of us expected. I did not know it at the time, but I was hit with the same frustration that the West Memphis Police interrogators must have experienced. Jessie Misskelley, despite confessing to witnessing the horrific crimes, could not seem to recall the order of events as they unfolded the day of the murders. He was unable to tell a cohesive story. He had no voice of his own and lacked any sense of narrative.

How can you watch three young boys get brutally sodomized and murdered and not remember the details of the crime or how the events unraveled? One of the boys had been savagely castrated, the skin of his penis ripped off. Why couldn't Jessie Misskelley remember this? Not only could he not recall that particular horror, but he got the victims wrong when it came to this most gruesome injury. Greg and I knew Christopher Byers had been sexually mutilated. Yet, Jessie Misskelley insisted to us that it was the "blonde" victim, Stevie Branch.

In the first hour we spent with Jessie, perhaps the only thing that we got out of him was that he admitted he was present when the young boys were killed. Even that was difficult information to obtain. He answered our questions with a series of "yahs" and "uh-huhs" without any elaboration. His lack of narrative, his complete inability to be engaged, was disturbing. *Something was very wrong.*

Jessie seemed frightened. As I studied his face, I thought that he looked more like the banjo-playing kid from *Deliverance* than a Satanic child killer. His crude haircut only emphasized his befuddlement—almost cleanly shaved sides with grooves, or stripes cut to his scalp meeting a Mohawk at the top of his head. Whoever his barber was had also cut out the shape of an "eight ball," like the black ball from a pool table, into his scalp. While it must have required some measure of talent to construct, the haircut made him look like a carnival freak.

Jessie, in his statements to police, had said that the murdered boys had been tied up with "a big brown rope." This was impossible and untrue since the eight-year-old boys had been bound with their own shoestrings. Jessie seemed to be the only person in the world who did not know that. Police interrogators simply glossed over this glaring inconsistency, like frenzied kids on Christmas morning unwrapping long anticipated gifts.

As the meeting at the jail progressed, an uneasy feeling returned once again to my gut. In my chosen profession, "gut" feelings are sometimes like a magical talisman. They can guide you and sustain you. But if you are not careful, they can also steer you down the wrong path.

Vic took notes, often pausing, confused, over something Jessie said. Jessie never made eye contact when he spoke, and he seemed unable to answer the most basic of our questions. I thought as I listened, *"Why can't this kid tell us what happened? How the hell are we going to get him ready to testify against his co-defendants?"* This was the only way that we could save him from the death penalty.

As we reached an uncomfortable end to our first meeting, I felt both frustrated and confused. I could not understand the genesis of either emotion. From looking at Vicky and Greg I could tell they felt the same way.

Suddenly, Jessie finally made his first real statement of the interview— something besides simply a "yes" or "no" answer in response to our questions.

"I don't wanna die in no electric chair," he stated in a terrified voice.

"What did you say?" I asked, confused.

"Them cops in West Memphis told me I was gonna die in a electric chair. I don't want to die in no electric chair," Jessie said with fear pulsating from his small frame.

My jaw dropped. I was more stunned than when I first entered the cell itself. Arkansas had not used the electric chair since John Swindler was executed on June 18, 1990. Furthermore, it was common knowledge that the electric chair was no longer used as a form of capital punishment. It simply was not an option. I knew that the police were certainly aware of this.

Our efforts to calm his fears by mentioning the approved lethal injection method failed miserably. Jessie could not seem to grasp the concept of a lethal injection. Apparently, the West Memphis police realized this as well and thought the idea of telling him that he was going to die in something that would cook the flesh from his bones was more terrifying. We tried to assure Jessie that there was no electric chair and that we were on his side. He seemed reluctant to believe either.

As we got ready to leave, I reached into my pocket and pulled out a wad of small bills. I gave Jessie $5 and told him to get a haircut, a real haircut from the jail barber before our first hearing. The Mohawk-mullet thing would have to go. It would be about as well received in court as his "*Fuck the World*" tattoo. Greg reached out and placed his hand on Jessie's shoulder. Jessie Misskelley recoiled in terror.

An overwhelming sense of insecurity flowed from this kid. As we were about to walk out, I faced Jessie one last time, to get something of real value from this interview.

"Which kid had his penis cut off," I asked.

"The blonde one," again was his reply.

"Okay kid," I said, "we will see you again soon."

Jessie said nothing. He just stared at the floor.

Once we got outside the jail and in the car, Greg said:

"What the hell is going on?"

"I don't know," I answered.

"Getting him ready to testify against the other two is going to be difficult."

"Maybe, impossible," I said.

The ride home was not silent. We had a lot to talk about. Meeting Jessie Misskelley had not helped clarify my mission. He was an enigma.

In our next meetings, Jessie Misskelley continued to tell us that he was present when the little boys were killed. But he remained incapable of providing any coherent narrative. It was as if he had thrown random information he had been given about the killings into a blender.

9

Two things were putting up major roadblocks to my ability to negotiate a plea for Jessie Misskelley and I really did not know which one was worse. Jessie's inability to form a narrative was making the prospect of him being able to testify against Echols and Baldwin nearly insurmountable. On the other hand, his father's daily news briefings were making the prosecutors as angry as I was. With his nightly show for the media, Jessie Sr. was literally destroying any chance at negotiating a plea to save his son's life. Frustrated, I could not make him understand that these public rantings were hurting his son's case not helping it. He did not see it that way.

A week into the Jessie Misskelley, Sr. Show, I got a phone call from a local deputy prosecutor. I had been expecting the call. But I was surprised that it did not come from deputy prosecutor John Fogleman, with whom presumably I would be working out a plea deal. The local prosecutor wanted to know if I was aware of "Big Jessie's" nightly press conferences. He, of course, was concerned about how they might affect any potential plea deal. I assured him that I would take care of it and as I hung up the phone, I wondered why Fogleman had used an emissary instead of calling me himself.

After that call and its all-too-clear message, I again instructed

Jessie Sr. to keep quiet and stay away from the TV cameras. He would not listen. I was tiring of running damage control between him and the prosecution. This had to stop.

The next day I called Jessie Sr. one last time and begged him, again, to stop. "My son didn't do this," he proclaimed. "Then why is he telling me he was there when it happened?" I countered. Jessie, Sr. said, "I don't know, but he was in Dyess wrestling that night and I have witnesses."

Then he read to me a short note his son had written shortly after he settled in his first jail cell in Cross County, Arkansas. When I saw the note, it nearly broke my heart and only deepened the confusion.

> Dear Dad and Lee,
> I miss both of ya'll I can not stand in here much longer I will go crazy Y'all know I did not do it I am not that crazy I miss ya'll a lot tell Susie I love her With all my heart ya'll tried to get me out I quit smoking I got a TV and I got a Bible and I quit cousing my stomach has been hurting me I watch the news last knight and I cry and cry...I hope that ya'll don't hate me because I did not do it I was with Rickey Deese the day it happen I was ruffin Please try to get me out I will die in here you that I can not stand it well I guess I will let you go for now but not for long I love ya'll Oh, I fixen to write Susie and give it to her please
> P.S. Write back I am in the cross county Jail I can see people on Sunday. I don't know what time I hope ya'll can come
> I Love ya'll,
> Jessie Jr.

I knew then why Jessie Sr. had become such a staunch defender of his son and why he had those press conferences. I also knew still that I had to get him to stop. And that I needed to get to the bottom of the confusion, and fast.

10

It has been said that winners earn the privilege of documenting their stories. Winston Churchill once wrote that "History will be kind to me for I intend to write it." He knew what he was talking about, having had his share of losing along the way.

In the years after those young men were locked up, Judge David Burnett was arguably one of the biggest winners. Before the trials had even started, Judge Burnett did everything he could to put himself in the proper light for a frightened public that saw only darkness. He made sure every day that the halo he seemed to have hung over his head stayed in place, admired by all. In his imagination, he was the good judge who threw the book at the Devil himself and won. He was a sainted figure who had preserved the integrity of the community, and perhaps more importantly allowed them to feel safe again.

He had selflessly done his civic duty and summoned the nerve to put those soulless creatures, the West Memphis 3, where they belonged. To emphasize this point, when imposing the death penalty against Damien Echols, he set the execution date on the anniversary of the murders knowing full well that it would not, and could not, happen quite that fast.

In a case that surely had no winners, the folksy no-nonsense

Burnett for years appeared to prop himself up as the clear victor, defender of all that was good in the criminal justice system. He allowed his history to shine, basked in it. Most people admired him. I was no fan by the time Jessie Misskelley was sentenced, and I had no interest in having an asterisk attached to my name in agate type in the never-read appendix of Burnett's epic fiction of the West Memphis 3 case.

I would imagine he was delighted when he learned he would be matching wits with a 30-year-old attorney with no jury trial experience. But he underestimated me. He mistook winning a battle for winning the war. I was prepared for war, even then, even after Jessie Misskelley was convicted and locked away. I had made a promise to Jessie that I would never give up and I intended to keep that promise.

David Burnett, a bright man, and former prosecutor knew the law well. He presided over the trial of Jessie Misskelley and the separate trial for Damien Echols and Jason Baldwin with a casual disinterest in proper jurisprudence and had manipulated the outcomes before they occurred. His favorable bias toward the prosecution seemed to have no boundaries, and the trials were nothing more than dog-and-pony shows. No one outside of the very few really cared. I cared, of course, and in the years ahead many others across the world would come to share my opinion.

Burnett, along with the prosecutors, whose reckless indifference to the fates of Jessie Misskelley, Jason Baldwin, and Damien Echols, had tried to bury me. What they did not know was that while they were doing so, quite successfully, I had managed to plant a seed during the hearing on my motion to suppress Jessie's dubious confession just weeks before the start of the trial. That seed would later grow and eventually turn the case around.

My passion for the law had been burning for twenty years by the time I first walked into David Burnett's courtroom. I had wanted to be a lawyer early on, and my mother, Eva, still recalls my standing on a tree stump in our backyard in Chicago honing my future oratory skills to imaginary juries. I was five years old when my family moved to Paragould, which sits approximately 90 miles north of Memphis,

Tennessee, 153 miles from Little Rock and a little more than 200 miles south from St. Louis. I still remember my five-year-old shock at watching the news of the assassination of Dr. Martin Luther King, Jr. in Memphis and the ensuing chaos that followed. Not even two months later I was transfixed again, watching coverage of the assassination of Robert Kennedy in Los Angeles. The nightly news accounts of the horrors of the Vietnam War, by then awfully close to its height, was a dose of hard reality even for a young boy. This was a chilling black-and-white television introduction to our increasingly violent world. Maybe that instilled in me a subliminal awareness of injustice.

By the time I was 10, I wanted nothing more than to become a lawyer. My mom showed me the wonderful power of words and speech, and their magic. My dad, a practical man, taught me how to deal with bullies, head on. "Hit them," he said. "Right in the mouth, and as often and hard as you can until they go away." He was right, of course.

I was a typical teenage Arkansas boy. I learned to hunt and fish wandering the woods and creeks that ran behind the family farm. In the late 1970s, I quarterbacked the Greene County Tech Junior Varsity Eagles football team and was a starting forward on its District Jr. Championship basketball team. I was an Eagle Scout. I was in the Science Club as well as the Future Business Leaders of America, but I sometimes chased girls more than books. I never wavered in my desire to be a lawyer, however. I had a calm sense of confidence, not cockiness, mind you, that came from my abilities and from the matter-of-fact reminders from my parents that I could do anything if I put my mind to it.

As a young boy I developed a strong religious faith that for the longest time saw me through the assaults I absorbed for my audacity in representing a devil worshipping murderer—an irony that is not lost on me today. Each day of Jessie Misskelley's trial, I would stop outside the First United Methodist Church in Paragould to pray. Too busy and consumed with preparing for the case, I had not been inside the church in some time. I would stop at the church and get out of my car and walk to the cornerstone that had been laid more than one hundred years before and rest my hand on it. I did not pray to win, for there were no winners in this case. Instead, my simple prayer was for truth and justice. I had not lost my faith in truth and justice. Not then, anyway. A few years later, I would begin to question my faith. How could God let something like this happen along with other atrocities like it? Once lost, it would be a long time before I would get it back.

I get weary thinking about it now, but in those days, I was a young man with a mission. I figured I could become a lawyer faster if I quit high school and jumped right in. So, I did. In September 1980, at the age of seventeen, I began my freshman year at Arkansas State University in nearby Jonesboro. Four years later, I was starting law school at the University of Arkansas in Fayetteville. I was married during my first semester of law school and by the time I butted heads with David Burnett I had three young children, Daniel, Christopher, and Kathryn, and was working my way up the traditional ladder. Everything was moving along the proper trajectory.

The year 1993 is the line of demarcation—a clear, defined, and indelible line that I crossed and from which I ventured out from a world of positive challenge and optimism into a darker world I was reluctant to become familiar with—though I did. I turned thirty years old in March 1993 and was entering just the fifth year of my law practice. My wife Kim and I had been married almost nine years. My children were, naturally, the center of my universe. By the time of our daughter Kathryn's birth, I was by choice and good fortune immersed in my work, spending a great deal of time at the office trying to build a successful law practice. Sometimes that compelled me to make a painful choice—work or children—that came with a substantial emotional price tag and tremendous guilt. I did not know it yet, but this feeling would only deepen in June 1993 and get even worse in the aftermath of the trial.

In the ethically porous and ambiguous worlds of business and politics—grandstanding and showboating and playing loosely with facts—alternative facts in the current argot—is often expected, even praised. In the law, in a case where three young, innocent lives were brutally taken and three more hung in the balance, such behavior is not acceptable. It is abhorrent. But national spotlights and mass hysteria can do strange things to shift the balance. And when the opponents are weak and defenseless and the call for justice immediate and unrelenting, justice can become a passing fancy.

Thank God for those cameras. I am gratified that the self-proclaimed modest and publicity-shy judge allowed cameras in the courtroom to preserve his wisdom and judiciousness for future generations. The cameras tell the story, every unblinking, strange bit of Jessie Misskelley's trial. It is all there—from opening statements to a quick cut of the numb, frightened, and convicted Jessie being hauled from the courtroom—looking like a lost child in chains beside his police escorts.

Over the years, Joe Berlinger and Bruce Sinofsky produced three films for HBO, *Paradise Lost: The Child Murders at Robin Hood Hills*, *Paradise Lost 2: Revelations*, and *Paradise Lost 3: Purgatory*. The HBO film crews shot every minute of both trials and recorded almost every word. The cameras and the microphones kept rolling even during the recesses and Judge Burnett either did not know they were still on, or he did not care. Joe Berlinger and Bruce Sinofsky and I became great friends. They had thought they were coming to Arkansas to film a story about troubled teenage killers. They left thinking that they were innocent. I miss Bruce Sinofsky, who died in 2015, but not before he got to see the impact of his work on this case and the criminal justice system. The films had an unrelenting influence on the case, not the least of which was the hundreds of hours of raw footage they shot during the pre-trial hearings and the two trials.

One day, years after the trials, I received an anonymous package that contained all this raw footage. I thought it would be great to watch it, and I put the first of dozens of DVDs in the player. It made me physically ill. I did not care to see myself flattened, again, by a runaway train. Who would? It was too painful to watch. It took me even more years to be able to sit down and finally take a serious look. Before that, it was just too much to bear.

If David Burnett had not invited those HBO cameras into the

courtroom, over the strenuous objections of both the prosecution and all three defense teams, I'd be sitting here today wondering if I only had imagined—perhaps with myopic hindsight—his heavy-handed management of Jessie Misskelley's case. The miles of footage I finally had the nerve to watch disabused me of that.

I had tried to re-watch *Paradise Lost* in 1997 when I attended a California conference of a group of criminal profilers, part of my continuing effort to get justice for Jessie. The profilers were viewing the film ahead of my presentation the next morning, but I had to walk out of the room. The memory of the trial was too brutal. To escape the film, I inadvertently walked into the home office of one of the profilers. The four walls were covered with photographs of cases he was working on. They were gruesome, but they still paled in comparison to the autopsy and crime-scene photographs from West Memphis, a good part of which were shown at Jessie Misskelley's trial.

One set of photographs in the profiler's office showed horrific photos of a woman who had been raped with a baseball bat. In another set of photos, a woman's nipples had been torn from her breasts with a pair of pliers. They were shocking and nauseating photos of repellant crimes.

But those photos were still not as bad as the photos from the West Memphis case that I had been spreading out on my conference table now for years, looking for something, anything, that would bring the West Memphis case to life again. I managed to find some courage in the past several years, and that has allowed me to finally watch all the DVDs of the trial. It seemed at first a surreal form of déjà vu looking at my thirty-year-old self. I still felt a twinge of pain, of being unable to kick that younger self into a fit of righteous indignation at what was happening all around him. I was a babe in the woods surrounded by wolves and loathsome characters who would soon be chewing me to bits. But I was too innocent, idealistic, and hopeful to realize what was happening. They say there is no substitute for experience, but I say that "bullshit and guts" will get you far. Never giving up, no matter what, can get you even farther. Perseverance can reap huge rewards in the end.

Part of my reluctance to watch was a still-strong sense of sympathy for that younger self. Seeing the trial again after all these years has made me realize that the way the case came to a legal conclusion in 2011 with an Alford Plea that set the West Memphis Three free had also robbed me of a victory that I should have gotten straight up in a new trial. No reasonable jury would have convicted any of the West Memphis 3 after the world's best forensic experts had given their testimony in 2008 and 2009. And the State of Arkansas knew it.

I suppose one could assert in David Burnett's defense—or for that matter that of the police and prosecution—that they simply got caught up in the panic and hysteria. But even if this was true, when it became glaringly obvious that the WM3 were innocent, they did nothing but dig in deeper to preserve their own legacies and their version of the truth.

I saw in February 2017 a small news article and shook my head. Some things never change. Karma can be vicious.

Ex-State Senator Agrees To Ethics Fine, Letter

Former state Sen. David Burnett, D-Osceola, has agreed to pay a $250 fine and receive a public letter of caution in a settlement of a complaint with the Arkansas Ethics Commission, according to commission records released Friday. "In the settlement, Burnett agreed with the commission's finding that he violated state law as a candidate for Senate District 22 by accepting campaign contributions from nine businesses and entities 'not listed as permissible contributors,' commission Director Graham Sloan said in a letter to Burnett. Burnett signed the settlement Jan. 27. Burnett said Friday that he agreed to settle the complaint because "it wasn't worth fooling with anymore." "I'll never be involved in it again," said Burnett, who lost his re-election bid in November to then-Rep. David Wallace, R-Leachville. Burnett served in the Senate from 2011-17 and previously served as a prosecutor and *circuit judge. Burnett said he felt like he could have defended himself against the complaint, but "it takes too much time and too much hassle.*

David Burnett sometimes danced a folksy and delicate jig over the fine line between "good ole boy" savant and questionable ethical behavior. It is an ambiguous line, especially in politics, where there is often no line at all. During the trial Burnett had no problem crossing the line. Many cheered him for doing so. I guess that truth and justice for the West Memphis 3 was just "too much hassle" as well.

When I watched the raw footage of the trial, I was astounded at David Burnett's disdainful facial expressions and hand gestures at anything Greg Crow or I said. His obvious favor toward the prosecution is displayed prominently in some scenes that did not make it into the *Paradise Lost* documentaries. The Freudian slips and the disparaging things he said about Greg Crow and me in the presence of the jury are astonishing.

I spoke to Greg and told him about some of the stuff I had been watching— both of us in action in 1994 and Burnett's antics. Greg was as surprised to learn of it as I was. He told me he had never watched any of the *Paradise Lost* films. He had made a conscious effort to not relive how badly we were railroaded. I understand this much better now than I ever had. "The deck was stacked against us from the beginning," he told me.

All these years later, the gross negligence, the automatic assumptions, the difficult legal realities, seem almost bizarre. But it was real, it was harsh, and it was what I had to deal with. In hindsight, the lives of Jessie Misskelley, Jason Baldwin, and Damien Echols had already been forfeited. Those inconsequential young men from inconsequential economic circumstances were tossed like dust into the winds of an Arkansas summer as soon as they were arrested. Those three poor boys were expendable as careers were made and reputations polished. Finally watching those DVDs and speaking to Greg about them, took me back to June 1993 when it all began.

11

As the trial date approached in January 1994, I was bolstered by what I thought would be the irrefutable testimonies of two of the world's leading experts in false confessions and police interrogation tactics, including the use of the polygraph to coerce a confession. My experts would be able to clearly explain to a jury that Jessie Misskelley's confession was nothing more than a contaminated fiction crafted and generated by Gary Gitchell. In addition, we had alibi witnesses, such as they were, who could place Jessie Misskelley in Dyess and not in West Memphis on May 5, 1993. I thought we could win this thing. I was beaming with confidence.

These assets would provide only a temporary and fleeting comfort, like a warming post-dinner cognac on the *Titanic* as it approached the iceberg. Burnett and his co-conspirators knew that these assets were formidable, and they seemed to collude to make sure that their testimonies would never be heard by the jury.

On the evening that the young boys disappeared, Jessie had been at home when a fight broke out between a child and an adult resident of the Highland trailer park. The Marion Police Department was called and most everyone who lived in the trailer park responded to the scene as well. After the officer arrived, Jessie Misskelley was seen by several witnesses leaning into the police officer's car on the passenger side, talking about the incident to the officer inside. According to the incident report filed by the officer, the fight took place at approximately 6:35 PM. Thus, a police officer became one of our alibi witnesses and his incident report became one of our exhibits. This was extremely important for a couple of reasons. First, Jessie had been working with a fellow named Ricky Deese on a roofing job but decided to not return to work after lunch. Jesse and some of his friends were about to leave Marion and travel to Dyess to practice wrestling when the trailer park fight broke out.

Stevie Branch, Michael Moore and Christopher Byers were last seen riding their bicycles on the service road near the Blue Beacon and the truck stop at approximately 6:30 PM. Jessie Misskelley could not have been at the scene of the crime when he was talking to a Marion police officer in his own trailer park several miles away at the same time. The Marion police officer would later claim that he never saw Jessie Misskelley in the trailer park on May 5, even though there were several witnesses who saw the officer talking to Jessie. *Was it perjury, or amnesia?* I could only shake my head. I suppose he might have rationalized that he was on "God's team" and had been granted benediction to forget about seeing and speaking to a no-good devil worshiping Satanist. Either way the officer was not about to provide an alibi for Jessie Misskelley. It was the classic struggle of good versus evil served up Southern Style. Around 7 pm on May 5, Jessie and his friends piled into a car and picked up the brother of another friend, then drove on to Dyess, where a wrestling ring inside an old movie theater had been rented by a man named Fred Revelle. There were many witnesses to this event.

Years later, after the Alford Plea, and after Jason Baldwin, Damien Echols, and Jessie Misskelley were released from prison, people would begin to approach and contact me letting me know the lengths to which the prosecutors went to stack the deck against us. One of those was the owner of the wrestling ring in Dyess who called to tell me that Jessie Misskelley had, in fact, been in Dyess on the evening of May 5, 1993, adding that he had left town at the request of a prosecutor so he could not be subpoenaed by us for trial. I suppose for him it was a cathartic apology, but it was years too late to help Jessie Misskelley avoid 18 years and 78 days of incarceration. Perhaps even more stunning was that the owner said he thought the prosecutor's name was "Davis." Normally, I would not give great weight or credibility to someone who called me to tell me a story like that. But it fit a pattern that emerged in the case post-trial. It seems that at least two other witnesses were told to make themselves unavailable to be served with a subpoena.

12

The scene where the bodies of the three eight-year-olds were recovered had not been properly secured and much potential evidence had been lost. After searchers found the first body, the entire crime scene was trampled, especially the creek bed. The bodies had been removed from the water too quickly. The coroner arrived nearly two hours later, which was an indication of how amateurish things had been handled. The bodies had been placed on the bank of the ditch in the hot sun, which destroyed evidence that could have been invaluable. Police also discovered the victims' clothing in the water close to where the bodies were found, but no other legitimate evidence was recovered.

For the most part the investigation was haphazard and chaotic. It would produce dubious "evidence" that was then misinterpreted by a grossly unqualified medical examiner and later the police. Arkansas uses a system in which county coroners are elected, but since the pay is so low, the local coroner is usually a local funeral director who has no training in forensics. The bodies were sent to Little Rock, and examined by Dr. Frank Peretti, a pathologist who was, and remains to this day, not board-certified. Dr. Peretti had taken the exam for board certification several times but failed each time before just giving up entirely.

There was no blood at the scene—an indication that the murders had taken place somewhere else and the ditch where the bodies were discovered was a dump site and not the primary crime scene. Luminol testing was conducted by the police some two weeks after the discovery of the bodies and revealed the presence of possible blood on the ditch bank where the bodies were laid by the police. Blood had seeped from the bodies into the soil. Luminol testing is not admissible in court because it is not scientifically reliable.

Before our trial, the medical examiner, Peretti, had informed Greg Crow and me that the time of death was impossible to determine because the coroner had done such a poor job in supplying the necessary data. A few weeks later, suddenly, Peretti had changed his mind and somehow, perhaps magically, could now testify as to a time of death. A stunning revelation would come many years later about Dr. Frank Peretti's magical abilities, and it would chill me.

As I look back at the trial now, I know that the clear and irrefutable examples of the poor and careless investigation simply did not matter. At the trial it was almost moot— because everyone from the judge to the prosecutors to the public cared not a whit about any of that.

13

Soon after I was appointed to represent Jessie Misskelley, the three defense teams and the prosecutors agreed to meet informally in Marion at the Crittenden County Courthouse to discuss how the discovery process would unfold, the all-important stage during which we would learn what evidence the prosecution had against our clients. As part of our discussions that afternoon, the topic flowed into who would preside over what was sure to be a tense, controversial and contentious case. The presiding judge would need to be cautious, even-handed, and impeccably fair. He would need to be thick-skinned and able to withstand the enormous pressure of adjudicating a trial that was sure to be covered in every medium across the country, day and night. Would pundits be offering their own opinions on the judge's rulings? Would they question his rulings? Would the intense media focus influence his decisions? I felt the judge in the case would need to be confident in his rulings and unaffected by outside pressures.

In the background lay another question that even in my naiveté I had some concern about: Politics. Whoever was chosen would need to be able to rise above the obvious temptation to curry political favor with the voters by presiding over a case in such a way that the guilty verdict that so many wanted would arrive quickly and forcefully. Even with my rose-colored glasses firmly in place I was worried. Still, I did not think personal interest and ill-formed intentions could possibly intervene.

We were not surprised to learn that the prosecutors wanted Judge David Burnett, but all six defense lawyers immediately and strenuously objected, for obvious reasons. Burnett had been a prosecutor in the Second Judicial Circuit of Arkansas for many years before taking the bench, and he never seemed to have forgotten that. His bias toward the prosecution in every case was legendary. It was common knowledge that he liked to inject himself into trial proceedings, not an endearing trait for a job that calls for impartiality. If he felt the prosecution was not doing an adequate job, he had at times started cross-examining witnesses himself at the trial. I had seen this phenomenon before with my own eyes.

One story making the rounds made sense to many of us. Once during a criminal trial, the story went, a prominent Jonesboro lawyer asked Judge Burnett, in open court, why he and the prosecutors did not just wear jerseys with their names on the back so the members of the jury could have no doubt that they were on the same team.

After much debate between defense and prosecution lawyers on this extremely critical point, only one name stood out. Everyone on both sides agreed: Judge Olan Parker. It was settled. We headed to Judge Parker's chambers to request that he accept the case and hear all the pre-trial motions in Jessie Misskelley's case and those for the separate trial of Echols and Baldwin.

"Gentleman, I am flattered that you would pick me," Judge Parker had told us. "But my health simply will not permit it." He was battling cancer and did not think that he could handle the rigors of this case. Then he added something that startled me. Judge Parker's offhanded comment would continue to haunt me for years. Someone else had claimed the right to preside and had already quickly inserted himself into the role, Judge Parker said.

"That red-headed judge from Osceola has already called the

case," Judge Parker told us, laughing, "and you will never get him to let go of it."

It was a highly unusual move, to say the very least. Within a few days, the grim news was confirmed. We received a letter in the mail containing an order signed by all the judges in the Second Judicial Circuit assigning Judge David Burnett to the case. We were in trouble and the case had not even started.

14

Our first taste of the turmoil waiting for us came at the arraignment for the West Memphis 3 in Marion. I had not been present in court the day that Judge Goodson called to ask if I would represent Mr. Misskelley. In addition to the palpable anger and fear in the courtroom that day, Judge Goodson's public pronouncement of my involvement on June 7, 1993, was the start of a perceived and dark stain that would follow me for years. In the uninformed public's eyes, I was defending an indefensible Satanic murderer.

At one point as Greg and I frantically answered the torrent of phone calls from the media, Greg asked me if people would understand the concept of everyone has a right to an attorney. Would people in Paragould and the surrounding areas who were so vocal in their hatred for Echols and Baldwin and Misskelley ever be able to understand that we had not asked for this? "What's not to understand?" I had told him.

When Greg and I walked into the courtroom in Marion to enter a not guilty plea, Jessie, Jason, and Damien were already there, tense and stunned and small in a sea of venomous observers. It was my first chance to gauge public reaction and I was unprepared for it.

The courtroom was packed, standing room only. All three sets of the victim's parents were there, as were the three sets of the defendants' parents. All were angry. The victims' parents wanted blood. The defendants' parents wanted the nightmare to end. The ugly mob seemed ready to jump the rail and hang the three defendants immediately. The crowd spilled over outside the courtroom into the foyer and even down the stairs to the first floor. Cameras were everywhere outside. Clearly there had not been much thought given to court security for such a high-profile case. The only protection from the seething crowd was an ancient and unarmed bailiff leaning sheepishly unconcerned and unaware against a side wall.

At the end of the arraignment hearing, murder victim Stevie Branch's father jumped up and lunged for Damien Echols, screaming for Echols to find justice in Hell, just as he had done at the June 7 hearing the day we were appointed as Jessie's lawyers in absentia. Somehow, the situation in Marion never got entirely out of hand. It could have been ugly.

To this day, I have never seen anything like it. After the hearing I immediately complained to Judge Burnett about the lack of security on such a high-profile case. Anticipating that the next hearing would be the same three-ring circus, I did something I had never done before. I secreted my Smith & Wesson .357 revolver into my briefcase. I did not want to be a sitting duck.

Instead of a circus, Burnett would have an army of police officers for security at the next hearing and for the others that followed. But that first chaotic appearance in Marion unsettled me. I had to question how a circuit judge could be so unaware, so completely unconcerned that he could let something like that happen. To me it seemed as if Judge Burnett was almost encouraging the antics in the court room. It was vaguely frightening, but it would get worse later, of course.

In January, shortly before Jessie's trial was to start, a fawning article on Judge Burnett appeared in the *Memphis Commercial Appeal*. It pointed out that he was an Eagle Scout, like me. He was a Vietnam veteran and a tough prosecutor. He told the reporter that he had "read a book on Satanism for information purposes" in preparation for the trial. My jaw dropped open by this remark. He was basically broadcasting for all to hear that the prosecution's motive was Satanism.

By then we were all playing a public relations game with the press, trying to use it to our own advantage. I certainly tried, and the judge himself was clearly no slouch. He was a master at spinning the media long before that term came into vogue. The article contained the following quote:

"Circuit Court Judge David Burnett is known around the Second Judicial District for common sense, often dispensed from the seat of his pants. The red-haired judge who will preside over the West Memphis child murder trials is a complex mixture of high energy, strong values, and sound judgment, colleagues say. They call him 'compassionate,' 'sharp,' and 'sweet.'"

Even in a game where there were few rules about putting your best face forward in the press, Burnett stunned me. He disingenuously expressed his irritation at the amount of press the case had received, calling the extensive national coverage in which he happily basked "a nuisance and annoyance to the court." I found that quite amusing coming from the man who had allowed documentary filmmakers into the court room. Perhaps more interesting was that the judge continued to put forth that he had been assigned this case and had, as a matter of duty and proper obligation, accepted the huge responsibility. Getting the case, he said in the interview, "didn't bother me one way or the other, but it's gotten to be a little more tedious than I thought it would be. I'll say that there's too much commotion, too much hullabaloo about it. But I can handle it."

The interview also provided an almost insane insight into his single-minded lack of judicial openness. He told the reporter that he was working on a master's thesis that asserted psychologists and psychiatrists "are no more capable of predicting future violent behavior than laymen, yet we use them as expert witnesses. Perhaps their opinions shouldn't be given the weight that is normally given by the courts and juries what have you. Future violent behavior is simply not predictable." This was a stunning revelation that would be a preview of things to come. One of the most glaring examples of Burnett's open and notorious bias towards the prosecution during the trials is his handling of "expert" witnesses and the admissibility of their testimonies.

In the Misskelley trial, he would not allow Dr. Richard Ofshe, a Pulitzer Prize winning social psychologist from the University of California at Berkeley to testify that in his opinion the Misskelley confession was "coerced," thereby robbing us of a crucial part of our defense. Weeks later in the Echols-Baldwin trial, Burnett would suddenly allow a retired police officer from Ohio with a mail-order Ph. D to testify, without restrictions, that the murders had the "trappings of the occult."

In making his ruling, Judge Burnett asserted that even the testimony of a third grader would be admissible if it assisted the jury in understanding the issues of the case. Dr. Richard Ofshe had a legitimate Ph. D from a prestigious university and was certainly not a third grader. I will never forget Prosecutor Brent Davis arguing to Burnett that Dr. Ofshe should not be allowed to testify because he was not a "real doctor" because he could not "fix a broken leg." I have always wondered if Davis believed that Dr. Dale Griffis, with his fake Ph. D could "fix a broken leg."

Going into the trial, I knew Burnett was no stranger to the concept of self-adoration. I knew he had trouble keeping quiet during the trial. I knew that eventually he would say something that an appeals court could jump on and jump on quickly. I would be there waiting.

15

I nearly choked on my coffee as I read the stupefying announcement that would once again draw unwanted national attention to Arkansas and its criminal justice system. Scanning the morning paper in March 2017 before I headed off to court, I saw that the State of Arkansas had announced plans to clean out Death Row for no other reason than its supply of lethal-injection drugs was about to expire on the shelf. Eight men were in line to be quickly and summarily executed in the name of fiscal expedience. It seemed the driving force behind the announcement was that it would be irresponsible to waste the costly drugs. The plan and its stroll-in-the park indifference ignited enough attention to briefly derail it, but it was soon back on track and four men were quickly dispatched. Most people around the nation and the world were stunned. I was not. Some things never change. Among the eight Death Row residents facing execution was Bruce Ward, who had, his attorney reported, "no rational understanding of the punishment he is slated to suffer or the reason why he is to suffer it." Sitting there at my kitchen table, I could hear it again, "*I don't wanna die in no electric chair.*" As much as I had fought being pulled back there, it was 1993 again. Bruce Ward is a latter-day incarnation of Jessie Misskelley, clueless and unambiguously intellectually challenged.

When I agreed to represent Jessie, I had believed his confession was real. Back in those days my view of the law and police procedures was untainted. Common sense dictated that no one would confess to a crime they did not commit. In 1993, my thinking, wrongheaded and uninformed, was that not even someone who was "slow" would confess to something that would quite possibly lead him to Death Row.

That was my first mistake. It would not be my last. Fortunately, I was nimble enough to learn from them. The Fall of 1993 gave me a lesson I had not received in law school. Much later, I thought about what a law school friend had told me about the advice his father had given him before he headed off to his first class. "Don't let your schooling get in the way of your education." Books were no substitute for the hard-knock education I got courtesy of the West Memphis police and the prosecutor's office. I had assumed Jessie's impressionable mind was, despite its weakness, still normal—that when confronted with the evidence he reacted as any guilty person would by confessing. Thinking his confession was earnest, I had assigned myself the task of stopping him from being executed, which was obviously where Burnett and the prosecutor's office were headed, despite Jessie's clear deficits.

The whispers of doubt began after that first meeting with the terrified Jessie at the Clay County Jail. I left confused. The poor boy, it appeared, was not capable of coherent thought—of constructing a flowing and logical narrative.

As that hot summer inched along, I would have further heated conversations with Jessie and his father. Each meeting produced nothing but anger. I admit to some petulance, but Jessie Misskelley was frustrating the hell out of me. For that matter, so was his father. The case was not proceeding the way I had planned. Unlike law school case studies, Jessie was the embodiment of real life—imperfect, flawed, and unpredictable.

I had a client who had confessed. I had a father who was adamant his son was innocent. We were spinning our wheels and going nowhere. I stormed from one meeting, upset over Jessie's ever-changing story, puzzled by his conflicting accounts of what he had said happened that day at Robin Hood Hills.

Jessie's father could barely control his anger at times. We were at odds as I kept pounding on the party line with "Little Jessie." Alone with me questioning him once again about what had transpired, Jessie would try but his story was never the same.

If his father was there, Jessie would tell his dad he was not at the crime scene at all. He had no idea of the consequences of what he had told the police, other than the terror so ably provided by police during the interrogation. Jessie had sat through 12 hours of coaching from interrogators, agreeing, changing, dodging, amending until hours of grilling fit neatly into what the police proffered as proof of guilt—though Jessie would immediately begin recanting what he had said.

Most people after being run over by a car crossing the street would tend to look twice before doing it again. It is called learning the hard way, assessing your bad luck, and taking steps to make sure it does not happen again. Jessie did not have a clue what he had done. He would have headed right back into traffic. Before the case was concluded with the Alford plea, Jessie would run back into traffic several more times.

As August turned into September, the light began to gradually reach me. I had been trying to fit the square peg Jessie Jr. into the round hole I thought he belonged in. They say that insanity is doing the same thing repeatedly and expecting different results. Several things outside Jessie's wobbly confession began to gnaw at me.

I had expected the prosecution would present all the evidence they had and allow us to see it during the discovery process leading up to the trial. I had assumed Judge Burnett, despite his reputation, would be impartial. I had expected the police had done their job and left no stone unturned in their efforts to find the killer. I was wrong on every count.

At first, based on media reports of what police had discovered about the case—which at the time was all I had to go on—I had assumed that Jessie had been a disconnected observer of the heinous crimes. I felt he had unwittingly been drawn to the crime scene by Echols and Baldwin but had done nothing but watch. I felt we could save him from the death penalty by arguing that fact, and that is what I intended to do. By getting him to testify against the other two, I knew I could work out a plea deal that would call for a prison term, but not a death sentence.

I was prodded constantly off my path to that end, thrown off balance. I was stubborn enough to resist at first, but eventually I opened my eyes. My understanding of Jessie and his uncomplicated mind began to cast doubt on my original assumption that he was guilty. The actions of the police and the prosecutor's office were so contrary to what I had expected in my naiveté that it snapped my head back. I was not in law school anymore. I was in the real world, and I was flunking an important course. Once the dance started as we prepared for trial—and it did very quickly after my first encounters with the West Memphis Police and Prosecutor Brent Davis— it became an awkward ballet of feints and false assurances and misdirection by our opponents, all of them.

My own dance with Jessie and his father was a separate matter, no less important. One steamy afternoon, after yet another heated and confusing meeting with Jessie and his father at the Clay County jail, I asked Jessie Sr. to stop by my office in Paragould on his way home. I wanted to know more about Jessie.

The drive back to Paragould gave me an opportunity to cool off, think, and try to solve the enigma of Jessie Misskelley. Maybe I was looking at all this with the wrong perspective, I thought as the now familiar rice fields flew past the car window. Jessie's scribbled letter to his father from jail made it clear that he could barely read and write. I needed to know more about him, and his father was the man to tell me. I had calmed down by the time I walked through the front door to my office, my anger had subsided and the lawyer in me was once again in charge.

I sat down with Greg Crow and Jessie Sr. in the library of our law offices. We started to piece together a short biography of Jessie Lloyd Misskelley, Jr.

I would learn that he had been abandoned by his biological mother at age four. I would hear his own struggles in school and of his profoundly mentally challenged brother. I quickly developed a new respect for the grizzled man sitting on the other side of the table. Jessie Sr. was a hardworking man who was doing all he could to make the best of a tough situation, one that included the growing enmity of the entire community. Jessie Jr. was the Devil's spawn and Jessie Sr. bore the brunt of it. I tried to soothe him as I struggled to find some comfort in what seemed like a hopeless situation. Later, I would see Jessie's mental health records that revealed a grade-schooler who had an I.Q. score of 68, far below what is accepted as "normal."

I would learn that Jessie Sr. had continually rebuffed pleas from school and mental health workers to allow them to help. They asked that Jessie be put in special education or resource classes, but his father had refused. Jessie simply could not function and yet he was instead passed from grade to grade, shuffled off for someone else to take care of the next school year. He had been bullied by his classmates, most likely tormented, and surely must have suffered greatly from it. He eventually dropped out of school.

Jessie Misskelley never had the best of anything: living conditions, education, support—he had never been given a decent shot at life. I was determined to change this. I became determined to get the best experts I could find to help my case, my shaky budget notwithstanding. I would start at the top and work my way down. All they could do is tell me no, right?

That was the spark that would lead me later to Ron Lax and Dr. Richard Ofshe, and then to Warren Holmes, three men who would become bright and penetrating lights in an otherwise overwhelming darkness. Before my clearer understanding of Jessie's mind, before I had ever heard of the concept of "false confessions" that would play so prominently at the trial and for many years later, I believed that Jessie Misskelley Jr. was guilty as sin.

16

By late September 1993 I knew Jessie Misskelley was innocent. It was an epiphany so clarifying and dramatic it would have impressed St. Paul himself on the road to Damascus. It was slow to arrive but electrifying when it hit. It was as if I had been buried under ten feet of distractions, blindfolded and comatose. The light that hit me kept me on a path that lasted nearly two decades.

There were several catalysts that would push me off my original intent to plea bargain and get Jessie away from Death Row and the needle. At one point early in pre-trial maneuverings, I mentioned to Greg Crow that I was surprised that Crittenden County Deputy Prosecutor John Fogleman had not yet called to discuss the terms of a plea offer. I knew he needed Jessie to testify against Damien Echols and Jason Baldwin. That was my ace in the hole. I could not figure out why he was waiting.

"Why don't you just call him," Greg asked.

"Because I want them to think they need us more than we need them."

The reality, however, was that we had no defense. We were just playing a game of cat and mouse. My solid belief in my client's guilt was further cemented when I finally did get the phone call from Fogleman in early August 1993. At last, I thought as I picked up the phone. Fogleman had a different message than the one I had expected. A DNA test on a bloody T-shirt found in Jessie's mobile home matched the blood of victim Michael Moore, Fogleman told me. My heart sank. Now they have got a slam dunk, I thought. This would make negotiating a plea an even more difficult task than it already was. They now had real corroboration of Jessie's shaky confession. Fogleman's revelation erased in my mind any trace of lingering doubt I had about Jessie's participation. *Or so I thought.*

DNA testing was still in its infancy in 1993. I immediately filed a motion for the State to provide us with our own independent DNA expert. I was not taking any chances with this news. I also made plans to speak with both Misskelleys. Fogleman's atomic bomb revelation was a game-changer, and it was time for Jessie Sr. to face the cold, hard truth that his son had participated in a gruesome triple murder. I phoned Jessie Misskelley, Sr. and informed him of the DNA match. I could tell even through the receiver that his spirit was broken. The defeated and disappointed father was in total disbelief.

"I can't believe it," he said weakly. "I have witnesses who say he was with them in Dyess when this happened."

"This DNA stuff is pretty solid evidence," I told him.

"I still can't believe it," he replied, suddenly indignant.

Jessie Sr. was not happy and still unwilling to admit that his son was a killer. When we hung up, I felt great compassion for the man and scolded myself for not being more understanding of his predicament. At the same time, it was my job to save his son's life and the facts were the facts.

Later in August, in the wake of Fogleman's phone call regarding the DNA match, Crow and I finally received the plea offer we had been expecting. The State was willing to take the death penalty off the table in exchange for Misskelley's testimony against Echols and Baldwin. Jessie would get life in prison with the possibility of parole.

On August 19, I made the drive to the Clay County Detention Center with two primary objectives. First, I had to communicate the plea offer to Jessie and get his response. Second, I had to address the bloody t-shirt.

Explaining the plea offer would be difficult enough, but how would I explain DNA to Jessie Misskelley? I decided that I would not even try. I would concentrate instead on the fact that the bloody T-shirt was found inside his home. I had learned that Jessie would agree with most anything you asked him if his father was not present. How I phrased the questions about the T-shirt would be of the utmost importance.

When I got to the jail, I spoke to Jessie for 40 minutes about a variety of topics and as was always the case, he could only answer my questions with a series of "yes" or "no" answers. I would ask him questions, and when I pushed him further, he would change his answer to something else. As always, Jessie could provide little or no narrative. He just seemed to try and guess the answer you wanted, and if he felt he got it wrong, he would try again. It was frustrating.

Next, we spoke about the plea offer. He was confused but expressed to me very clearly that he did not want to accept the offer or spend the rest of his life in prison. I agreed to see if I could get a better offer from prosecutors that would be a specific term of years as opposed to life in prison.

When I asked if he knew anything about a bloody T-shirt found by police in his trailer, Jessie answered my question without a second's hesitation. I was surprised at how quickly and confidently he had replied.

"I always—every time I get mad at my daddy for something—I always go out and hurt myself."

"Hurt yourself?"

"Bustin' bottles, and stuff. I usually hurt myself."

"Hit them with your fist or something?"

"Uh-huh."

I decided that the first real conversation that I had ever had with my client was just too intense to ruin with my usual and unrelenting cross examination of him about the murders. So, I moved on to something else. After we finished talking about the plea offer and as I was preparing to leave the jail, Jessie spontaneously told me that the blood on the T-shirt was his.

Suddenly, and quite proudly, he displayed fists and knuckles that were littered with scars. I gazed at the young man's hands. He seemed proud of the scars, like they were shrapnel wounds from a battle defending his country instead of self-inflicted and meaningless injuries. I left the jail bewildered as usual, but for a different reason this time.

The answer would come on September 27, 1993. That day, in my mind, marked the beginning of a case to save Jessie Misskelley from both himself and the State of Arkansas that so desperately wanted to kill him.

At a pretrial hearing in Marion that day, suddenly and without warning, John Fogleman walked up to me in the courtroom and announced that he had been misinformed about the DNA match. "The blood on the T-shirt did not belong to Michael Moore after all," he said. Without preamble or an apology, he said the blood on the T-shirt was Jessie's. His tone and demeanor were the same as if he had been arguing with me over a parking ticket. Then he calmly walked away, as if the whole matter was inconsequential.

Those words from Fogleman, coming on the heels of hearing Jessie finally producing a competent narrative about hitting those bottles and wiping his hands on his shirt were electrifying and empowering. The jolt was tremendous. Everything suddenly became clear to me.

I realized that my frustration about Jessie Misskelley's inability to tell the story of how the murders had taken place had a simple yet profound explanation. Jessie Misskelley did not know anything about the murders other than what he had been told by the police.

Jessie Misskelley was innocent.

He had not been anywhere near Robin Hood Hills that day, or night. He certainly had not been with Damien Echols or Jason Baldwin, wherever they were that day and evening. Jessie's father had been right all along, and according to him there were witnesses who could prove that. It now would be a simple matter of interviewing these witnesses and finding the right experts to prove that Jessie was innocent.

When we interviewed those alibi witnesses, we discovered another horror had emerged from Jessie Misskelley, Sr.'s nightly news conferences. He had spouted the names of the alibi witnesses, which the news crews duly recorded and broadcast. Police were then dispatched to interview most of these witnesses, who each in turn denied that they were with Jessie Misskelley on May 5th out of fear of being dragged into the case themselves. Who could blame them? By the time that they were ultimately willing to tell the truth, their prior inconsistent statements had severely crippled our alibi defense.

17

Before Christmas 1993, the jailers had begun a peculiar ritual. As Greg and I arrived to meet with Jessie, the jailer would slide the key along the floor to Jessie's cell down at the end of the long hallway. The huge key bounced and slapped the walls on either side like a hockey puck until it slid under the cell door and disappeared. Seconds later Jessie's arm would emerge through the food slot in the massive cell door, and he would carefully insert the key into the lock and let himself out. Then Jessie would emerge from his cell wearing the giant teddy bear slippers his family had purchased for him as a Christmas gift. Hardly the grim and menacing image of a Satanic killer.

On one of those visits before Christmas, the Sheriff of Clay County, Darvin Stow, stopped me as I was leaving the jail and he said to me something I will never forget.

"Dan, I don't think your boy is guilty. He wouldn't hurt a fly."

"That's because he is not guilty," I told him.

Jessie Misskelley had become the official mascot of the Clay County Detention Center. I was hoping that the jury would share the Sheriff's sentiments about "Little Jessie" at trial.

Not long after that conversation with the Sheriff, I again went to visit Jessie Misskelley as part of my continued preparation for the trial. As soon as I went into his cell, he told me that a preacher had come to visit him that morning and gave him a book. He handed me a small pamphlet. On the cover was a picture of the Devil in caricature, complete with horns, hooves, and a forked tail. It sat under a boldface heading that asked, "Do you know Satan?"

"Dan, who's Satin?" Jessie asked, pronouncing it as the fabric, not as Lucifer.

Here was this kid accused of being a Satanic Child Killer, yet he had no idea of the concept of Satan, nor of his own dire predicament. The irony was not lost on me.

By the time Jessie finally told me that he was not there when the little boys were killed, he also told me that he thought Greg and I were cops and that is why he tried to parrot to us what he had told Gary Gitchell and Bryn Ridge. Jessie did not understand the concept of a lawyer or that we were on his side.

After his wrongful conviction on February 4, 1994, Jessie would still not understand what had happened to him. He could not draw any conclusion about what he had done to bring the entire thing about. All he knew, and all he could say tearfully to his father afterward, was that he did not want to spend the rest of his life in jail.

My epiphany of September 27 had opened the door, leaving enough of a gap to let in a little light on what I had thought was a hopeless case for my hopeless client. Ron Lax would push it wide open, and Warren Holmes and Dr. Richard Ofhse would knock it down, leaving no doubt, in my mind at least, that I would win the trial and could get Jessie Misskelley acquitted of the charges manufactured so cleanly and cynically by the West Memphis police and tied up so viciously by the prosecutors and Judge Burnett. Again, I had lost a battle, but not the war. My promise to Jessie that I would get him out of prison started a long chess match that took until August 2011 to reach checkmate.

18

On a gusty April afternoon in Baltimore in 2014, a young high school student who had not yet been born when those young boys were murdered in 1993 asked me an earnest question that jolted me from the place, I had been hiding for over twenty years.

"How has this case really affected you?"

I smiled wanly, taken aback. "A great deal," I told her, but I did not go into details, preferring instead to deflect the question. I was not quite ready to reveal the psychological scars I had accumulated during those decades to a group of inquisitive 16-year-olds.

The kids, along with their teacher, Joel Brusewitz, had invited me to their juvenile justice class to hear about my role in the case that had become universally known as The West Memphis 3 Case. The students at Catonsville High School were using the case as part of their curriculum. Their zeal for it and all its facts and circumstances were as acute as my own. Their questions about what had happened were probing and insightful.

By then Damien, Jessie and Jason had accepted the Alford Plea and were free from prison, though not necessarily from life. They were out of jail but not cleared, in a limbo they still live with today. I could have spoken for hours about the case, yet that single question had rendered me mute. Avoiding any deeper analysis about what the case had done to me was the easier path.

On the way home, that student's question hung heavily on the plane as I settled into my window seat next to my fiancé, Lea Ann Vanaman. By the time we hit cruising altitude the creeping anxiety that I had tried to keep at bay for so long hit me hard. Indeed. *What exactly had this case done to me?*

I had over the years since the trials developed chronic insomnia. When I did sleep, I would be visited by nightmarish visions of those three dead boys. In that realm between sleep and consciousness, the young boys would stand at the foot of my bed beckoning me, but to where? My health danced precariously on the edge, tension and stress threatening to do me in. I had gained far too much weight, teetering very close to becoming diabetic.

My marriage broke slowly apart after the trial in 1994 and then finally splintered in 2008. My kids, who I loved more than anything, wondered what had happened to their father. I was, on too many nights, a dazed man going through the paces, exhausted from trying to free Jessie and keep up my law practice. Escape became a survival mechanism—simply withdrawing whenever I had a chance and not engaging in anything with anyone. It was not a healthy habit, but I got by. Of course, getting by is not the way one should go through life.

On the flight back to Memphis that April in 2014, I wrestled with the question asked of me by that student in Baltimore. I could not deny it. Those murders and that case had altered my life forever and on more than one occasion had nearly caused me to self-destruct. How could I explain this to a group of enthusiastic high school students, and how do I encourage them to get involved—to speak truth to power, to stand up for what is right? The true measure of my pain was unlikely to encourage them, so I said nothing. There was turbulence on that flight back to Memphis from Baltimore and it had nothing to do with atmospheric conditions.

But as I sat there, I was heartened by several other things. Next to me was a woman I loved deeply who had stood by me and abided my distractions and encouraged me to keep fighting. Lea Ann knew my demons and loved me back, nonetheless. I still had things to do. I wanted the killer, badly. I wanted his confession, and some corroboration, because that was the only thing that would clear Jessie, Jason and Damien from the Alford plea that still adhered to them like so much old and caked-on rust. I also wanted the redemption that had been stripped from me by the Alford plea. I reminded myself that if it were not for those struggles, I would not have found my strengths.

It was much warmer and humid when Lea Ann and I stepped off the plane in Memphis from Baltimore. As we took the shuttlebus to our SUV, I asked if we could take a little detour before we headed back to Paragould. I wanted to see the crime scene again in West Memphis—the place where it had started. I had not been there in many years.

I had first visited that hellish place just a few days after Christmas 1993. I had not visited sooner because I wanted to make sure that all the leaves were gone from the trees so I could get a feel for the scene and how it sat in relation to the Blue Beacon, and the large and always busy truck stop next door. I wanted to get a sense of how close the interstate was to the exact place where the bodies were found.

I walked around the crime scene in what seemed to me to be a surreal juxtaposition with reality. We were close enough to the interstate that I could have thrown a baseball to the service road and with a little luck might be able to bounce it into the outside lane of the interstate. What really caught my attention in December 1993 was the vast parking lot of the truck stop that backed up to the crime scene from the west.

It would have been easy for anyone to dispose of the bodies from there. My survey of the crime scene that day was captured in perpetuity by Berlinger and Sinofsky's cameras. In *Paradise Lost* you can see a kid lawyer looking beleaguered with Metallica's song *Sanitarium* playing in the background. That song, and that scene in the film are still difficult for me to hear and see even now.

In December of 1993, when I left the crime scene, I drove over to the office of the *West Memphis Evening Times*. I had been told that the local paper had run a story before the arrests about the FBI assisting the West Memphis Police with a profile of the suspected killer or killers. It did not take long to find it in their archives. The story had appeared in the May 10, 1993, edition of the *Times*— five days after the murders— with a headline at the top of the front page that read: PROBE CONTINUES INTO MURDERS; FBI LENDS A HAND ON SUSPECT PROFILE.

The story reported that the West Memphis Police were starting to get information from the FBI relating to a possible profile of a possible suspect or suspects. Inspector Gary Gitchell was quoted as saying that "the behavioral sciences division of the FBI faxed us some information this morning that may help the investigative team develop suspects."

The article went on to state that the "profile" was based on evidence that had been collected by the West Memphis Police Department and quoted Gitchell saying that the evidence had been "compared to information from similar cases across the country." Gitchell also told the reporter that the community was still on high alert and that people should be wary and keep their children close to home.

"I'm scared," he said in that article. "People should be concerned."

A few days after I read that piece, I would meet face to face with Inspector Gitchell and ask for a copy of the FBI profile that Quantico had sent. Surprisingly, he said it did not exist. I gave him a copy of the article in which he mentioned it. He denied it again and said the newspaper simply had gotten the story wrong. "Fake news," it would be called today.

Interestingly, and too late to help, just weeks after Jessie Misskelley's trial in 1994, I finally got my hands on a copy of the fax that Gitchell had received from the FBI. It was what the West Memphis Police Department had used in their neighborhood canvas.

Questions 10 and 11 are a glimpse of the first criminal profile in the case. I have always called it the "Rambo" profile.

QUESTIONS TO ASK PERSONS

1. ASK: NAME, ADDRESS, PLACE OF EMPLOYMENT, TELEPHONE NUMBERS FOR HOME & WORK.
2. ASK: HOW LONG THE HAVE LIVED THERE.
3. ASK: WHO ALL LIVES IN THEIR HOME AND WHAT THEIR RELATIONSHIP IS AND WHERE THEY WORK.
4. ASK: HOW MANY KIDS THEY HAVE, WHERE THEY ATTEND SCHOOL, AND NAMES AND ADDRESSES OF THEIR FRIENDS.
5. ASK: THE TYPE OF VEHICLES THEY OWN AND GET COMPLETE DESCRIPTION: COLOR, YEAR, MAKE, MODEL, TAG NUMBERS.
6. ASK: NAME AND ADDRESS OF ANY VISITORS THEY HAVE HAD BEFORE, DURING OR AFTER THIS INCIDENT.
7. ASK: ABOUT ANYONE NORMALLY SEEN IN THE AREA THAT HASN'T BEEN SEEN SINCE THE INCIDENT.
8. ASK: ABOUT ANYONE THAT LIVES IN THE AREA THAT APPEARS STRANGE OR HAS BEEN ACTING STRANGE.
9. ASK: WERE THEY AT HOME ON WEDNESDAY EVENING.
10. ASK: IF THEY OR ANYONE THEY KNOW IN THE AREA IS A *VIETNAM VETERAN*.
11. ASK: IF ANYONE IN THE AREA WEARS A UNIFORM, ANY KIND OF UNIFORM.

MAKE SURE THAT ALL THIS INFORMATION IS WRITTEN DOWN!!

. . .

A Harvest of Innocence

THE FBI THRESHOLD PROFILE—THE CRAZED VIETNAM VETERAN—USED by the West Memphis Police did not fit the three throwaway kids—Misskelley, Echols and Baldwin. This would also explain why Gitchell would be less than honest about the fax. He did not want me to point this out during the Misskelley trial.

As I was standing there that day in April 2014, at what was once the crime scene, with that young girl's haunting question still dancing in my head, the chaos of those early days came crashing back to me. I recalled my Sisyphean task back in 1993. That the more I pushed, the larger the boulder grew. Then I recalled what Judge Olan Parker had said in 1993 about Judge Burnett and how we would never get that "red-headed judge" to let go of the case. It is no coincidence that when Judge Burnett finally became Senator Burnett and was then compelled to finally let go of it, the West Memphis 3 would have the stage set to be released from prison within just a matter of months.

By that April day in 2014, the physical place had changed. After twenty-one years, what had been a scene of great and wrenching horror was barely noticeable or recognizable. The small, wooded patch next to the third busiest interstate highway exchange in the nation had been gone for years. So was the narrow creek that had meandered through it. With the trees gone and the creek replaced with culverts, the only real sign of the evil that lurked there is the old concrete driveway that once served the old Blue Beacon Truck Wash, the building itself long gone as well. Just west of the crime scene now stands a couple of typical interstate motels, lacking personality and offering nothing but bland efficiency. As I glanced at the motels, I could not help but wonder if the guests there that April day on their way to somewhere else knew of the horrors that once terrorized and tortured the peaceful place just outside their windows.

Of course, West Memphis wanted to forget those dark days that began on May 5, 1993, when fear and panic ruled the day. Perhaps it was no accident that the crime scene had been bulldozed and the old businesses hopelessly associated with the terror had been replaced with new ones that were free from the horrible grime.

I have never considered this to be the location where the boys were killed. It was merely a dump site. It seemed to me that if the killer were familiar with the geography of the area, he would have chosen to dispose of the boys' bodies a few miles east in the Mississippi River. If he had dumped the boys in the river, they might never have been recovered at all. This was a clue to what I now think happened on May 5, 1993.

Why I stopped there for the first time in so many years, I am uncertain. In the many years that I have been compelled to drive through West Memphis on my way to or back from somewhere else, I have never been able to shutter my mind from the evil that had besieged it, or even remove my gaze from it as I drove by. But I never stopped at that signature spot.

Lost in my own thoughts at the scene that April day, I was startled by the sound of a car's horn. It was my own GMC, and inside was Lea Ann, perhaps the one person who knew where a lot of my scars were hidden. She was giving me that little mischievous smile of hers as she rolled down the window and pleaded with me to get us home before an approaching storm hit. I climbed in behind the wheel and told her that I had to make one more stop.

"Why are you doing this to yourself?" she asked.

"It's okay," I assured her. "I just need a minute."

As I drove down Highway 77 from West Memphis to Marion, the county seat and home to the Crittenden County Courthouse, she busied herself with her iPhones and laptop. I stopped and got out, walking up to the courthouse. Built in 1910, it stood in an old oak grove. I walked slowly to its most prominent feature, the huge pillars that adorned the front entrance. I found it oddly unchanged from the way it appeared twenty-one years earlier—with one exception. There were no yelling mobs seeking blood and vengeance for the infamous crimes of May 5, 1993. The Arkansas Witch Trials had begun here. I looked up as the skies darkened from black to green. It began to rain. I anticipated the second honk from the car just before I heard it, and Lea Ann yelled "Come on let's go home."

As I turned to walk back to the SUV, I glanced up at the large inscription just above the big pillars that read "Obedience to the Law is Liberty." I wondered how things might have been different if those managing the case—the police, the prosecution, the trial judge, and the appellate courts had simply adhered to this simple creed. It was time to go home.

19

If I were inclined to commemorate each September 27th to honor my epiphany that Jessie Misskelley was innocent, I would light a candle to Ron Lax, whom I met for the first time that day in 1993. The news that he had died in Memphis in 2013 hit me hard. I had known it was coming but I was not prepared for the finality. I felt as if I had lost an older brother. I kept thinking he would somehow shake off the brain tumor that was slowly killing him, that he'd beat it and be back at work the next day. He was that sort of guy. He handled his final struggle like everything else he did, with dignity and without fanfare. Ron's contagious confidence and his unfettered way of going after what he wanted had been a source of strength for me for years. Without Ron Lax, we would not have found our key witnesses at the trial, but that was just the beginning. I miss my good friend a great deal. As hard as his death was to accept, I knew he had at least lived to see Jessie Misskelley, Jason Baldwin, and Damien Echols walk out of prison. Ron Lax, a vocal opponent of the death penalty, provided me years of invaluable service and never charged a cent. Introducing me to the work of Dr. Richard Ofshe was just the first step. Ron played a key role in getting those young men freed. Ron Lax never gave up and this made us kindred spirits. My only regret is that we did not get the killer before Ron passed.

It was Ron who first pursued and then clandestinely obtained the DNA of Terry Hobbs, the stepfather of Stevie Branch. Ron Lax had been the one who had told Terry Hobbs in 2007 there was a DNA match on a hair found at the crime scene. Long before that, another stepfather, John Mark Byers, had been skulking in the background of suspects.

Ron Lax came into my life on September 27, 1993, like he stepped from the pages of a Raymond Chandler novel. For all his toughness, Ron Lax was a sensitive man with a deep intellect. Ron had approached me at the preliminary hearing in Marion while I was still reeling from John Fogleman's announcement that the blood on Jessie's T-shirt was Jessie's, not Michael Moore's. Ron slipped me a business card embossed with Inquisitor Inc., his Memphis private investigator's office. He invited Greg Crow and me to lunch after the hearing to discuss the case.

I had gone into that hearing still basking in an appellate victory that Crow and I had just achieved against none other than Judge David Burnett—a 7-0 reversal, and dismissal, on another criminal case before the Arkansas Supreme Court. That victory had given me hope that the system worked, and that if Burnett were again inclined to disregard the law, the Arkansas Supreme Court would not. I cannot tell you how much this reversal and dismissal of Burnett's ruling in that earlier bench trial boosted my confidence heading into the Misskelley trial. Fogleman's revelation had amped it up even more. Lunch with Ron Lax would burst things wide open, and by the end of that day, I was a confident young lawyer with a different mission than the one I had when the sun came up.

After Fogleman dropped his bombshell about the DNA, I went immediately to Greg Crow, who was sitting at the counsel table with Jessie. In the noisy courtroom, I leaned in and whispered Fogleman's revelation into Crow's ear. His face lit up. "Damn," he said. "The kid was telling the truth." We nodded at each other as the bailiff entered and announced that the Honorable Judge David Burnett was entering the crowded courtroom. I handed Lax's card to Greg.

During the first recess, I went over to Fogleman and told him that with his news, I would not need to present my motion for the assistance of a DNA expert, since the point was now moot. "That's right," he said, "no need." I was both relieved and haunted by the implications that this remark would have. Ron Lax was about to add yet another pleasant surprise to a day full of them.

During those early pretrial days, I had been taking halting half breaths, fearing I was in over my head, feeling I was dealing with a case that had nothing but a bad ending waiting. There were already signs I was about to get more grief than I had bargained for. By that day in Marion, I had already seen enough to know that my client's life was in danger—that people who were fighting the Devil would have no qualms about killing him, or me for that matter— in the name of righteousness. Worse, I was afraid they might hurt my family— Satanic Panic was in full bloom by then. Ron Lax and the efforts he brought with him—to say nothing of the generosity—allowed me to start breathing deeply again and to start planning my defense. He had an uncanny sensitivity for sniffing out cases that to him seemed too far afield from normal police practice to make sense.

The convenience of Jessie Misskelley's confession and the arrest of the three young men so upset the hard-boiled Lax that he took an immediate personal interest in helping me. Unlike several other experts I would seek out later to no avail, Lax did not want money. He had plenty of money, and his interest in the case was based on truth and justice—not on fattening his bank account. Lax's innate curiosity had led him to Dr. Richard Ofshe, a sociology professor at the University of California at Berkeley whose groundbreaking work in the field of "false confessions" had among other things elevated him to becoming a sought-after expert witness and to a Pulitzer Prize. Lax had read about Ofshe's work—and news of the West Memphis murders and the arrests of Jessie Misskelley, Damien Echols, and Jason Baldwin prompted him to come to Marion and invite me to lunch.

Ron Lax was really one of the unsung heroes of the case who sought no attention but drew it anyway. He had offices in both Memphis and Nashville and primarily did investigations for insurance companies looking for ways to deny tort claims. He made a lot of money doing it. He started doing death penalty work in Tennessee for the public defender's office, specializing in mitigating death sentences. His introduction to me of Ofshe's pioneering work, I thought, might just level the playing field, and give us a shot at winning at trial. Looking back, I realize that all it did was take the death penalty off the table, but I was unaware of that at the time.

After the Marion hearing, we found Ron Lax waiting for us outside the courtroom. He was standing next to one of the most attractive women I had ever seen. Ron made the introductions, and we descended the winding staircase of the old courthouse together and outside into the parking lot. Lax suggested that we follow him and his brand-new BMW to a restaurant back in West Memphis. I retrieved my minivan, and we did just that. During lunch, Ron quickly proved he was a friendly and likable guy, but also very professional—all business. After we finished eating, he pushed a *New Yorker* magazine across the table to me. In the magazine, he told me, was an article about Dr. Richard Ofshe. "I think Jessie Misskelley's confession is false," Lax said. "There are too many inconsistencies and things that he just got dead wrong." "We've had the same concerns," I told him.

Then Lax told me that Ofshe had shared in a Pulitzer Prize for his work on a religious cult in California. He said if we could somehow get Ofshe to assist us, we would be getting two experts for the price of one. Lax was also assisting the Echols defense team. "We're in this mess together, and we should work together to see that the right thing happens," Lax said. "I agree," I told him. "And we could use all the help we can get."

I still wanted to proceed cautiously. I did not know Ron Lax from Adam. Picking up the check for lunch, Ron told me to call him any time I needed anything. We walked back out to the parking lot and he and his assistant, Cheryl, climbed back into his BMW. I walked over to his window. He rolled it down. "Why are you doing this," I asked. "Why are you helping us out for free, you know I can't pay you?"

"It's not about money. I don't believe in the death penalty, and I think these kids are innocent."

I thanked him for both the lunch and the tip on Ofshe. Ron Lax was a godsend. He would soon become our eyes and ears on the ground in West Memphis, all *pro bono*.

20

The drive back to Paragould was not nearly long enough, so after I dropped off Crow at the office, I just kept driving. Going nowhere in particular, I wanted some time to myself. I pulled the minivan over and read the *New Yorker* article. Dr. Richard Ofshe was a groundbreaker in his field. The wheels in my mind were spinning. I drove on. Methodically, I tried to wrap my mind around all the facts that I knew at that point. My client had confessed to watching three murders take place and described a satanic ritual to the police. Other than his statements, and because the bloody T-shirt was now off the table, there was no physical evidence to connect him to the crime.

My mind was still wandering, and I soon found myself standing on the banks of the Black River with my hands jabbed deep into my coat pockets. The scent of the water and the sounds of the river flooded my senses and calmed my thinking. River-bank trees stood guard around the waters' edge acting as sentinels for my solitude. I was alone and that comforted me.

The river had always been a place of solace for me. I duck-hunted here with my father and sons, and that special place had always been a welcome escape from everyday life. Many cultures believe that a river can speak to a persons' soul, and so do I. The answers to many of life's most important questions had revealed themselves to me as I stood silently on this riverbank. Crouching down on my knees to a squatting position I focused on the waters slow passage. A few early fall leaves were floating in the current.

Ron Lax and Jessie's bloody t-shirt floated by, as well. Ron seemed absolutely convinced that Jessie's confession was false. The *New Yorker* article talked of suspects telling the police what they wanted to hear just to get them off their backs. This would explain the "yes and no" answers, the inconsistencies and impossibilities and the lack of narrative in Jessie's confession. I had to admit to myself that up until now nothing else could even come close to explaining the questions that had been nagging me regarding my client.

Still staring into the river my mind began to process this new possibility. With my own background in sociology and psychology, what Dr. Ofshe said in that article made sense. Then I thought about Big Jessie and his insistence that I interview those alibi witnesses. We had just lost 116 days of valuable preparation time, and for all intents and purposes we would be starting all over again with a completely new focus.

I picked up a flat rock. Bolting up from my crouched position, I skipped the rock across the surface of the river. The rock landed firmly in the dark mud on the opposite side. So did my mind. The kid was innocent and there was no turning back.

I began cataloging the tasks I needed to complete if the scenario was going to be a feasible defense. First, I had to learn everything I could about Dr. Richard Ofshe and the science of false confessions. Next, I needed to speak with each of the potential alibi witnesses. Having an expert evaluate Jessie's mental capabilities became a top priority as well, and that process would begin the next day, September 28.

Turning back to the minivan, I took one last glance back to the rolling river. A wood duck screamed in the distance. I felt the desire to pay homage to God's amazing creation that had, once again, given me the answers I was seeking. I jumped back in the van and headed back east to Paragould. I wanted to get home and see my kids. The next day would again be the start of some exceptionally long days with little time at home. But that was tomorrow.

My former wife Kim's journals still reveal the look on my face that evening when I got home and told her the news. According to her journal, she, the kids, and I ate dinner, and then I helped her get the kids bathed and in bed. Everything seemed remarkably normal except the look on my face. She described it as "dazed."

"Kim, Jessie Misskelley is innocent. He did not do it. I don't think any of them did."

The words took her breath away and she sunk into a chair beside me. "Explain this," she said. The kids were in bed, and I began talking. I poured months of unanswered questions and the strong lack of evidence against the accused on her that evening. This was strangely therapeutic for me. Kim's expression could not hide her surprise.

"You really think that they are innocent?"

"I do."

"But he confessed, why on earth would he do that if they're innocent?"

"That's the last piece of the puzzle."

She stared at me, dumbfounded as I explained the inconsistencies and impossibilities of Jessie's statements to police, his immediate recantation, the lack of DNA evidence, and Jessie's explanation of the soda bottles. I told her about Ron Lax and Dr. Richard Ofshe and the theory of false confessions and all I had been considering since the epiphany earlier in the day. When I finished laying out my case before her, I slumped back into my recliner, exhausted. "Well," came Kim's cautious response. "You'd better get some rest then."

After September 27, I did little else except prepare the chessboard for the epic battle to come. Greg Crow and I had taken Christmas Day off to spend time with our families, but I have no memory of it. According to my billing records, I spent 3.25 hours doing research at the office on Christmas Eve, and I spoke to Jessie Misskelley Sr. on Christmas Day. I know that there had been a Thanksgiving and a Christmas that year. The family pictures show that I was there physically, but they also reflect a young lawyer in over his head. The vacant stare that I have in those pictures is hard to look at now.

My epiphany changed things forever and changed them in a way that as I sit here now over thirty years later and recall that day, I am filled with a mixture of both regret and immense pride. Pride in the fact that I never gave up on my client, and regret at the naiveté of my thirty-year-old self. Very few lawyers have ever had the opportunity to literally view their past selves in action. I have. I have because much of what I went through, during the trial, my first jury trial, and years of appeals afterward were caught and preserved on tape in the film *Paradise Lost*.

Now there are times when I wish I could step back into those 1993 and 1994 moments and shake my thirty-year-old self, tell myself to take a good deep look at what was really going on. But of course, I cannot. Look back at your past, they say, learn from it. Just do not stare at it. If you do, you might very well never return.

The State of Arkansas had adopted its regime of truth for the case, and they would stop at nothing to defend their version of this "truth." It did not seem to matter much that the facts surrounding the crime and the confession itself did not match the physical evidence and the real facts of the case. Hysteria and panic will do that to you if you let it. History reveals that this has happened many times before. All it takes is the occurrence of something so evil and so monstrous that it cannot be explained in rational terms. What cannot be explained in logical terms is then often met with religious and dogmatic scrutiny.

That is exactly how Inspector Gary Gitchell put it to Jessie Misskelley on June 3, 1993, when he drew a crude diagram on a piece of copy paper depicting a small circle in the middle with three "dots." The dots, he explained to Misskelley, represented Damien Echols, Jason Baldwin, and Jessie himself. Gitchell then drew many dots outside the circle and told Misskelley that these dots represented the police and the people of West Memphis. The inference was clear even for a mentally challenged kid like Jessie Misskelley: You do not want to be in the circle of "evil," or part of a murderous Satanic Cult.

For Jessie, the only way out of a horrific situation where the truth was not going to help end his nightmare was to tell the police what they wanted to hear.

At the end of the interrogation, Inspector Gitchell asked Jessie if he would be willing to go out to the crime scene and show them where all the events, he spoke of in his confession had occurred. This is standard police procedure. Jessie's response to this simple request was, "I guess I don't have a problem with that." Apparently, the police had a problem with it because they never took Misskelley out to the crime scene. Why would they not follow standard police procedure?

It must have felt good for them to know that they had just defeated and broken the will of an intellectually challenged teenager with no parent or advocate present—even though Arkansas law at the time required that a parent sign the Miranda waiver form. Did they know Jessie was intellectually challenged? They had to know, otherwise they would not have had to ask Misskelley during the interrogation if he knew how to tell time, or even more astonishing, if he knew what a "penis" was.

21

Today, I hate the long hot Arkansas summers. For me, they begin on May 5th, that horrible anniversary of the deaths of those three boys, when rain-filled ditches start the inevitable flashbacks and the nightmares all over again. The trigger is usually a mud-filled ditch, and even the creek in my own backyard is not immune to reviving those horrible images of those dead eight-year-olds flickering in my mind like an old movie. I accept that those uninvited horrors are now part of my life. The nightmares of those three kids standing at the foot of my bed are far less frequent. They keep me on edge, which is good. It boosts my energy and reminds me there is still a killer lurking out there, a killer who I will search for until I am dead.

Ron Lax had obtained for me Dr. Richard Ofshe's telephone number in California. By the first week of October 1993, I knew it was time to reach out to Ofshe. I needed to convince him to help when I had no money to pay him. That night, still at work, drained and needing a break, I peered at the clock on my office desk, 3:30 a.m. I laid my head down on the blotter for a quick break. What seemed like just a few minutes later a tap on my shoulder snapped my head up.

"Have you been here all night?" Vicky asked.

"Um, yes," I mumbled, trying to pull myself together. "I hope you aren't working too hard," she said.

I started rubbing my eyes. Straightening my shirt, I was already looking toward the phone.

"I've got to make a phone call," I said. "What time is it in California right now?"

"About 6:30 a.m."

"Well, I've got time for a shower and some breakfast first. I will see you in a couple hours."

"Okay," said Vicky. "Get some rest."

When I got home, I realized I had not called Kim to tell her I was working late. Her look when I walked in was not pleasant, but she said nothing. I grabbed a shower and put on fresh clothes. The house was empty by the time I emerged from the bedroom. I hit McDonalds on the way back to the office and bought Egg McMuffins and some coffee for everyone at the office. I went directly into Greg's office. On the way in, I asked Vicky to join us. I briefed them both on my research on false confessions and Ofshe. They agreed it was a spark of hope.

By then the sun had been up in California for hours. I dialed Ofshe's number and gave myself odds of him even talking to me. Slim, I thought, 100 to 1. Dr. Ofshe picked up, his voice quite soothing. I made my pitch. He was cordial and asked me to do two things. First, I was to FedEx him a complete copy of the transcript of Jessie's confession along with the police officers' notes from the interrogation, which were sparse. Then he told me, to buy and read a book by Dr. Gisli Gudjohnson, to which he had contributed. It was the first scholarly work completely devoted to the concept of interrogations and false confessions; he told me.

"I don't have any money to pay you," I explained.

"That's okay. We'll worry about that later," he replied.

"Thank you so much."

I immediately handed the confession and officers' notes to Vicky to copy and send to Dr. Ofshe. I waited almost a week for Dr. Gudjonsson book, and when it arrived, I immersed myself in everything it had to offer about false confessions. Suddenly, the concept of a false confession was not that opaque. In fact, it made perfect sense. The theory was not some abstract notion, but empirically and scientifically proved. It was good stuff.

A few days later Dr. Ofshe called my office. "Well, what do you think?" I asked. I will never forget his reply. "That's the stupidest fucking confession I've ever read," he told me. "I want in on this case. I will consult for you for free and I'm coming out to Arkansas to visit with Jessie Misskelley myself."

I held the phone in my hand in silence. I was skeptical that a man with such prominence would do all of this for us pro bono. "We don't have any money to pay you," I reminded him. "Doesn't matter," he said, "What is being done to this kid is wrong and I want to help."

The money did not matter, he said, because working on the case would be research. If the Court reimbursed him for his time and expenses, then that would be fine. I suddenly did not feel all alone in defending my client, and it was an incredibly good feeling. Dr. Richard Ofshe was one of three or four people on the entire planet who understood the dynamics of a false confession, and he was now on our team. In the end, Dr. Ofshe would fly in and out of Memphis and come to Arkansas three times. I eagerly awaited his first visit. I would wait patiently for six weeks.

On December 15, 1993, Dr. Richard Ofshe flew to Arkansas to debrief Jessie Misskelley. He rented a car at Memphis International Airport, and drove nearly 100 miles to Paragould, where we met at my office on North Second Street. After becoming acquainted, we set out for the Clay County Detention Center. I have no real memory of our conversation on the way up to Piggott, but I will never forget the conversation on the way back. Ofshe met with Jessie Misskelley for close to two hours. By design, I was not a part of the conversation. It goes without saying that this was a long and quite anxious wait for me. When Ofshe finished his interview, we got back in the car to drive back to my office in Paragould. Ofshe was incredibly quiet and contemplative, not saying a word. Finally, I could not stand the suspense any longer. I stopped the car.

"Well, what do you think?"

"Dan, your client is innocent."

Naturally, this was the news I had hoped to hear. This would sit at the center of our defense. Ofshe suggested that I retain an expert to look over Jessie's polygraph charts.

"What if I don't like what he has to say?" I asked.

"Dan, don't worry, your client is innocent," was his reply.

He was right and I began my search for a polygraph expert immediately.

22

I found out about Warren Holmes while reading a Florida case where a judge had the courage to suppress a confession. The polygraph expert in that case was a man named Warren Holmes. When I read about his credentials, I knew that this was the guy I wanted to review Jessie's polygraph charts.

I was only one for three in trying to acquire the best experts in their field. I had called Park Dietz, a renowned forensic psychologist who had worked on the John Hinckley case and his attempted assassination of President Ronald Reagan in 1983. He also worked on the Jeffrey Dahmer case. Reputable and well-known for his expertise, Dietz was at the top of his profession and would have been among the best to evaluate Jessie Misskelley. To my dismay, Dr. Dietz would not even speak to me on the phone unless I paid a consultation fee of $15,000. I told his secretary that we could petition the court after the trial to get the doctor's fee paid, but this did not change the outcome. I did not even have fifteen hundred dollars, so the search for a forensic psychologist continued. I put the odds of convincing Warren Holmes at 15,000 to one.

I called Mr. Holmes in December 1993, not long after Dr. Richard Ofshe returned to Berkeley. The gruff and close to inscrutable

Warren Holmes came across as completely disinterested and, frankly, almost rude. But I was as persistent and charming as I could be. Warren Holmes was a much sought after and highly respected polygraph expert, a literally world-class discerner of the complicated tests and reading them. Holmes was the most qualified expert in the world in the field of polygraphs. He was a retired Miami homicide detective and had administered polygraphs in the investigations of the JFK and Martin Luther King Jr. assassinations, and the Watergate scandal. Holmes had also consulted and taught polygraph methods to the FBI, CIA, and the Royal Canadian Mounted Police.

When he answered my call so gruffly, my worst fears rose to the top: another high-priced expert who would do nothing until he saw a check in his hand. Holmes seemed to have little interest in getting involved in an Arkansas murder case. I told him, "My client is innocent, just 17 years old and facing the death penalty. Could you please just look at the charts and the confession?"

He did not say yes, but he did not say no either. He finally agreed, quite reluctantly it seemed, to just take a look without making any commitment to consult on the case. I sent the WMPD polygrapher's charts and notes, and the confession to him via Fed Ex.

Two days later, Holmes called back, and his entire demeanor had changed. Holmes suddenly seemed eager to help. First, Holmes explained that the WMPD polygrapher did not ask proper "control" questions for the exam. Second, Holmes said that

Misskelley had passed all the questions about the murders showing no signs of deception. The one question that he showed signs of deception on concerned his past drug use. Then Holmes asked me if the police detectives had ever taken Misskelley to the scene of the crime to ask him where all the events described in the confession occurred. I told him that they had not. "If they had," Holmes said, "even they would have known he didn't know anything about these murders. Any good detective knows to do this. I will consult on this case."

Then, as I had told Ofshe, I explained to Holmes that I had no money to pay him, and we would have to ask the court for funds after the trial.

"I don't care, this kid is innocent," he said.

And just like that, I was batting .500. I had two of the finest experts in their fields lined up to assist me in defending Jessie Misskelley. At that point I thought I had assembled a formidable army. I had thought I could demonstrate to a jury that Jessie's confession was coerced by police and littered with key errors. I genuinely thought that I could win this thing. Of course, I was wrong. I underestimated Burnett's ability to manipulate the outcome.

23

As the trial date loomed closer, we continued to file motions and briefs. The three young defendants continued to make court appearances, though in most everyone's mind the trial was a foregone conclusion. Some folks did not even think that a trial was needed at all. Stepping far outside the constant news coverage that painted the defendants as everyone imagined, one Arkansas newspaper reporter wrote a bravely sympathetic account:

"These three kids didn't look as though they would hurt anybody. One of them looks like a scared rabbit [Baldwin]. Another [Misskelley] looks at nothing and nobody—he just keeps his chin in his hands and stares at the table. The third [Echols] has dark, hollow eyes and often seems oddly disconnected from the attorneys surrounding him. Beneath his thick dark hair, slicked back to reveal a widow's peak, is a soft doughy frame. But the most striking thing about them, the characteristic they all share, is their white skin. I don't mean race, but—literally—their color. Youngsters their age in this season should be bronzed by baseball and summer jobs. These three missed last summer's sun entirely because they have been locked behind bars since spring."

In 1993, Arkansas had just passed a new a law making it impossible to execute an inmate who had been deemed "mentally retarded" by the court, a term now seen as pejorative, but 29 years ago that was the exact language of the statute.

The statute barred the execution of defendants with an I.Q. of 65 or lower. While the law created a presumption of "mental retardation" at 65 it left open the possibility of introducing additional evidence to the court that tended to show someone with an I.Q. score above 65 could still be placed in the realm of "mental retardation."

I intended to demonstrate that Jessie's childhood score of 68, his recent score of 72 and the totality of the circumstances he had experienced in life put him squarely in this realm despite his I.Q. scores. Judge Burnett seemed put off that we would even ask for a hearing on the issue.

We were hoping for the best, but as always with Judge Burnett, expecting the worst. Four days before Christmas, 1993, there was not much quibbling to be had at the hearing. Judge Burnett—using his latitude and discretion, conveniently so, I would assert—ruled that Jessie showed clear and strong evidence of "street smarts" and was, first, not mentally impaired, and second, could be executed if convicted.

Our psychologist –a man I would come to regret hiring— had testified that Jessie was at the borderline of intellectual functioning and was functioning at the level of a five-year-old child. But at least he had "street smarts" according to Judge Burnett.

Among the biggest "what ifs" for me today is what the outcome might have been if we had been able to find for the case the services of a forensic psychologist with much better qualifications and credentials. In my search for the best, I had done the same as with Ofshe and Holmes. I started at the top and worked my way down.

And that is exactly what happened. I would learn very quickly certain things about experts that would test my long-held Eagle Scout abhorrence of cynicism. Expertise has its price. After being rejected by Park Dietz, we called several local psychologists to no avail. No one was willing to get involved. The case and its attendant publicity were simply too dark for doctors to be associated with.

Running out of options, I called a psychologist in Jonesboro who I had previously worked with in a domestic relations case. He had seemed competent to me at the time. By this time, my status as a public defender had essentially relegated me to begging for help and being grateful for any scraps people would toss in my direction. The psychologist agreed to meet with Greg Crow and me at his office.

After a perfunctory but cautious discussion given the rabid hatred and public rage that still festered, the psychologist agreed to evaluate Jessie with the assurance that he *might* be compensated by the court after the trial. At the time, it seemed like a sound decision. At least we had our own psychologist, not one provided by the State of Arkansas. In my limited experience no state-appointed psychologist had ever declared anyone incompetent to stand trial, unable to appreciate the criminality of their conduct, or unable to assist their counsel in their own defense.

We provided the doctor copies of Jessie Misskelley's mental health and school records and scheduled a day for him to go to the jail and conduct the mental evaluation with Jessie. As a result, Jessie's mental status during the pre-trial and trial was left in the care of a local novice. I had to play the hand that was dealt me, and the result was not all that much different than had a nuclear bomb gone off in that small courtroom in Corning, Arkansas, during Jessie Misskelley's trial. I came up short. It is just one of the several falls I took during the pre-trial hearings and the trial itself and I am not the least bit squeamish about saying so.

On the eve of his testimony at trial, I discovered that our doctor did not even have a license to practice psychology in Arkansas. When confronted about the issue, he lied to us and claimed to have a license. And once we did become aware of the lie and the issue, Judge Burnett refused us time to get a replacement to evaluate our client, and as such, the blast itself and the resulting fallout of this explosive development was devastating. Jessie Misskelley was a seventeen-year-old kid facing the death penalty, something that would not even be possible in today's jurisprudence, and despite my inexperience and missteps on this key issue, I still question the motives and the ethics of the judge who would deny us time to obtain a new psychologist.

Much later, long after Jessie Misskelley was in prison, we were able to secure post-trial a qualified doctor that we so desperately needed back in 1993 and 1994. Dr. Tim Derning proved to be everything I would have hoped for back then. Derning would prove invaluable in pushing the case forward during the appellate process.

24

With less than a month before the trial was set to start, and the day after Judge Burnett ruled that the seventeen-year-old Jessie would be tried as an adult, Arkansas State Police divers were summoned to the Lakeshore Trailer Park to look for something believed to be in the lake behind Jason Baldwin's mobile home. Someone had alerted the media, who were there, cameras ready.

According to witnesses, the Arkansas State Police diver put on his gear and walked straight out behind the Baldwins' trailer into the lake, bent over, and picked up an ominous-looking knife and quickly put it into a plastic evidence bag. Strangely enough the knife fit the FBI profile of the crazed Vietnam veteran. It looked like *John Rambo's* knife, large and threatening. I was not there but witnesses at the scene would later recall that it looked as if the diver knew exactly where he was going and what he would find. Photos of the diver with the knife appeared the next day on the front page of none other than the *Memphis Commercial Appeal*.

Oddly, or perhaps not so oddly in this odd and troubling case, another knife would come into play right before the trial. In late December 1993, Crow and I were in West Memphis interviewing witnesses and just happened to meet up with Bruce Sinofsky, Joe

Berlinger, and their HBO film crew at a West Memphis restaurant. During dinner we discovered we were all staying at the same interstate motel.

I had gotten to know Berlinger and Sinofsky very well during the months they were in Arkansas shooting *Paradise Lost*. They both seemed a bit unsettled about something and as we walked out of the restaurant, they told us that that they believed that John Mark Byers, the stepfather of victim Christopher Byers, was the real killer. They implored us to look closely into this.

They also told us about how strangely Byers had been acting in some of their film shoots. They described one scene in which Byers and Todd Moore, the father of Michael Moore, took target practice with a handgun at some pumpkins, pretending to kill the three defendants in the courtroom. At one point in the segment, Moore asks Byers what he thinks the range would be in the courtroom for him to shoot the three defendants. Byers's response was "about ten feet."

Mark Byers' often bizarre statements on the news and in the presence of the HBO cameras were a long and common thread over the years since the convictions. In *Paradise Lost*, Byers cited Bible verses and enacted bizarre scenes of him dancing on the graves of the WM3 after they were executed while pouring lighter fluid and lighting it at the crime scene. He also recounted to the HBO filmmakers an incident of being tied up, sodomized, and thrown in a ditch at the age of eighteen or nineteen.

That same night, the production crew told us about the knife Byers had given their cameraman as a gift. The cameraman went on to tell a creepy story of how Byers had given him a folding lock-blade knife that appeared to have blood in its hinge. When I asked where the knife was, they told me they had turned it over to their attorneys in New York, who had in turn given it to Inspector Gary Gitchell.

We were less than a month away from trial and the prosecutors had not told us anything about this knife. We decided to see how long it would take them to tell us about it if they would tell us at all.

I looked around at the nervous faces of the film crew as we talked outside the restaurant in the damp cold. They were alarmed, and we were fast becoming that way. Having agreed to meet again for breakfast, we went back to our motel room. The more Greg and I discussed it, the more concerned about Byers we became. It was obvious that the HBO crew was convinced Byers was the killer. Before turning in for the evening, Greg and I stacked every piece of furniture we could in front of the door to our room for safety's sake. At breakfast, Bruce and Joe said they had done the same thing. We all enjoyed a nervous laugh about it.

Later, at Jessie's trial, after prosecutors finally admitted they had the bloody knife, there was a delay in the trial while the knife was sent for potential DNA and blood typing to see if it was used in the murders. Whether or not there was any DNA on the knife is still unclear because the lab that conducted the DNA test was not accredited. I was told later by one of the appellate attorneys that the lab had fallen under serious suspicion and was closed. The blood was the same type as both Mark Byers and Christopher Byers. Over twenty years later, retesting of the Byers' knife would still yield no results. It seems that the sample had been depleted during the previous testing in 1994.

Greg and I had struggled for a short time about whether to put Mark Byers on the stand to discuss the knife in an attempt to create reasonable doubt. We decided against it, knowing that mere innuendo with no physical evidence pointing directly at Byers would almost certainly lead to a death sentence for Jessie. The lawyers for Echols took that risk at their trial and their client did receive the death penalty. I can't say for sure whether this risk was a contributing factor or not, but I have never regretted my decision not to point a finger at Byers at trial.

The lawyers for Baldwin, in their closing arguments, tried to convince jurors that Jason should not be guilty "by association," thereby implying that Damien Echols was guilty. I found this both moronic and ironic because their impotent efforts to secure a separate trial for Jason Baldwin led to his "guilt by association," and to his life without parole sentence.

The first time I spoke to John Mark Byers was in 1998, when I was being interviewed live on *Court TV* during Damien Echols Rule 37 hearing. I am a big guy but standing next to Byers I was barely noticeable. Standing about six feet eight and weighing more than 350 pounds, he was a presence even before he opened his mouth. When he shook my hand, his was so large it seemed to wrap around mine twice. He squeezed my hand so hard that I thought he broke it. I took the handshake to be a warning to back off. I did not.

Mark Byers would always dance on the fringes of being a real and viable suspect. The HBO filmmakers decided to make a sequel to the first *Paradise Lost*, implying strongly that he was the killer. I felt the same way about the possibility. An alleged bitemark on the face of Stevie Branch had by 1997 raised even more suspicion against Byers because he had mysteriously had all his teeth removed after the murders and had several different accounts about the circumstances about why he had undergone the curious procedure.

By this time, Damien Echols had a new appellate attorney named Ed Mallett from Houston, Texas. We also had some support from Barry Scheck of the *Innocence Project* in New York. Due to the generosity of some benefactors who wished to remain anonymous, we were able to retain the services of a bitemark expert to compare the bitemark to the dental impressions of the West Memphis Three. Each of the WM3 were excluded. Of course, we had no way to compare Byers' teeth since they were now gone. Byers strange behavior made him a convenient suspect, and his later brushes with the law and the circumstances surrounding the mysterious death of Melissa Byers in March of 1996 did little to quell those suspicions. I had tracked Byers' every move on the night of May 5th, 1993, and the morning of May 6th. I could find nothing in the timeline that would have given him the opportunity to commit the murders. Soon, human bitemark evidence would fall into the same realm as hair and fiber evidence, not scientifically reliable enough for admission into evidence in court. Thus, we abandoned this area of inquiry from our defense strategy as we moved forward on appeal.

25

Things do not arrive in a linear fashion when you are preparing for a trial. Attorneys do not often have the pleasure of setting daily goals and knocking them off neatly, one at a time, as the trial approaches. Rather, there are often dozens of items, each with its own independent timetable which often injected chaos into every waking moment. We had to deal with many of these items, with the added anxiety of knowing that a missed opportunity or an excursion down a path in the wrong direction could mean death for our client. It was not a pleasant thing to consider.

Our primary goal as the trial date grew ever closer was to build an arsenal with which we could get Jessie Misskelley's unreliable and coerced confession thrown out at trial. And our arsenal for that endeavor would have been the envy of any lawyer. Ofshe and Holmes were world class experts.

Judge Burnett had set the date for the hearing on our motion to suppress Jessie Misskelley's confession for January 13, 1994, just days ahead of the trial. The odds were against us, this we knew. But I had a strategy in place that would allow us to fight another day if we had to.

There were other things afoot as well. Greg Crow and I also filed a motion with the court trying to prohibit the introduction of the horrific pictures of the victims. Those pictures were beyond gruesome and included both crime scene and autopsy photos for each of the three victims. I was greatly concerned about these photographs being viewed by the jury and what their reaction would be. We knew we would never be able to keep them all out, but we wanted to remove all we could from the jury's view.

The crime scene photos and autopsy photos I looked at in the first murder case I worked on in law school kept me from sleeping for almost two weeks. Photos from the second and third murder cases I worked on kept me up for a few days. When I saw the hundreds of color photos of the crime scene and the autopsies of the three victims in the West Memphis case, I knew I would never sleep well again for the rest of my life. The jury would want to punish someone for these gruesome crimes after looking at these photos and the only person on trial would be Jessie Misskelley, Jr. The damage would be incalculable.

Judge Burnett had some other rather annoying habits and hang-ups that would make young lawyers cringe. His biggest and most vexing habit was that during a trial, a proceeding that he was supposed to be acting as a neutral and detached magistrate in, he would often fall back into his old role of prosecutor, sometimes cross-examining witnesses from the bench. This was improper and considered a "comment on the evidence." Burnett would also make gestures with his hands, arms, and face that the jury would see on display. These gestures could manipulate the outcome at trial as the jury looks to the judge as the final arbiter on important issues before the case.

On January 10, 1994, three days before the suppression hearing was set to begin, I filed a motion with the Court simply entitled "Motion." It contained the following language:

"That the Defendant hereby specifically requests that the Court refrain from engaging in language or conduct, or permitting conduct in the presence of the jury, which would amount to a 'comment on the evidence,' as prohibited by the Arkansas Constitution. That the Defendant respectfully requests that the Court refrain from any interrogation of witnesses, in the presence of the jury, that would negate the presumption of innocence, violate the due process rights of the Defendant and amount to a comment on the evidence by the Court."

His Honor was not impressed with the subject matter of our motion and was not bashful in expressing his feelings on the matter. We knew it would not curtail all of Burnett's attempts in injecting his thoughts and gestures in front of the jury. I felt, however, that he would make a mistake eventually, something that an appellate court would notice.

26

By the time the suppression hearing was upon us, all three defendants had received death threats. Jessie Sr. had his fair share as well. On one evening, Crow and I had returned extremely late from a day of interviewing witnesses in Marion and West Memphis. When we pulled off the street into the office, we noticed a car sitting in our parking lot with the engine running. Rather than pull in alongside, we circled the block and drove to the Paragould Police Department to ask for assistance. The driver of the car told the police that he was just waiting for a friend, but this did little to calm our fears.

The next morning, Kim mentioned to me that people were beginning to approach her at work and at church, questioning why I would represent a satanic child killer. Crow and I decided to install alarm systems in our homes to protect our families, especially since we were often away.

Security was on everyone's mind it seemed. The Sheriff of Clay County decided he would hold a meeting with all the participants in the trial in Corning, including Judge Burnett. Because of the death threats against Jessie Misskelley the sheriff said he was installing metal detectors at the front entrance to the courtroom and Jessie would be wearing a bulletproof vest coming in and out of the back of the courthouse. The sheriff also said that a police sniper would be posted on the roof of the courthouse during the trial. I decided quickly that I would not wear a bulletproof vest but would be carrying my 9mm submachine gun with me in the car each day going back and forth to the trial.

On Wednesday, January 12, 1994, Crow and I drove across the Mississippi River over the Interstate 55 bridge and picked up Warren Holmes and Richard Ofshe at the Memphis International Airport. I had decided since both these wonderful men were footing their own expenses flying in and out of Arkansas, Holmes on two occasions and Ofshe on three, that I would try to lessen the impact of this by putting the name-brand motels in West Memphis, close to the Crittenden County Courthouse on my Visa Gold card.

Richard Ofshe had other ideas about the lodging for the evening. He pointed over at the Airport Marriott Hotel as we were exiting the airport and said that establishment would do just fine. I nervously drove over and went in alone to inquire about reserving four rooms. The place was busy with pilots and flight attendants coming in and out constantly. I asked the receptionist if he had four rooms available for the evening and without even checking his computer, he answered that he did not. I went back out to the car to give the bad news to the guys, Ofshe was more than a little skeptical about the situation. "Come in with me," he said. "I will show you how this is done."

The two of us walked back into the hotel, and Ofshe walked right up to the very agent who had just turned me down. In what seemed like some kind of *Jedi* mind trick out of *Star Wars*, Ofshe plopped down his membership rewards card and told the young man that of course he had four rooms available. "Of course, we have four rooms available, Dr. Ofshe."

I threw down my gold card and said a little prayer in hopes that it could withstand the transaction. It did. It was $792.55 for one night's lodging, and that was twenty-nine years ago. I could not argue that it was perfect for our preparations for the hearing the next day.

Ofshe and Holmes got to work immediately pouring over their files. I would be conducting the examinations of them both, so I spent time with each in preparation for their testimonies at the hearing. Meanwhile, Greg Crow concerned himself with the legal arguments that we would be making. Soon we would be ready.

Later in the afternoon, Dr. Ofshe asked if I would take him across the river back into Arkansas to get a look at the crime scene and the courthouse. As we arrived at the Crittenden County Courthouse in Marion, Ofshe noticed a sign taped to the front door announcing that the courthouse would be closed the following Monday in celebration of Dr. Martin Luther King Jr. and Robert E. Lee's birthdays. At first, he asked me if it were someone's idea of a joke. After I explained that it was not, he insisted that I acquire a copy of the sign for him to take back to UC Berkeley to hang in his office on campus as a strange token of his trip to Arkansas. Then we went upstairs to the courtroom and took a quick look around. The hearing would start at 11:00 a.m. the next morning.

Walking into the courthouse that Thursday morning I was both exhilarated and confident because I was flanked by two of the leading experts in their respective fields, but with one caveat. I had no confidence in Burnett and his ability to suppress the confession. We were going to have to win this issue on appeal.

27

Wrapped snugly and indelibly within the suppression hearing, we were hoping to get an admission, or perhaps the better word would be an omission, from Detective Mike Allen that would give us an excellent issue on appeal. It began with a series of motions that we had filed literally begging Judge Burnett to allow us to conduct the depositions of the police officers who had interrogated Jessie Misskelley to produce his fictional confession, including Mike Allen. Burnett had repeatedly refused to allow us to conduct the depositions of the officers but did order them to talk to us about the circumstances surrounding the confession. They refused.

The suppression hearing began with a spirited discussion between Judge Burnett and I regarding the officers who had disobeyed his order requiring them to meet with us. Burnett had already indicated back in Chambers that he would deny our latest motion to conduct the officers' depositions, and when I asked for a ruling on the record, the following colloquy took place:

"MR. STIDHAM: Today we are before the Court to argue a motion to suppress the statements that were given by Mr. Misskelley on June the third. In a civil matter when you walk into a courtroom, you know

what the witnesses are going to testify because of discovery. Unfortunately, we don't have the luxury in this case and, therefore, we were not able to prepare for what the officers might testify...
BURNETT: I ordered the officers to make themselves available at a specific time and place to discuss the case with you not in the nature of normal discovery but to make themselves available to talk to you about what they knew about the case. If they chose not to, they have the right to do so...
MR. STIDHAM: One point further I would like to make since we have not had the opportunity to discover what the officers are going to testify to — obviously we are going to know after they testify — Mr. Crow and I have not had an opportunity to brief the law as to the facts because we don't know what the facts are. So, we would like to ask the Court to take the motion under advisement after completion of the hearing and then give Mr. Crow and I at least twenty-four hours to submit a brief prior to you making your decision.
BURNETT: I'll consider that after I hear it. It may not be something I need a brief on. If I think I can rule with the evidence that is before me, that's what I'm going to do. I will listen and if I think I will need a brief on a point of law that might be raised...if it is necessary, I will consider that."

Obviously, Burnett had no intention of making the officers follow his Order. This is exactly what I expected he would do. So, our discovery deposition of Detective Mike Allen began on Thursday, January 13, 1994, in the old courthouse where the words "Obedience to the Law is Liberty" are inscribed on the huge pillars outside. Of course, it really was not a deposition at all. It was the actual suppression hearing itself, but at least the officer would be under oath. When it was Mike Allen's turn to testify, I was particularly interested in whether he had complied with Rule 2.3 of the Arkansas Rules of Criminal Procedure mandating that a police officer makes it clear to anyone whom he asks to come to the station for questioning that they are under no compulsion whatsoever to do so. If the Rule 2.3 warning is not given, then *anything* that the person tells the officer at the station is *automatically excluded* from evidence with *absolutely no exceptions.*

I suspected that Mike Allen had not advised Jessie Misskelley of his Rule 2.3 rights, so I was looking forward to our first conversation about it. Once he was sworn in, I asked Detective Allen, "what, if any, rights," he had advised Jessie Misskelley of before taking him to the police station for questioning on the morning of June 3, 1993. To my absolute delight, Officer Allen answered as I hoped that he would.

"Misskelley was not a suspect, so I didn't advise him of *any* rights."

Then I moved on quickly to other questions during my cross examination, none of which were more important than the one I had just posed.

The prosecution would play the tape of Jessie Misskelley's confession, and the second for clarification purposes, for the first time for the frenzied media. Newspaper, television, and radio reporters sat in the jury box, tape recorders in hand, salivating like Pavlov's dogs, and ready to bolt out of the courtroom to meet their deadlines for the 5 o'clock and 6 o'clock news. They had previously been unable to report on the gruesome yet muddled details of the confession because the *Memphis Commercial Appeal* had a copyright to the story about the confession. Once it was played in open court, it was fair game for every media outlet, and many bolted out of the courtroom to make their breaking news. Once the State rested, it was time for me to put into evidence the most powerful testimony in the entire case—the testimony of Warren Holmes and his opinions regarding the interrogation of Jessie Misskelley including the use of and his interpretations of the polygraph exam that were used to facilitate the confession itself.

As I began my examination of Mr. Holmes, those few members of the media who had remained in the courtroom, heard the story of Misskelley passing the polygraph he was given by the West Memphis Police Department even though their in-house polygrapher had told Jessie he was "lying his ass off." They heard also that the officers had told other lies to Misskelley in order to obtain the confession.

The playing of the confession in open court was front-page news, but Holmes' testimony was relegated to section "B" of the papers, if even mentioned at all. Even more devastating was the fact that the HBO cameras were noticeably absent too. They chose not to make the trip and Holmes' testimony about the polygraph evidence would never make it into any of the HBO documentaries. The best evidence of Jessie Misskelley's innocence would never make it into the public realm. But there would be a transcript of it in the record of the case.

Holmes testified that Jessie Misskelley did not at any time during his confession attribute any conversation during the crime to the victims. Nor did Misskelley express any feelings about how he felt while the horror of the murders was unfolding. Both issues were very unusual, Holmes said, and it caused him grave concerns about the validity of the confession. In addition, Holmes testified that he did not like the discrepancies Misskelley gave about the times the murders occurred. "It would seem to me," Holmes said, "that despite his IQ level, he should know the difference between 9 AM in the morning and 5 PM, and he should know the difference between a rope and shoelaces, and those things bother me a lot."

When I asked Holmes if a polygraph examination can contribute to a false confession, Holmes' answer was "unfortunately it can." I was amazed by Holmes' testimony and afterward felt that he had completely dismantled prosecutor Brent Davis' case. Davis and Burnett recognized this as well. However, I did not have high hopes that the jury would ever hear most of it at trial. As Holmes left the stand, I asked for a moment from the court to visit with Dr. Ofshe who had been sitting in the courtroom absorbing the testimony of the officers and Mr. Holmes.

"You can't put me on the stand today," Ofshe told me. "Why the hell not. You are the star of the show," I told him. "My opinion has changed as to what happened in that interrogation room. After listening to the officers' testimony, I must regroup and revamp my conclusions."

"Okay," I said, "but we are about to rest our case in the hearing."

This is just another example of how crucial it was for us to conduct the depositions of the officers before the hearing, but Burnett would not permit it. Ofshe was compelled to change his theory of the confession that had been completely hidden from us until now by the prosecution just six days before the trial would begin.

28

All the television reporters who had left the courtroom during Holmes' testimony were now back in attendance as the hearing wound down, satellite trucks at the ready outside preparing for their live reports for the 10 o'clock news. The only person more excited was Judge Burnett. He could not wait to make his announcement that the confession would be admissible and that the jury would be allowed to hear Misskelley's confession at trial.

As he started, I quickly jumped to my feet and interrupted him. He was not amused, but the returning reporters were about to save me. I told Burnett that an issue had come up during the hearing that we could not have possibly anticipated because we had been refused the opportunity to depose, or even talk to, the officers in advance of the hearing. I said it diplomatically, but I made sure to point out that this was, of course, his fault. Burnett did not like it at all, but he was cornered because the media were there watching this take place.

I asked for twenty-four hours to brief the new issue and submit it to the court. I quickly added that the State would not be prejudiced in any way by this development. Judge Burnett finally relented and gave us the 24 hours.

Burnett told us to fax a copy of our amended motion to suppress along with the accompanying brief to prosecutors. The prosecution would have until noon on Saturday to respond. Burnett then announced to the media that he would reveal his decision at a press conference in his living room on Saturday, January 15, 1994, at noon. There he would have the media to himself with no interruptions from me. I shook my head at Greg and said, "Let's go."

We raced back to our office eighty miles away to amend our motion to suppress, adding a violation of Rule 2.3 of the Arkansas Rules of Criminal Procedure, something we could not have done until *after* Detective Mike Allen's testimony. We amended our motion and brief to suppress and then faxed them to the prosecutors and Burnett the next day.

Rule 2.3, with at least a half century of case law behind it, was crystal clear. If a police officer does not inform anyone, suspect or not, that they are under no compulsion to accompany them to the police station for questioning, then any subsequent statement they may make at the station cannot be used against them under *any* circumstances.

This is not a right found in the U.S. Constitution, it is an enhanced right given to Arkansas citizens through the Arkansas Rules of Criminal Procedure. Detective Mike Allen had clearly testified that he did not advise Misskelley of "any" rights prior to taking him to the station for questioning. We had the prosecution on the ropes, and we knew it.

Then the waiting began. One last hurdle to clear. I tried to sleep, but I did not have much success. The next day I went to the office early and waited by the fax machine. The Rule 2.3 issue was so clear and damaging to the prosecutions' case against suppressing Misskelley's confession, I knew that Fogleman and Davis would surely ask Burnett to reopen the hearing for further testimony so they could convert their acolyte. Back on the witness stand, I suspected that Detective Mike Allen might somehow *miraculously* remember that he did give Misskelley his required Rule 2.3 warning.

To my huge surprise and great relief no fax or any kind of response ever came in from the prosecution to rebut the Rule 2.3

issue by the noon deadline. I was in shock that they had not even bothered to reply at all.

Within a couple of minutes, however, the phone rang. It was Judge Burnett.

"Dan, you did a great job on that amended motion and brief. You will probably get me reversed by the Arkansas Supreme Court, but there is no way I can suppress that confession. Surely, you understand I can't let this kid go."

I was stunned by his candor, but not his decision. Judge Burnett then held the press conference in his living room announcing that Misskelley's confession was voluntary and could be used as evidence against him. I had never seen any judge give a press conference about any issue in a case pending in their court from their living room either before or since. Even more disturbing was the cryptic nature of the last thing Judge Burnett said to me. Its implication was clear. Politics and the next judicial election seemed more important than the life of a mentally challenged 17-year-old facing the death penalty.

When I drafted the Order denying our motion and amended motion to suppress Jessie's confession for Burnett's signature, I made it a *glaringly obvious* point to include language that Burnett had, in fact, considered the issues that Greg and I had raised in our amended motion and brief, which of course was the Rule 2.3 issue. The record was now entirely closed on this issue. I knew I had just planted a seed that would become a giant oak tree in the case someday. I just did not know how long it would take to grow.

29

After the arrests and initial appearances of the three defendants were complete in the summer of 1993, the satellite trucks disappeared as quickly as they had arrived, and the national media disappeared, at least for the moment. Other breaking stories took the big trucks and news anchors far from West Memphis and on to the next big thing.

In the summer of 1993, Vince Foster, deputy White House counsel and former member of the prestigious Rose Law Firm in Little Rock, was found dead in Fort Mercy Park off the George Washington Parkway in Virginia outside Washington D.C on July 20, 1993. His death was ruled a suicide by five official investigations. Controversy and conspiracies swirled when it was learned that Clinton aides entered his White House office within hours of his death. In California, the father of a thirteen-year-old boy accused Michael Jackson of sexually abusing his son. And all over the country that summer, people began to be worried about syringes found in cans of Pepsi Cola. Such was life in the national media.

But the West Memphis murder case was like a hot ember. The flames had disappeared temporarily, but they were more than capable of starting a major conflagration at any time. With the national folks gone, the local media seemed empowered, and the various outlets covering Memphis—newspapers, radio, and television stations—were competing full time.

The talk of satanic cults had put them into a virtual feeding frenzy. They were like piranhas during the day and a pack of rabid wolves at night roaming the streets of Marion and West Memphis for any scrap of information about the case. On days that they could not find anything factual about the case to report, it seemed to me that they would not hesitate to simply generate something. The truth seemed unimportant and with rumors swirling of satanic cults killing children, holding sexual orgies, and eating the flesh of dogs it was not that hard to generate something that at least vaguely resembled news.

One short scene from *Paradise Lost* captures the stench of the aggressive and emotionally tone-deaf reporting that characterized much of the local media frenzy—sensationalizing for the sake of sensation. In the scene, a smug on-air reporter asked victim Stevie Branch's mother, Pam Hobbs, who had on her head the Cub Scout neckerchief her son had been wearing when he was murdered, if she "had contemplated joining Stevie before [her] natural time . . ." Pam Hobbs did not understand the question, which the reporter then clarified by asking simply if she had considered suicide given the circumstances. It was a callous ambush on an unwitting parent of a victim whose pain and shock only days after the murders was all too visible. In my mind that was not reporting. It was not providing information the public has a right to know. It was nothing short of repulsive and insensitive pandering, a way to get a story that perhaps no one else would have.

The cloying reporter who had asked Pam Hobbs about suicide was a smarmy minion I would soon nickname, the "Maggot." He worked for a television channel out of Memphis and quickly became an annoying and aggravating source of tension. He was not atypical among the hordes of reporters looking for an edge on the competition. The Maggot was not the only reporter buying Jessie Sr. beer by the case, then waiting for the inevitable and eminently quotable lines after the beer kicked in.

One of the T.V. news reporters out of Memphis at one point got Jessie Sr. drunk, had him call his son at the jail, then recorded the exchange for the evening news. It made for compelling television viewing, and it really annoyed me. My calls to the assistant news director at that channel about what to me was clearly unethical behavior did no good.

Nor did Maggot have a spasm of conscience when he learned my nickname for him—in fact, he seemed emboldened by it. He announced later that he was writing a book about the case. His meddling got worse when he reported that he had found an eight-year-old, a playmate of the young victims, who allegedly witnessed the murders from a tree house in the woods where the victims' bodies had been recovered. Of course, there was no treehouse in the woods, but Maggot took the child, the son of Vicki Hutcheson, out there anyway and had him point out where he saw the murders take place for the evening news.

After the segment aired, the West Memphis Police began interrogating the boy, soon followed by the prosecutors themselves. Under pressure that surely rivaled the vise they applied to Jessie Misskelley, the young boy finally revealed that he had seen John Mark Byers, stepfather of victim Christopher Byers, at the crime scene that day directing Damien Echols to kill the boys. This was even too much for the prosecutors.

I later decided that the best interests of my client demanded that I remove the Maggot from the playing field so he could no longer taint the jury pool with his reckless reporting. I simply added him to our witness list. Because he had been injecting himself into so many stories as he cloyed for attention, in my mind he had become a part of the investigation, and we could not discount the possibility that he could be called as a witness. Potential witnesses, of course, are excluded from the courtroom and what was happening inside. The news director's response, quite predictable, was to send another reporter to cover the trial. The Maggot's response was not so predictable. He quit his job.

He would later attend every day of the trial for the purpose of writing his book. Even more unpredictable was that I later heard that his wife ended up having him out of the house and filed for divorce. What I know to be certain, and perhaps the most unpredictable, was that the Maggot ended up living with Jessie Sr. in the old, dilapidated trailer, sleeping on his couch after Jessie's trial was over. He moved away from Memphis after both trials were over, landing another reporter's job somewhere in the Midwest, I believe. He never wrote his book. And all the while, the people of West Memphis and the Mid-South wanted nothing more than to feel safe again.

30

Satanic Panic was very real in Arkansas in 1993 after the murders. On August 1, there was a "Witches March" in Jonesboro. According to news reports, a Wiccan bookstore owner was run out town by the Jonesboro Ministerial Alliance for being a "pagan." The Wiccans protested and took to the streets. Stevie Branch's biological father was there to counter-protest and slung Bible verses at the "white witches" as they marched in the street. As the trial date grew nearer in Corning, the chief of police there became concerned about a rumor that the witches would be marching in Corning during the trial. Of course, this never happened.

The First United Methodist Church in Paragould, my church, did something in October that angered almost all the other churches in the county—sponsoring a "Trunk or Treat" celebration for the kids to safely celebrate Halloween. The idea, which made sense from a safety point of view if not from a spiritual one, called for church members to park their cars in the church parking lot and offer treats to the kids from their open trunks. The event was for church members only and was held at 3:00 in the afternoon, safely before dark.

Pastors from the other churches blasted the Methodist Church for its celebration of a "Pagan" holiday, but the Methodists would not back down. The other Churches held "Fall Festivals" instead of celebrating Halloween apparently in hopes of avoiding the wrath of God. I guess God has a sense of humor, however, because it snowed Halloween night turning the Fall Festivals into Winter Festivals the next day, at least until the snow melted by the afternoon. That is how crazy it was, traditional Halloween was cancelled because of those pesky Wiccan Witches running around Jonesboro and the fear of Satanic Cults that did not exist.

The deeply rooted Christianity in the entire Mid-South played a large role in the spread of rumors and the insidious gossip that was conveyed to the media. Soon after the arrests, West Memphis Pastor Tommy Stacy told a reporter that a youth minister at his Baptist church informed him that he once had a conversation with Damien Echols who told him that he had made a "pact with the devil and was going to hell." Despite this being double and triple hearsay, it was accepted as cold hard fact, and it only increased the fear and anger.

When a Memphis television reporter asked Pam Hobbs, mother of victim Stevie Branch, if she thought Echols, Baldwin, and Misskelley were Satanists, she replied, "Yes." When the reporter asked her why, she replied, "Just look at the freaks. I mean just look at them. They look like punks."

John Mark Byers would quote Psalm 23 to a reporter while also expressing his belief that there are "angels and demons on earth," and the demons "do the devil's will," implying that Baldwin, Echols, and Misskelley were demonically inspired. The murders and the grisly circumstances surrounding them were compellingly lurid, a rich motherlode of a story propagated daily by the media.

It did not take long for me to realize that I had failed to adequately gauge the fear and the hatred that my representation of Jessie Misskelley would inspire. It would soon be spreading outside the borders of West Memphis and Crittenden County. It could not be contained.

It was like a virus, and it would find its way to Paragould, miles from West Memphis and the courthouse where the initial legal skirmishes were taking place. Paragould was the town where I had grown up. It was a community that prized and cherished family. I saw that my neighbors and friends did not see this admittedly horrendous crime as just a normal murder case with a defendant who is presumed innocent and constitutionally entitled to a lawyer to defend him. They viewed it as both a religious and human atrocity. One day my phone rang. It was the father of one of my cub scouts from Pack 99. Before the murders, I had been recruited to serve as a Pack Master because of my long association with Scouting. I welcomed the opportunity to spend time with my sons Daniel and Chris and to get involved in my community. My defense of Jessie Misskelley, however, ended my short stint as Pack Master.

"Some of the decisions you have made are not liked by the parents of the Cub Scouts and we think it would be better if you just stepped down. This would be best."

"Sure," I told him, "I understand."

At least that was my immediate response, but his words rang sharply in my ears. I knew that my decisions regarding the Cub Scouts had less to do with the Pack and more to do with my defense of Jessie Misskelley. One of the victims in West Memphis had been wearing his Cub Scout uniform at the time he was killed and this, no doubt, had fueled the request for my resignation. I did not have time to be angry anyway. Disappointed would have to suffice. I had a job to do despite the grumblings of my community.

After Kim and I took our kids to "Trunk or Treat," I began in earnest preparing for the trial of Jessie Misskelley. In fact, by then it was the only case I was working on. I left it to Crow and the paralegals to run the office and take care of all our other clients. As I reviewed the numerous bits of information emerged from discovery from the police and prosecution, it reflected how much the West Memphis police department looked only for evidence to meet and solidify their belief that this was a satanic crime which of course was an exercise in fiction.

I found a letter dated May 26, 1993, from Inspector Gary Gitchell that had been sent to Dr. Frank Peretti and the State Crime Lab that put this tunnel vision on full display. Gitchell, who had not yet received the written autopsy reports, was both frustrated and frantic. "We need information from the crime lab desperately," he wrote. "We feel as though we are walking blindfolded through the case."

One question among the many Gitchell asked in that letter was whether the three young victims had been sodomized or possibly forced to perform oral sex—a strong indication that police had already created a scenario and needed, or wanted, evidence to back it up. I did not think that it was a coincidence that these themes suddenly appeared in the "confession" that Gitchell crafted for Jessie Misskelley just seven days later.

Gitchell had in his May 26 letter to the crime lab also asked whether there was "anything" that would demonstrate the involvement of a black male? Was this a reference to "Mr. Bojangles," the man who stumbled into the restaurant on the night the boys went missing covered in mud and blood? *As sinister as it may sound, did the arrests of the West Memphis three just days later have anything to do with the police losing the blood scrapings collected from Bojangles?*

That same day, May 26, police interviewed a local man named William Winfred Jones, who stated that a drunken Damien Echols had told him after the murders that he had raped and cut up the little boys. This only served to energize the police in their tunnel vision. Jones would later recant his story just moments before his testimony was to begin in the Misskelley trial despite the threats of Davis to prosecute him. In one of the strangest ironies of the case, Brent Davis accused Ron Lax of "coercing" Jones not to testify.

Peretti appeared more than willing to provide the information that Gitchell wanted in his May 26 letter. After police finally received the written autopsy reports, they seemed to misinterpret the information. Police noticed that Peretti had mentioned that the victims' anuses were dilated, which they immediately and mistakenly mistook as a sign of sexual assault when in fact that dilation occurs naturally when bodies are submerged in water. The macabre injuries to the young boys' bodies were taken as signs of Satanism, sexual assault, and sexual mutilation when as it would emerge later nothing could have been further from the truth. After the trials, it would be revealed that these injuries were caused by something else entirely, evidence that I would not discover until 1998 that would change everything.

I gave a reporter a copy of Warren Holmes' analysis indicating that Jessie Misskelley had passed the polygraph test given to him by the West Memphis Police. During this polygraph exam police had told Jessie that he was "lying his ass off" and that the test showed he knew something about the murders.

When this hit the papers, Brent Davis was furious. Judge Burnet took me to the woodshed and threatened to jail me for contempt of court if I did something like that again. What was "good for the goose apparently was not good for the gander." Someone close to law enforcement could leak a copy of my client's false confession to the press, but I would be jailed if I talked to the press about anything that showed Jessie was innocent. Burnett would not call it a gag order, he just ordered me to stop talking to the press, a proclivity that he could not control himself.

We would win a pyrrhic motion to have the location of the trial moved away from the poisonous air of West Memphis and Crittenden County. Judge Burnett moved the trial to Clay County where Jessie Misskelley was being held. I have often said that this motion and a second one to take an early lunch during the trial were the only two motions we won in the entire case. It is not that much of an exaggeration.

31

Judge David Burnett chose Corning, Arkansas, in Clay County, as the site for the trial of Jessie Misskelley. Clay County is situated in the furthest corner of northeast Arkansas and is surrounded by the "Bootheel" of Missouri from the north and the east. The County is divided into two Districts—Corning in the Western District and Piggott in the Eastern District.

The two towns are divided by the Black River, which is why there are two courthouses, one in each town. Early in the last century, there was a tremendous need for two courthouses in the county because the Black River routinely deserted its banks and flooded the county, thereby separating the two sides for weeks and months at a time. The U.S. Army Corps of Engineers has all but eliminated that problem now, but there are still two court houses, but only one sheriff and tax collector and one circuit clerk. The courthouses were built in the 1960's and are almost identical in layout. The Clay County Detention Center was virtually brand new in 1993 and was built in the Eastern District in Piggott serving both sides of the river. The Second Judicial Circuit of Arkansas is the largest geographically in Arkansas serving six counties and at one time ten courthouses. Clay and Crittenden counties are the farthest apart from the other in the Second Judicial

Circuit both geographically and demographically. Clay County is far removed from the Mississippi River and the bustling city of Memphis and the two busy interstate highways in West Memphis. There were people in the jury pool in Corning who stated under oath that they had not even heard about the triple murders in West Memphis, something that I still find hard to believe to this day.

CORNING IN 1994 HAD TWO SMALL MOTELS AND TWO RESTAURANTS, A family-owned diner and one pizza chain restaurant. The Misskelley family was hard hit by the change of venue because of the distance and the fact that they could not afford to stay in a motel even if a room was available. The media snatched up those rooms immediately after the announcement of the trial date. The victims' families were embraced by the Corning community and offered private cabins along the river as accommodations. The Misskelley family had planned to stay in a camper on the bed of the family truck in Corning until the local First United Methodist Church opened its doors to them. The Rev. Jim Roper was quoted as saying he offered the sleeping quarters to the Misskelley family:

"...because that is what Christians are supposed to do. Jesus Christ died for everyone not just victims or defendants. I don't know anyone whose closets are free of skeletons. They were in dire need for God's grace. We are here to give them that."

The good grace of the Methodists in Corning was especially important due to the unusual cold that January. It was so cold the Mississippi River in Memphis was covered with huge chunks of ice, a rare site, a photo of which appeared on the front page of the *Memphis Commercial Appeal*.

Leading up to the trial I had already begun playing that long game of chess. I tried to make every move thinking three moves ahead. Without even realizing it, I had been taking a deliberate Zen-like approach, trying to keep pieces on the chessboard, so I could live to fight another day.

The night before jury selection was to begin, I visited John

Fogleman in his motel room in Paragould. I know he must have thought I was insane, but I felt a driving need to reason with him somehow, to try and convince him that these three kids were innocent and that he did not have to prosecute the wrong persons for these murders. Fogleman was both kind and compassionate. He applauded me for my passion but said that he believed that the right people were on trial.

Judge Burnett set aside a week for jury selection beginning on January 19, 1994. To the surprise of most, the jury selection was over by the end of the day on January 20.

A few weeks earlier Greg and I had received a call from a jury consultant in Little Rock eager to offer their services for free. Together, we had developed a "profile" of the best possible jurors for the case. The consultants concluded, and I agreed, that female jurors were less likely to impose the death penalty. The small courtroom was full of potential jurors. When the Clerk pulled the numbers from the hat for the first set of potential jurors to be examined, they were almost all females. One woman stated during *voir dire* that under no circumstances could she impose the death penalty. Knowing that the prosecution would strike her and perhaps use up one of their strikes in the process, I casually told Burnett that this juror was "good" for the defense. I immediately felt something was wrong, however, when Brent Davis said that she was "good" for the prosecution, and she was seated on the jury. *Why would Davis want someone who would not consider the death penalty on the jury since he was seeking the death penalty?* It did not make any sense, but I had to move on.

The next juror was a man. He looked like he was a hunter and a fisherman, like me. Despite the objections of the jury consultant, I picked this man because I knew a hunter would seriously question the lack of blood found at the crime scene. Anyone who had ever killed a deer knew the enormous amount of blood involved. This man would become the foreman of the jury of seven women and five men, with two male alternates.

Then, as I had predicted back in October when I tried to warn

Burnett that January was not a good month to conduct a trial, northeast Arkansas was paralyzed by a severe ice storm. The trial was delayed for almost a week. It would be the first of two delays in the trial. The other was for the testing of the Byer's knife.

32

On January 26, 1994, after both delays, the Misskelley trial was finally set to begin. Literally, as opening statements were about to begin, the State tendered an offer to try and make the trial go away. Joe Calvin, the deputy prosecutor for Clay County asked to speak with Greg and me. The State offered 50 years in exchange for Jessie Misskelley's *truthful* testimony against Echols and Baldwin. The decision, of course, was not mine to make. Greg Crow and I sat down the senior and junior Misskelleys to explain the offer. Jessie said that he just could not "tell any more lies on Echols and Baldwin." Jessie Sr. agreed and we walked back into the courtroom and the battle unfolded. Jessie's use of the word "lies" would come back to haunt me ten years later as I learned for the first time why he used that specific term. They would come back to haunt Judge Burnett 15 years later for the same reason.

From the State's perspective, the case was relatively simple. They would play Jessie Misskelley's confession, show the horrific autopsy and crime scene photos, and while doing so they would phrase everything in such a way to compel the jury to want to punish someone. It was a crude approach, lacking subtlety, or nuance, but it produced devastating results for Jessie Misskelley, Jr. and for me. The prosecution had only two witnesses who could have conceivably corroborated Jessie Misskelley's confession. The first, William Winfred Jones, the man who had previously told police that a drunken Damien Echols had confessed to him that he had killed the kids, recanted just prior to his scheduled testimony, and thus was not called by the State. The second, Vicki Hutcheson, would recant her testimony shortly after the trial—too late to have any impact, of course— but would not do so under oath out of fear of being charged with perjury. A decade later that would change. Prosecutors presented no physical evidence to link Jessie Misskelley to the murders. Of course, none has ever existed to this day.

Our entire case, aside from pointing out the fundamental and astounding police mistakes at the crime scene, was to put on our alibi witnesses, as tainted as they were, and then attack the confession with Holmes and Ofshe. As Ofshe began to testify, Judge Burnett finally took off his robe, and joined the prosecution team, and cut us off at the knees. I had Ofshe and Holmes ready to shatter the foundation on which the prosecutors' case had been built.

Judge Burnett, agile as always, limited their testimony. At one point during my attempt at convincing Burnett to allow Dr. Ofshe to testify that the confession was involuntary, Burnett stated that he had already found that the confession was voluntary and retorted on the record: "What the hell do we need a jury for?" What the jury did not get to hear, and it was powerful, we put into the record of the case in the form of what is known as a "proffer" so that the appellate courts could see just how Burnett had abridged Ofshe and Holmes testimonies and how vital it was to the defense.

After the proffered testimony of Dr. Ofshe, spectators in the courtroom, mostly reporters, approached me at the counsel table during a break and told me that they felt his testimony was so compelling that we had won the case. I reminded them that the jury did not get to hear the proffer. Still, I felt that we had a chance. That was all I could hope for.

The evening before I was to give my closing arguments to the jury, I had a wave-break of all the emotions I had been keeping at bay for the previous nine months. The ups and downs of the trial itself were like an emotional roller coaster, and that ride never seemed to end. And yet, there I was near the end of the struggle with nerves completely frazzled. It was a surge set loose, I presume, by knowing that it would all be over one way or another within twenty-four hours. In that moment I knew only that I was gripped, and temporarily overcome by the pressure of having that young innocent man's life totally and completely in my hands. It hit me suddenly and powerfully, like a blindside sucker punch.

Was I afraid of failing? I am not sure. But I was certainly overwhelmed. In my bedroom at home that night preparing for the end of the trial, facing what would be my first-ever jury summation, and one that was a matter of life-and-death, I had sunk to the floor and sat paralyzed for an instant, staring, and thinking about what would happen the next day. I felt cold and weak, almost unable to breathe by the awesome responsibility at hand. I could not bear the thought of Jessie Misskelley getting the death penalty for something that he did not do. *Could I save him?*

Minutes later, the warm and consoling touch of my wife, Kim, brought me back to reality and back to my normal yet solid state of nervousness that I had become accustomed to, and the quiet confidence eased back into my soul. "You'll do fine," she said.

I knew quickly after that backwash of anxiety that any fear that might be lingering in my system would simply have to go. For the past hour or so, it had been sucking the energy out of me that I needed to prepare for the closing argument that would be the most important that I would ever give and that was distracting me from what I had to do—what I had worked so hard to do. I would have to face this fear down, crush it and banish it from my thoughts so it would not return. I knew I had to exude confidence for the jury the next day if they were to believe all I had tried to make them see during the trial.

Looking back now, I remember taking Warren Holmes back to Memphis to catch his flight back to Miami after his testimony in Corning. On the way to trial that morning I pulled a volume from my law library entitled *Cross Examination in Criminal Trials* co-authored by F. Lee Bailey. I had admired Bailey's work and I knew that he and Holmes had worked together several times on cases. On the way to Memphis, I pulled the text out of my briefcase and asked Holmes if he could get Bailey to autograph it for me. This was his reply:

"I'll get it if you want, but you are ten times the lawyer he ever thought about being."

I told Holmes never mind, and I put the book back into my briefcase. It would be the last time I ever saw him.

The jury began their deliberations on the evening of Thursday, February 3. At 12:10 am. Shortly thereafter, they asked to be excused for the night and begin their deliberations again in the morning. Burnett told them to be back the next morning at 9:30 am. When I arrived the next morning, Sheriff Darvin Stow, without telling me the source of his information, told me that the first vote in the jury room had been four votes for outright acquittal. This sort of gave me hope. Later, I would learn from one of my criminology students at Arkansas State University, whose uncle was the jury foreman, that the first straw poll for the jury had been five votes for acquittal.

One incident demonstrates Burnett's heavy handedness as well as the indecision of the jury. A long deliberation usually does not bode well for the prosecution and Burnett knew this very well. As the morning wore on, Burnett's fears about the jury and their deliberations seemed to get the best of him. What happened next still shocks me.

About an hour before lunch on that second day of deliberations, Judge Burnett came to the counsel table and summoned me and prosecutor Davis to the hall outside the jury room. The Court reporter was not present. Burnett then knocked on the jury room door. The deer hunter foreman opened the jury room door. Judge Burnett told the foreman that he was going to send the Sheriff out to get the jury lunch and asked them what they would like to eat. No one spoke but the foreman. "We don't need lunch," he said. "We are almost finished." I was floored by what Burnett said next. Burnett casually told the jury that he was going to send out for food anyway "because you will still have to come back after lunch for sentencing."

I was stunned. I could not believe that the judge had just told the jury that they were now mandated to find my client guilty. The jury foreman's response to Burnett's casual statement suddenly turned the tide. "What if we find him not guilty?" the foreman asked. "Will we still have to stay?" Now even more stunned, I looked for any sign that the foreman might be kidding or not taking the grim matter seriously. The foreman of the jury seemed quite serious and not another juror had uttered even a single word. The look on both Burnett and Davis' faces confirmed that my assessment of the situation was a good one for the defense. Both Burnett and Davis looked very pale and genuinely concerned. Davis appeared that he might even faint. Without another word spoken, the jury room door was shut again by Burnett, and I quickly reported the news to Crow.

"The judge had just created a clear mistrial by telling the jury that sentencing would be required even before a finding of guilt. He just told them what they had to do," I said.

The foreman was clearly insinuating that Misskelley would be acquitted. We were both joyous and anxious as we huddled to decide what to do. It was an excruciating choice. We agreed that if we asked for a mistrial, there was a good chance we would get it. The prosecutors were looking completely dejected. They may not have even objected to a motion for a mistrial at that moment. Countering that and strongly influencing our decision, we knew if Burnett granted the mistrial and we found out later that Misskelley would have been acquitted, we would not have been able to live with ourselves. Lawyers with more experience would have handled things much differently, but we honestly thought we were about to win the case. We decided not to ask for a mistrial and take our chances. This was perhaps my biggest blunder in the case.

The next hour was grueling, but at 11:54 a.m. on Friday, February 4, 1994, the jury returned with a guilty verdict, but not for capital murder. It seemed that the seven jurors wore the other five down reaching a classic compromise verdict. The five who had voted first to acquit Misskelley outright, obviously felt that there was a reasonable doubt as to his guilt. My theory is that the seven jurors agreed to take the death penalty off the table and the jury was finally able to reach a compromise.

In addition to finding Misskelley not guilty of capital murder, the jury found him not guilty on two of the three counts of first-degree murder opting instead for the least serious possible classification of murder, murder in the second degree. Regarding Michael Moore, the jury came back with a guilty verdict on murder in the first degree. Jessie Misskelley had been spared the death penalty. When the jury retired for the sentencing phase, people in the Courtroom walked up to me and told me that Greg and I had done a tremendous job in defending our client. This included both prosecutors, one of the police detectives who had interrogated Misskelley—and even Judge Burnett. Some observers in the courtroom were even calling it a "victory," but it did not seem like one to me. I was especially devastated when Burnett sentenced Misskelley to life in prison for one count of first-degree murder and an additional forty years, twenty years each, for two counts of second-degree murder. *What would the jury have done had it not been for Burnett opening that jury room door?* After Burnett pronounced his sentence, I leaned down as he stood silently next to me, and I made a promise to Jessie Misskelley:

"I will never abandon you no matter what, and I will get you out of prison one day or die trying. This isn't over, I promise."

As he left in the police car that would take him to his first day in prison, I warned him, sharply, that under no circumstances should he talk to the police. He nodded that he understood. Back in Paragould, confronted with what I saw as my failure, I wept.

33

I suspected Jessie Misskelley's promise to keep quiet was empty. Jessie Misskelley lived in a black-and-white world void of nuance. The true nature of his disability would not be revealed to me for some time, but I knew Jessie would struggle with his promise not to talk to the police. As a concrete thinker, incapable of considering what the long-term consequences of any decision might be, he would not learn anything from his first encounter with the police and how devastating that encounter was—no matter how many times I told him to not to talk to anyone about his case. I was counting on the fact that law enforcement knew that I represented Jessie Misskelley and that they were not allowed to talk to him without my consent and my being present.

These vulnerable traits would become the major focus in the seesaw battle between Davis and myself, who needed Jessie Misskelley to testify in the upcoming trial of Damien Echols and Jason Baldwin. I would soon find out that Brent Davis would go to extraordinary extremes to accomplish this goal and, of course, that he would find an ally in Judge David Burnett.

After the conviction Jessie made his requisite "perp" walk to a waiting squad car, cuffed, shackled, and befuddled, guided by the sheriff and the chief of police. A scrum of dozens of reporters scrambled alongside on the icy, snow-covered pavement, gripping their cameras, microphones, and tape recorders, fighting for the best angle. "Why did you do it?" one reporter yelled. Jessie shook his head "no" and ducked into the police car. I walked up to the front passenger side of the cruiser and rapped my knuckles on the window to get the attention of the two Clay County Deputies whose task it would be to transport Jessie to prison in Pine Bluff. When the deputy rolled it down, I reminded them both that Jessie was still my client and that they were not to talk to him about the case under any circumstances. They nodded in agreement, but their faces and body language had changed since the days I visited Jessie at the jail before the trial, the lighter times when Jessie would unlock his own cell door and prance around the jail in his teddy bear slippers. The deputies' faces showed a new presence had taken hold.

I had a feeling where this new presence was coming from because I had noticed one of the two officers huddled with Brent Davis just before they began their journey. This did not instill confidence that the officers would heed my warnings. As soon as Jessie settled in the back seat, one of the deputies offered Jessie a cigarette and lit it for him. Jessie accepted it and inhaled deeply; hands bound. As the car drove off, I felt a chill.

I went back into the courthouse and found Greg Crow and Vicky Krosp. We loaded our file boxes into the car with a furniture dolly. It was a long and empty ride home back to Paragould. No one wanted to talk about what had just happened.

The once hot and hazy rice fields along Highway 135 between Corning and Paragould were frozen and white. What open water we passed was filled with thousands upon thousands of now camouflaged snow geese, sitting amidst the remaining mallards and pintails about to head back north to prepare for nesting in Iowa, Nebraska, Minnesota, the Dakotas, and Canada. I thought briefly about the duck hunting I had missed while preparing for the trial. There is always next year, I told myself, though my time would soon be focused on Jessie Misskelley's appeal.

When I arrived home on the evening of February 4, I was not sure if my wife and kids would recognize me. Still lost in the highs and lows of the past nine months, I was drained. I have extraordinarily little recollection of my first evening home. According to a journal Kim had kept during the trial, she and I and the kids went to Walmart. I do remember that part well. The boys were elated to have me back and expressed their enthusiasm by running up and down the aisles. As Kim went to the checkout, I played with 15-month-old Kathryn, setting her down and letting her wander through the maze of clothing racks, disappearing briefly as I watched her intently.

Kim mentioned that the checkout lady had seen the results of the trial on TV and told her that she thought I had done an incredibly good job. Kim wrote in her journal of the oddity of watching the big man dressed in jeans and a flannel shirt play with his young daughter, so glaringly different from the Dan on TV wearing a suit and tie and looking so busy.

The thing I remember most was the strange feeling that I had nothing to do the next day. There was no trial to attend, no witnesses to prepare, and no judge or prosecutor to joust with. I had been in combat mode for so long I had forgotten the comfort of simply sitting down, relaxing, and having a beer. I would later learn that this down time would come to haunt me in ways I could not have imagined. I slept the entire day Saturday, finally rolling out of bed Sunday at about noon.

Sunday morning's *Commercial Appeal* ran a front-page story recounting a conversation between Big Jessie and Little Jessie as he was about to leave the courthouse for prison. According to the article, Jessie wept as he told his father that he would not survive in prison. Jessie Sr. reminded his son that he was strong and would get through it. Jessie Jr. expressed his fear that he would never come home, but the elder Misskelley again reminded his son of his strength. Reading this only deepened the sadness that was beginning to settle over me. I had to get this kid out of prison. Little did I know at the time, but Jessie Misskelley, Jr. was not the only person involved in the case who was panicking.

Because I had told prosecutors we were appealing Jessie's conviction and that he would not be testifying against his codefendants, his confession automatically became inadmissible in the second trial. The jurors would never get to listen to it. This put prosecutors in a tailspin. A deeply concerned Brent Davis and John Fogleman would express both their plan and their fears to the parents of the victims, explaining to them that they needed Jessie—and they needed him badly.

Jessie, they told the shattered parents, would not testify against Echols and Baldwin "out of the goodness of his heart" but would need to be enticed to do so. They asked the victims' parents for their consent to negotiate a deal for less prison time for Jessie in exchange for his testimony.

In a scene captured in *Paradise Lost*, which would not be revealed to me until two years later at a private screening in New York, Davis tells the victims' parents that "unfortunately, we need his testimony real bad." In the same scene, Fogleman explains to the victims' parents that without Jessie's testimony "all is not lost," but the odds of a conviction "are reduced significantly." In a stunning and illuminating assessment, the nervous Davis responds to a question about the odds of convicting Damien Echols and Jason Baldwin without Jessie's testimony at "fifty-fifty." Two things continue to trouble me about Davis's comments. First, it showed the prosecutors' frenzied desperation to get Misskelley to testify. It also demonstrated the prosecutors' willingness to go to trial and seek the death penalty against Echols and Baldwin based on "fifty-fifty" evidence. Two teens were facing the death penalty with nothing more than a flip of a coin to determine their fate.

34

The near-inquisitorial practices of the legions of law enforcement available to Brent Davis did not miss a beat after Jessie Misskelley was sentenced to life plus forty years in prison on that bitterly cold February day. They began in the police cruiser taking him to prison before I had made it back into the courthouse to gather my belongings. They continued without interruption as prosecutors and police pursued their mission to get Jessie to testify in the upcoming trial.

Three days after Jessie Misskelley's sentencing, Brent Davis called me to reveal that Jessie had "confessed" to the Clay County Deputies on the way to Pine Bluff after they asked Jessie if he wanted to "talk" about the case, assuring him that nothing he said could be used against him later. I was livid. The macabre loop that had started the case in June the year before was beginning anew. Police were still preying on an intellectually challenged kid. Jessie Misskelley would not be able to match wits with even the ineptest of police officers. By law, those officers were prohibited from talking to Misskelley about the case at all.

After dropping his bomb, Davis asked if I would travel down to Pine Bluff with him the next day to determine whether Jessie intended to testify or not. I was outraged, telling Davis that I had specifically told the officers who drove him to Pine Bluff that they were not to talk to him about the case under any circumstances. Davis seemed cavalier over the breach of my client's rights even though their misconduct was directly imputed to him. I suspected that one of the deputies had been directed by Davis to perform this task in the first place. But I was eager to put this issue to rest and agreed to make the long ride down to Pine Bluff with him the next day, February 8, 1994. Fogleman and Gitchell were to meet us there.

Davis faxed me a copy of the report by one of the Clay County Deputies dated February 5, 1994. When I read it, I was struck immediately that Jessie obviously had been paying attention during the trial. Things that Jessie allegedly told the deputies in the squad car –the alleged new "confession" — were nothing more than a muddled stew of things brought up during the trial by both the prosecution and the defense. Taken as a whole, they still made no sense, but that was how Jessie Misskelley processed information.

It is a three-to-four-hour drive from Paragould to Pine Bluff and there is no good way to get there. As soon as we arrived and passed through security, deputies brought Jessie out to the assistant warden's office. As I started to follow him into the office, I turned to see Brent Davis and John Fogleman coming in behind me. I stopped them. Jessie was my client, and I would speak to him alone and learn his intentions. They were not pleased.

Inside with Jessie, my first question was to ask why he had spoken to the officers after I had told him specifically not to. "I don't want to be here for the rest of my life," he said, eyes glued to the floor. He then told me what I can only describe as a repulsive story of how the officers who drove him down to prison told him that if he did not testify, Echols and Baldwin would go free, and Jessie alone would bear the entire blame for killing the three little boys. Whether for emphasis or only plain sadistic revelry, the deputies then told him while he was locked away in prison, Echols and Baldwin would soon be having sex with his girlfriend.

Recounting what he told the officers in the car, Jessie told me, "I made it all up. It was a lie." I then asked Jessie if he wanted to testify against Damien and Jason, and that if he did, he would have to testify *truthfully* in court.

"I want to testify so I can get out of here," said Jessie.

Clearly, he had run right back into traffic again, learning nothing from his previous encounters with the police.

I walked outside to talk to Davis, Fogleman, and Inspector Gitchell. They wanted to know when they could come in and talk to Jessie. Dodging that question, I told them I needed two things, a Bible, and a map of the crime scene, the one that a West Memphis police officer had drawn. I explained that I needed the location of the bodies whited out. The two prosecutors went in search of a Bible and Gary Gitchell called the police department to have them fax over the map of the crime scene. I went back into the assistant warden's office and renewed my conversation with Jessie. Little did I know at the time, but I had just set into motion something that later would become both a legend, and a myth, known as "The Bible Confession."

There was a knock at the door. When I opened it, I realized that one of my wishes had been granted. Someone handed me a Bible. I thanked them and shut the door again. I walked over to where Jessie was sitting and asked him to place his hand on the Bible. I then opened my briefcase and pulled out a small micro-cassette tape recorder. The resulting transcript from that afternoon is sixty-five pages long.

When you pour this now mythological "Bible Confession" through the filter of what we know now as the true extent of Jessie's intellectual disabilities coupled with what we now know was the source of the injuries to the victim's bodies, as we say in Arkansas, "that dog just won't hunt."

The most crucial part of his statement to me that day in Pine Bluff was his complete unfamiliarity with the crime scene. I tired of waiting for Gitchell to bring me the crime scene map, so Jessie and I drew our own. I was doing exactly what the West Memphis Police Department did not do. I took Jessie to the crime scene so he could tell me exactly what happened, and where it happened, the very thing that Warren Holmes said was so important to do in order verify his story. Jessie failed miserably.

He could not seem to find the truck stop just west of the crime scene despite it being so massive. He also said that there were no ponds or lakes nearby. And four days after telling the Clay County deputies that he Damien and Jason had smoked two marijuana joints, Jessie then insisted that they did not.

Eventually, I got the crime scene map from the police. It was more to scale, but Jessie's identification of key and crucial points did not improve despite most of the landmarks now being clearly labeled apart from the location where the bodies were placed in the water. Jessie immediately said that this map was wrong.

"That don't look right. This don't look right," he told me, "To my knowledge it don't look right."

With the police diagram, however, Jessie had no problem gravitating to that large pipe that crosses the Ten Mile Bayou that had been mentioned often during his trial. This was the place that the police recovered the victims' bikes. I asked him to take a green highlighter and indicate on the map where the victims' bodies had been placed. Jessie placed green marks at the big pipe, nowhere near where they were placed in the small creek inside the wooded area where the water was only waist deep, not over anyone's head as Jessie had insisted to me. If the West Memphis police had taken Jessie out there on the night of his June 3, 1993 "confession" and asked him to point out where everything occurred, even they would have known he had never been there. At the end of the taped session, this issue of whether Jessie wanted to take a plea deal and testify against Echols and Baldwin came up again. Jessie's reply now was "I-I-I really don't know."

And with that the interview was over. It ended just as it had begun, with Jessie vacillating over what was true, and what was not, and expressing serious doubts about testifying against Damien and Jessie. The prosecutors were disappointed that I would not let them talk to Jessie.

On his way to prison after the trial, as part of his so-called "police car confession," Jessie had told the Clay County officers he had downed a bottle of *Evan Williams* bourbon after the murders and smashed the bottle near an overpass. "Let's go see if we can find it," I said to the prosecutors and Gitchell.

We made the long trek back to Interstate 40 and then east on to West Memphis to the overpass where Jessie first said that he had smashed the bourbon bottle. We got out and using Gary Gitchell's flashlight began a search under the overpass. The first thing we did was roust a sleeping homeless man. I noticed immediately that this was the place where all whiskey bottles in West Memphis came to die. There was enough broken glass under there to fill the bed of a small pick-up truck. None of the bottles were intact, and it felt as if we were looking for the proverbial needle in a haystack.

We picked up several pieces of what we thought could be part of an *Evan Williams* bottle. We drove to a local liquor store, went inside, found an Evan Williams display, and compared the pieces of glass to the full bottles. One of the pieces we found appeared to be the bottom of an *Evan Williams* bottle. To me it seemed like going to the beach and getting excited about finding some sand.

We had all agreed that there would be no possibility of obtaining any type of fingerprints off any broken bottle we might have found. I explained to Davis, Fogleman and Gitchell that I would need time to let all this soak in and that of course I would have to speak to Jessie Sr.

Davis and I spent the hour-long drive to Jonesboro with him trying to convince me that this one broken piece of glass sitting among thousands of others was the "Holy Grail" of the case and that Jessie should testify at the second trial.

Brent Davis and I have differing accounts about our conversations that night. I remember distinctly that Davis shared with me what he said was his latest evidence. It would later be found to be totally fabricated, as was much of the evidence in Jessie Misskelley's trial, but Davis did not know that as we drove toward Jonesboro.

Revealing his new information, Davis had hoped to convince me of the need for Jessie Misskelley's testimony. Davis told me that a kid named Michael Carson, a jailhouse snitch, had come forward with some startling information. Carson said that while he and Jason Baldwin were incarcerated in the Craighead County Juvenile Detention Center together, Jason had confessed to the murders and the sexual mutilation of one of the victims.

As I made the last leg of the journey home to Paragould alone, I decided Davis's latest news even coupled with mountains of glass, did not change anything for me. Any plea deal would be the Misskelleys' decision, not mine.

The next morning, I dialed Jessie Sr.'s number. I took him through the entire litany of events the previous day and night. Jessie Sr. advised me, as had become his custom, that his son was innocent and should not take any plea offer. Ultimately, Jessie Jr. also agreed that he would not, under *any* circumstances, testify against Echols and Baldwin. I reported this information directly to Brent Davis by leaving a message with his secretary. I thought the craziness was finally over. It was far from it.

35

Brent Davis' next move was to essentially kidnap Jessie Misskelley, aided and abetted by Judge Burnett. On February 16, 1994, Davis submitted an order signed without my knowledge or consent, nor that of Greg Crow, to have Jessie Misskelley brought back up from prison to the Craighead County jail. The order stated the transfer was necessary for the "purpose of giving testimony" in the Echols and Baldwin trial.

When I finally figured out what had happened, it became clear that Burnett and Davis would stop at nothing to coerce Jessie Misskelley into testifying in the upcoming second trial. I knew this ploy would give another deputy sheriff, this time a Craighead County Deputy, three or more hours alone with the bewildered Jessie Misskelley, Jr. trying to convince him to testify.

Davis would use this to his advantage. This deputy had made it clear to Jessie on the transport back up from prison that if he didn't testify against Echols and Baldwin the only way he would get out of prison "was on a stretcher after he died." It was clear the prosecution was first, tone deaf, and second, more than just a little desperate. They simply would not take no for an answer.

The next afternoon, February 17, 1994, the phone rang at my house around 6:15 p.m. It was Greg Crow. He had just gotten a phone call from deputy prosecuting attorney Joe Calvin from Clay County. He had advised Crow that Jessie Misskelley was at his office in Rector, Arkansas. I hung up the phone and immediately called Calvin at his office. "We got Misskelley down here at my office in Rector and he is about to give a statement," Calvin said, "Do you and Crow want to be here?"

I asked Calvin how in the hell Jessie had ended up at his office, but he responded by saying only that Jessie was ready to give his statement. I told Calvin in no uncertain terms that no one was to take a statement from my client or speak to my client unless I was present. He asked me if I was coming to his office in Rector to which I replied, "I am on my way." Crow and I took off on a high-speed drive to Rector, about 20 miles north of Paragould.

At Joe Calvin's office we found Brent Davis. Fogleman was conspicuously absent, in my mind because, perhaps, he did not want any part of what was about to unfold. We asked to speak to our client immediately and were led into a conference room to do so. Fifteen minutes later Davis and Calvin burst in and demanded to take a statement from Jessie. I objected to their intrusion and informed Davis and Calvin that I would finish visiting with my client uninterrupted. They left the room but returned a few minutes later to express their fear that Crow and I would convince Jessie to decline to make a statement to them. *Really?*

Jessie, as always, was bewildered and wanted only to solve the problem at hand –to do something so these men would let him out of prison. He was unable to think about the long-term consequences that giving a statement would have on his appeal. What Brent Davis was trying to do to the befuddled Jessie was depraved, to put it kindly. As we all stood around him, Jessie stood up and announced he was ready to make a statement, despite our advice to him to remain silent.

In a move I now realize was something akin to calling an arsonist to help put out a fire he had just set, I immediately telephoned Judge

Burnett at his home from Calvin's office strenuously objecting to what was happening. What Davis was doing was unconstitutional, I reminded the judge. Judge Burnett did not seem too interested in Jessie's constitutional rights. Judge Burnett advised me that he had earlier granted "use immunity" to Jessie and that the prosecutors did not need my permission to speak to my client. I could not believe what I was hearing and what was happening.

I walked back into the conference room in total disbelief. Just as he did in his June 3, 1993, confessions, the "police car" confession, and the "Bible confession," Jessie's new version of events was just that, a new version.

As in the statement I recorded on February 8, 1994, Jessie used the phrase "I can't remember" more than a dozen times. He could not remember the clothing Damien and Jason wore on the day of the murders, among many other things. He could not remember whether he could remember. In most situations, a prosecuting attorney interested in justice, would be taken aback by Jessie's malleability, his stunning lack of coherence, and his continued lack of narrative, but not Brent Davis. He was buoyed by it, like a hungry wolf stalking his prey.

Bizarrely, Jessie explained to Davis that he left the crime scene after Damien and Jason had thrown the bodies in the water because he was going wrestling. The whole statement was laughable, if not impossible, but Davis seemed focused on every word as if it were finally what he needed to avoid those "fifty-fifty" odds of winning convictions against the other two evil teenagers.

At the end of the statement, I explained, on the record, that as an officer of the court it was my duty to state that in my opinion Jessie Misskelley had just perjured himself. I asked Mr. Crow if he had an opinion, to which he replied, "I have a very strong opinion that he is perjuring himself."

And with that, it was over. Just like the West Memphis police officers before him, Brent Davis, with the full consent of Judge David Burnett, had just outwitted an intellectually handicapped kid. I was ashamed for them.

In the short time that we could speak to our client, Jessie had revealed that the Craighead County Deputy Sheriff who had brought him up from Pine Bluff had promised Jessie that his girlfriend would be brought to the jail so that he could have sex with her after he gave his statement. These men were evil, I thought, during the drive back to Paragould. By the time I got home the 10 o'clock news was coming on with a lead story noting that Jessie Misskelley had been brought back up from prison in case he wished to testify against his co-defendants.

It dawned on me that the police and the prosecutors had, again, manipulated the media. The minds of every potential juror in Craighead County had just been poisoned by this choreographed reminder that Jessie Misskelley had confessed. I did not think it could get any worse, but it did.

I began fielding phone calls from the nervous lawyers who were representing Damien Echols and Jason Baldwin. I told them what had happened at Joe Calvin's office, and they shared my disbelief. When I called Jessie Sr. to let him know the most recent development, he was as angry as I was. I suggested to Jessie Sr. that he drive over to the Clay County jail and immediately meet with his son. He agreed.

When he arrived at the Clay County detention Center, he was told that he could not see his son. Davis now had effectively cut little Jessie off from his lawyers and his father, all with the full consent and knowledge of Judge Burnett. This was so patently wrong in so many ways I could not begin to wrap my mind around it.

Over the course of the next several days, I met with investigator Ron Lax and the attorneys who represented Damien Echols to begin a joint effort in drafting motions for prosecutorial misconduct. Our collective anger deepened when we discovered that Brent Davis had begun covertly meeting with Jessie Misskelley at the Clay County detention Center. This of course was done without my knowledge or consent on Friday, February 18, Saturday, February 19, and again on Sunday, February 20, 1994, in direct violation of Jessie Misskelley's constitutional rights. Ultimately, we decided that each defendant —

Echols, Baldwin and Misskelley — should file his own separate motion for prosecutorial misconduct because the issues were slightly different for each of our clients. I would later learn that each time Davis dropped by to see Jessie, he brought with him a carton of cigarettes as a token of their new friendship.

36

Davis's frantic, unrelenting, and panicked mission still had me dumbfounded. Our motion, filed on February 23 in Clay County, requested three points of relief for the blatant prosecutorial misconduct that had occurred. First, we requested an order from the court directing the prosecution to have no further contact with Jessie Misskelley without my knowledge and consent. Second, we asked Judge Burnett to hold Brent Davis in contempt of court and punished accordingly. Finally, we requested that a special prosecutor from outside the Second Judicial Circuit be appointed to investigate the allegations contained in our motion.

The day of the hearing on the three separate motions, Burnett moved all the lawyers and the court reporter out of the courtroom in Craighead County and outside the earshot of the media. In even tones that I hoped would disguise my anger, I explained to Burnett each allegation contained in our motion. Under Arkansas law and the U.S. Constitution, police misconduct was imputed to the prosecutors, I told the judge. Because I had notified Davis that Mr. Misskelley would not be testifying and would instead pursue his appeals, no further contact should have been made with him. What the prosecutors had done was nothing less than kidnapping, I told the judge.

Davis, standing nearby, did not deny any of the clandestine meetings he had with Jessie without my knowledge. Instead, Davis told the judge he had not taken notes, as if that would somehow exonerate him. Throwing more gasoline on the fire, Davis told Judge Burnett that he believed that I had lost my perspective on the case and was not pursuing the best interests of my client. What happened next surprised me, even at a time in the case when nothing should have surprised me. Judge Burnett fired me.

He appointed Jonesboro attorney Phillip Wells to meet with Misskelley to determine whether Jessie wanted to testify against his co-defendants after all. Clearly, I could not be trusted to perform this task on my own. The order revealed just how desperate

Burnett and Davis were to secure Jessie's testimony. Wells would meet with Jessie alone, then later and separately with his father and stepmother. Then Crow and I would join the discussion. Prosecutors had baited the trap again with a reduction of Jessie's sentence to forty years, down from the life plus forty he already had been sentenced to.

In the end it came down to one simple thing. Jessie told his dad and stepmother, in the presence of Phillip Wells, and then Crow and me, that he did not know whether Damien and Jason were guilty or not. "I can't lie on them no more," Jessie said. These were the same exact words that Jessie had used to turn down the 50-year offer just as his trial was about to start. Phillip Wells reported to Judge Burnett and Brent Davis the same thing that I had been telling Davis for the last three weeks. The Echols and Baldwin trial would proceed without testimony from Jessie Misskelley. Brent Davis then asked Judge Burnett to deny our motions for prosecutorial misconduct, not in a back room where they had been heard but publicly before the media. Judge Burnett was happy to oblige. In 2008, during an attempt at cross-examination of a defense witness during the Rule 37 hearings, Brent Davis would suddenly and without preamble confess that what he did to the mentally challenged Jessie Misskelley to try and obtain his testimony in the second trial was wrong. Luckily, there is a transcript for posterity.

The next morning, I got to the Craighead County Courthouse

early because I wanted to catch Burnett before they got started with jury selection for the Echols and Baldwin trial. Knowing that I could not trust Davis or Burnett, I found Burnett alone in his chambers. I pointed my finger at him and said, "If one more cop or prosecutor talks to my client, I swear to God I will hold a press conference outside the courthouse and I will tell the whole world everything that has been going on." Burnett offered no reply. At the very moment I was talking to Judge Burnett, Brent Davis had another deal in the works that would demonstrate just how desperate he was to win a conviction in the second trial, and at any cost. Even 30 years later the wickedness of it still disturbs me.

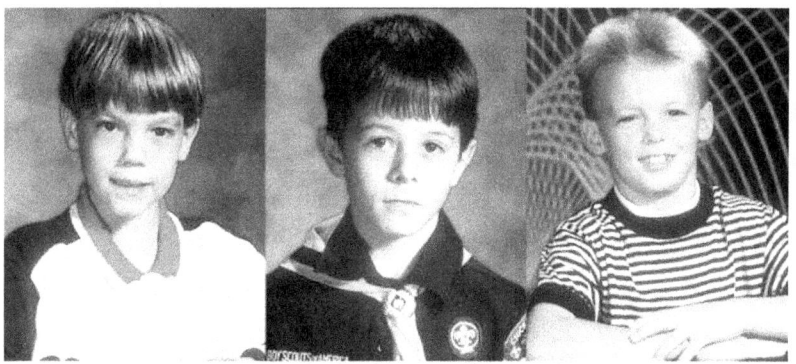

Christopher Byers, Michael Moore, Stevie Branch. Author's Collection.

Iconic mug shots: Damien Echols, Jessie Misskelley, Jr., and Jason Baldwin.
Author's Collection.

Aerial view of the crime scene. The bodies of the three boys were recovered in the wooded area to the east (above) of the large truck stop. Robert Richman photo ©

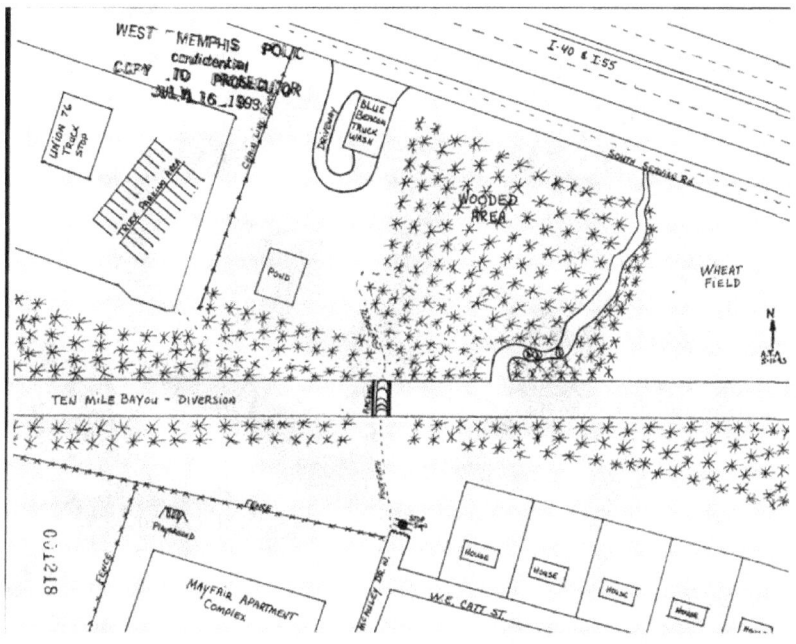

Crime scene drawing by West Memphis Police (not to scale). The bodies were recovered by the black arrow. The dotted lines denote trails leading to the area of the bodies. Author's Collection.

At the Bench with Judge David Burnett. Robert Richman photo ©

Jessie Misskelley, Jr. being escorted into court wearing a bullet-proof vest. Robert Richman photo ©

The Author with Jessie Misskelley, Jr. in the Corning, Arkansas courtroom. Alamy ©

A Harvest of Innocence

Paradise Lost *Director of Photography Robert Richman (left) and the Author inside the Corning courtroom.* Robert Richman photo ©

Dr. Dale Griffis, a retired Ohio police officer whose credentials included a fake mail order Ph.D. from a university he had never attended, testifying as an "expert in the Echols-Baldwin trial that the murders had the "trappings of the occult."
Robert Richman photo ©

Dr. Frank Peretti holding the infamous lake knife. Robert Richman photo ©

Warren Holmes testifying for the defense. Robert Richman photo ©

Dr. Richard Ofshe testifying for the defense. Note what appears to be Judge Burnett's indifference. Robert Richman photo ©

Jessie Misskelley, Jr. being transported to prison after being convicted in Corning in 1994. Robert Richman photo ©

Prosecutors Brent Davis and John Fogleman advise the parents of the victims that without Misskelley's testimony their chances of securing a conviction in the second trial were only "50-50." Robert Richman photo ©

Live on Court TV during the Damien Echols Rule 37 Hearing outside the Craighead County Courthouse in Jonesboro, Arkansas. Robert Richman photo
©

Courtesy of Alan Leveritt and the Arkansas Times ©

With actress and host Winona Ryder at the "Cruel and Unusual: An Exhibition to Benefit the West Memphis Three" at Sixspace Gallery in Los Angeles. Photo by Chris Weeks / Getty Images ©

A Harvest of Innocence

Winona Ryder and the Author in Los Angeles. Photo by Burk Sauls / Enigma Photos ©

August 19, 2011, just after the Alford pleas were entered freeing the West Memphis Three after 18 years and 78 days of incarceration. Jessie Misskelley, Jr. on the left and the Author on the right. Enigma Photos ©

The Author, Misskelley, and George Collier at Macy's Department Store in New York purchasing new attire for Jessie in October 2010. Enigma Photos ©

Bruce Sinofsky-Headshots for the Gentlemen's Quarterly (GQ) *article "Three at Last" that was published in the December 2011 issue.* Peter Hapak / Trunk Archive ©

The Author-Headshots for the Gentlemen's Quarterly (GQ) *article "Three at Last" that was published in the December 2011 issue.* Peter Hapak / Trunk Archive ©

Joe Berlinger-Headshots for the Gentlemen's Quarterly (GQ) *article "Three at Last" that was published in the December 2011 issue.* Peter Hapak / Trunk Archive ©

A Harvest of Innocence

Author and Lea Ann Vanaman at the screening of Paradise Lost 3: Purgatory *during the 49th Annual New York Film Festival at Alice Tully Hall on Monday, October 10, 2011. Photo by Evan Agostini / AP ©*

With John Philipsborn at the Paradise Lost 3: Purgatory *film screening at the 49th Annual New York Film Festival. Enigma Photos ©*

A Harvest of Innocence

From left: Gail Zimmerman, Jason Baldwin, Erin Moriarty, and Dan Stidham. Gail produced the 48 Hours/Mystery: "A Cry for Innocence" and Erin was the investigative journalist for the show. This production really pushed the case forward and featured Johnny Depp showing his support for the WM3. Enigma Photos ©

With Damien Echols and Jason Baldwin at the Nashville Sundance Screening of West of Memphis. *Enigma Photos ©*

Actor Michael Gladis who portrayed me in the film Devil's Knot *based on Mara Leveritt's book of the same title. Gladis wore the same glasses that I wore during the Jessie Misskelley trial. Later Gladis sent me this shot from the set. Enigma Photos ©*

Metallica drummer Lars Ulrich with Jason Baldwin backstage at a concert.
Courtesy Jason Baldwin ©

Holly Ballard, Jason Baldwin, and Eddie Vedder of Pearl Jam. Courtesy of Jason Baldwin ©

Natalie Maines and Jason Baldwin at a Voices for Justice Rally. Courtesy of Jason Baldwin ©

With Sir Peter Jackson at the 2012 Sundance Film Festival for the screening of the film West of Memphis. *Peter and his partner, Fran Wash, were instrumental in reigniting the investigation into the West Memphis Three case.* Enigma Photos ©

Jessie Misskelley, Lea Ann Vanaman, the Author, and West of Memphis *Producer/Director Amy Berg in Chicago.* Enigma Photos ©

A shot taken during the shooting of a scene from the film West of Memphis. *Producer/Director Amy Berg is in the foreground. Seated with her back to the camera is Laura Nirider and to her left Steve Drizen, Co-founders of the Center for Wrongful Convictions at the Northwestern Pritzker School of Law in Chicago. Next to Drizen is Dr. Tim Derning, Jessie Misskelley, and the Author.* Enigma Photos ©

The Author in front of the "Wall of Truth" was taken during a break in shooting West of Memphis. Photo courtesy of Amy Berg and photo by Olivia Fougeirol ©

Criminal Profiler John Douglas was brought in to assist the defense in its re-investigation of the case by Peter Jackson and Fran Walsh. His colleague, Ken Lanning, debunked the theory of Satanic Ritualistic Homicides in the late 1980's, but there are still people hosting seminars for law enforcement agencies about this topic even today. Photo Robert Richman ©

Joe Berlinger and Jason Baldwin at a Cinema for Peace event in Berlin. Photo courtesy of Jason Baldwin ©

When Gary Gitchell was asked by reporters how strong the case was on a scale of 1-10, he replied "Eleven." Photo Robert Richman ©

Free at last. Photo courtesy of Robert Richman ©

37

In the Spring of 1994, the eye of the hurricane passed slowly over Corning, Piggott, Paragould, West Memphis, Jonesboro, and all points between, providing a brief respite from the trials and the appeals that lay ahead. Soon after Damien Echols and Jason Baldwin were locked in prison, to the relief of most people, Ron Lax invited Damien Echols' attorneys Val Price and Scott Davidson, and Greg Crow and I to his office in Memphis for a post-mortem of the trials. We looked at everything, unblinking, grilling ourselves and each other on what went wrong and what we could have done differently. At the heart of the grim exercise was a simple question: Had we done as well as we should have or could have? We made lists of things we would have done differently.

In *Strickland v. Washington* the U.S. Supreme Court in 1984 established a two-part test for establishing a claim of "ineffective assistance of counsel." Under this test, a criminal defendant cannot obtain relief unless he can show that, first, his lawyer's performance fell below an objective standard of reasonableness. Second, did that lawyer's performance give rise to a reasonable probability that if he had performed adequately, the result at trial would have been different? These were tough questions to face. We knew the day would come when we each would be on trial ourselves, and we wanted to be ready. It is not easy to dissect one's performance, especially when I believed I had never wavered in my attitude and that my client's interest always came before my own.

I wanted more than anything to return to something close to normal life, to my family, to cases that did not spark interest from outsiders or draw national attention and death threats. The next eighteen months would provide bursts of joyful distractions filled with enticing family moments—a Siren's song that had begun its seductive call my first night home after the trial. These would prove intermittent over the next 18 months as Greg Crow, and I, prepared our arguments for Jessie Misskelley's case before the seven-member Arkansas Supreme Court. We knew we had two key arguments in our favor and were guardedly confident.

In addition to the Rule 2.3 argument from the original trial, we knew police did not obtain a waiver of Jessie Misskelley's Miranda rights from his father, as required by state law. He was seventeen—a minor—when they brought him in, questioned him, and produced the confession that both opened and closed the case for the State. In addition, with a third grade reading level, Jessie could not fully comprehend the meaning of his Miranda rights in the first place. Surely the Arkansas Supreme Court would see the confession was involuntary, we felt. The appeal would be a two-year process.

Writing our Arkansas Supreme Court brief would be laborious. It would take close to a year for the court reporter to produce the lengthy transcript from which we would work, two thousand six hundred pages from a trial that had lasted three weeks. We would use the time to craft a brief that would, after page number restrictions by the Arkansas Supreme Court and requests for more pages, be eighty-eight and a half pages. After that, we would have oral arguments before the court itself.

The pressure would prove unrelenting and the pull between my desire for normalcy and my need for justice for Jessie Misskelley erupted one afternoon in a scene that still saddens me. One morning my son Daniel asked me to sit with him and play a video game. I told him I had to go to the office to work on the case. "You love Jessie Misskelley more than you love us," he said as he jumped up and ran to his room in tears. I stood briefly staring at his closed door, then burst into tears of my own. I took the afternoon off and played with the kids, but Daniel's comments stung me deeply.

Greg Crow and I would not be ready for the Supreme Court until July 1995. After months of intense work and writing, delays, more writing followed by further delays, we filed our Abstract and Brief with the Arkansas Supreme Court and then sat back to await the response of the attorney general. By Fall, the briefs and reply briefs were all in and we requested oral arguments before the Arkansas Supreme Court, which were scheduled for Monday, December 18, 1995.

I expected a favorable decision. We had gotten Burnett reversed and dismissed by the Arkansas Supreme Court in a 7-0 decision in 1993. So naturally, I was expecting the same result again with Jessie Misskelley being set free. Knowing Jessie Misskelley would have to endure prison for two years was a hard pill to swallow, but I could do nothing to accelerate the process. The wheels of justice turn slowly, but they do turn.

With the huge task of the appeal to the Arkansas Supreme Court looming, the Law Offices of Stidham and Crow were flirting with bankruptcy. After the trial, working on the appeal left us little time for other clients. Our top-notch paralegals, Vicky Krosp and Karen Nobles kept the doors open. We still had our meager salaries as public defenders, though neither of us had handled a Greene County public defender case in months. By April of 1994 things had gotten so tight that Greg and I had to re-finance our office building to pay our federal income taxes. We had to pay our state income taxes in installments. Things were edgy, and to make matters worse we had not been paid for our work on the West Memphis case, but we began to see our practice come slowly back, and we began to recover.

On Friday, April 22, Judge Burnett presided over a hearing in Paragould, in the old historic 1888 Courthouse, concerning the payment of attorneys' fees in the cases as well as expenses. He awarded more than $140,000 dollars in defense attorney's fees, with Val Price getting $30,500; Scott Davidson his second chair $26,000. Paul Ford was awarded $26,000; his second chair, Robin Wadley got $20,000. Greg and I had more than 2,000 hours in the case —far more than any of the other defense teams. We were awarded a joint fee of $40,000—the least amount of any defense team. With interest, when we finally received payment, it worked out to about $21.73 per hour. Burnett had promised $40 per hour for out-of-court time and $60 for time spent in hearings and trial. Warren Holmes got his airfare, as he had requested; Richard Ofshe received $1,500; Ron Lax received nothing for his many hours of assistance in our case, though he did receive $7,000 in the Echols case. As the hearing ended, I asked Burnett what formula he had used to arrive at the figures. He refused to respond. He awarded us $3,500 for out-of-pocket expenses, despite us presenting receipts for $4,049.11.

To add insult to injury, the County of Crittenden and the State of Arkansas continued arguing over who should pay us and we had no idea how long it would take to get paid, adding more misery to an already miserable situation. When the State of Arkansas put a lien on my house, I wrote the head of the State Income Tax Section telling him that I would pay my taxes when the State paid me the $20,000 it owed me. He was not impressed, nor did he care.

38

While we were waiting for the trial transcript, I was enjoying the benefits of being a real father again. Daniel, my oldest was eight and a half and my second son, Chris, would be seven in just four months. My daughter Kathryn was still a toddler—perfect ages for children to love their father unconditionally. That first week of April 1994, I became mesmerized by the Arkansas Razorbacks—who had a stunning and impressive regular season and were hot during the 1994 NCAA Men's Division I Basketball Tournament. They had improbably worked their way through their bracket, into the Final Four, and then into the final scheduled for April 4 against perennial favorite Duke.

Like a disgruntled magistrate, Kim ruled that the nationally televised game at 9:00 pm was too late for me to watch with the boys on a school night, and she forbade them to sit up with me at home for the game. I could not talk her out of it and the more I tried, the more the boys cried.

Reluctantly, I left the house and drove over to Roy's Last Chance in Paragould to watch. They had a big-screen television, and much to my surprise, the crowd was sparse. Coincidentally, my long-time friend Brad Broadaway, a huge Hogs fan, was there. The game was close, but Arkansas prevailed in an upset win 76-72.

After I went home, I snuck into the boys' room and was surprised to find Chris still awake. "I did it Daddy, I watched it," he told me, still amped up from the excitement long past his bedtime. "I just couldn't listen to it. I turned it all the way down so momma wouldn't hear it." I laughed so loud; I thought I would wake up Kim myself. Life seemed almost normal.

The next day the news was filled with stories about the Razorbacks taking the National Championship, but there was also the disturbing story of *Nirvana* front man Kurt Cobain committing suicide at age twenty-seven in Seattle.

Two weeks after the championship dust had settled, I turned down an offer to appear on the *Maury Povitch Show*. Povitch's producers wanted me to debate the victims' families, the same sort of cringingly tasteless drivel that the *Geraldo* people had wanted me to do during the Echols and Baldwin trials. Producers from the *Geraldo Show* invited me to appear on a segment they would call *"When Kids Kill Kids: Did the Devil Make them Do It?"* They planned to include a Catholic priest.

Years later, Geraldo Riviera would apologize for his role in creating and promoting the satanic panic, but at the time he had only inflamed it. Later in 1994, I would turn down the *Maury Povitch Show* again, for the same reason. I could be the record holder for the number of free trips to New York ever turned down by a single person. I wanted no part of it.

Despite the distractions and the teasing warmth of normality, Jessie Misskelley's case was still there, like a cancer in remission—forgotten but always threatening to erupt once again. It seemed lonely out there, but Greg Crow and I were confident that once we got a chance to take our case to the Arkansas Supreme Court we could win and find an answer to my prayers, "truth and justice" after all.

On May 22, 1994, Cheryl Adcock, Ron Lax's assistant, faxed me a troubling note. Diane Moore, the mother of victim Michael Moore, had called Cheryl and told her that during the trial in Corning she had been having lunch and other meetings with the members of the jury. Mrs. Moore, it seemed, had also taken to calling the Misskelley household in the early morning hours, very intoxicated— berating Jessie's stepmother Shelbia one moment, then expressing doubt about Jessie's guilt the next.

"I don't know what to believe anymore," she had told Shelbia.

We could never confirm her stories of meeting with jurors, and I doubt very much that it happened. I felt sorry for her and her enormous grief. Later, Diane Moore would be sentenced to five years' probation for negligent homicide because of a June 1995 drunk-driving accident that killed a pedestrian.

In June the focus of the national media moved quickly off West Memphis and placed it squarely and rabidly in Southern California. Football hero and cultural icon O.J. Simpson was charged with the murders of his ex-wife, Nicole Brown Simpson, and Ronald Goldman, in what can only be described as gruesome circumstances.

At approximately 6:45 p.m. on June 17, 1994, shortly after the charges were announced, police saw Simpson on the LA Expressway in a white Ford Bronco driven by his best friend and former teammate, Al Cowlings. Simpson was riding in the back seat, and he reportedly had a gun. With the huge motorcade of police cars in pursuit, TV helicopters swooped in to join the chase. The 60-mile, low-speed pursuit through southern Los Angeles would go down in television history. This story took the spotlight off the West Memphis 3 case, at least temporarily.

There is a strange irony, to me at least, in O.J. Simpson's ultimate acquittal. He was found not guilty in some part by a jury that was selected from a community that largely did not trust police in a case rife with alleged police misconduct. In our case, we argued police misconduct, but people in northeast Arkansas believed firmly in the integrity of the West Memphis police. Today, most people, I believe, think three juries got it wrong.

39

Duck hunting has always been a Stidham family tradition. I went on my first hunt on a crisp November morning at the Dave Donaldson Wildlife Management area, just south of Corning, when I was twelve years old. Since then, my sons have done the same, using the single-shot .20-gauge Winchester Model 370 shotgun I used. Good Lord willing, my grandchildren will use that ancient Winchester when it is their turn. The comfort of a well-worn tradition means a great deal to me.

Normally, duck season in Arkansas begins around Thanksgiving, but in 1994 hunters—and there are plenty in Arkansas—were allowed under special circumstances to shoot Teal two months earlier on two selected weekends. The feel of the September hunt was different because the trees were still green and full. I drove my old 1977 Ford Bronco to the edge of a field on a bright, sunny afternoon and began unloading the supplies Chris and I would need into a pirogue, a flat-bottomed canoe we'd use to collect our game.

Summer had not yet surrendered its grip to cooler weather and the September air felt stuffy and oppressive. Freshly cut rice stubble stood knee high in the field we needed to cut across to get to the water. After pulling the pirogue from the truck, I sat Chris inside.

Shielding my eyes from the sun, I spotted the cypress tree standing at the edge of the field to our west. A state game officer had offered the tree as a landmark that sat near the duck-hunting area he promised would be fruitful.

I threw the tow rope over my shoulder and smiled at Chris, telling him to hold on, then began pulling the fiberglass pirogue through the stubble to the cypress. As we neared the landmark the foliage became fuller, and we would easily find ample cover to hunt.

As we edged into a thicket, I saw we would have to cross a ditch filled with dark, imperceptibly moving water to reach a suitable spot to hunt. The murky water in the ditch appeared thick and muddled, with a surface film that would cling to anything that passed through it. My nostrils flared with the odor of rich earth dampened by a rain shower that morning. The trapped stand of water reeked from runoff from field chemicals and the putrid heat combined to create a perfect breeding ground for mosquitoes. The wafting stagnation proved irresistible to swarms of flies as I stepped into the water.

I stared deeper into the pool and my skin began to prick and crawl as a chill swept through my hands and feet. Every hair on my bare arms stood quickly to attention. Despite the sweltering heat I felt a penetrating cold. I broke my gaze from the stagnant water to see what surrounded us. The land was completely still. Ditch-bank trees, still full of leaves, stood frozen. Their roots breaking from the bank looked like snakes slithering quietly into the water.

Shivering, I felt my heartbeat quicken, pounding loudly in my chest. A new sensation I had been unaware of began to overtake me. Other than my rapid breathing the woods were eerily silent. No birds chirped; no trees rustled—not even a squirrel ran for cover. It was deathly silent. I was overwhelmed by a sense of urgency.

I quickly glanced over my shoulder to make sure Chris was safe from whatever imminent danger had gripped me, although I had no idea what that threat might be. Chris smiled up at me with the excitement of a seven-year-old boy on a duck hunt with Dad. "Pull it together," I thought to myself.

Standing motionless on the side of the ditch, my legs shook. I could not move. My head swirled and I feared I would pass out. Pushing past the tightness in my chest and throat I choked out an "Alright let's go," praying I would not break into a panicked run. Soon I would be immersed in the filthy water. I was overcome by the thought of it. My only concern at this point was for Chris, still excited and blissfully unaware of my paralysis. I had to get him away from the danger.

My paralysis broke and I lunged in. Gripping tightly on the pirogue rope I pulled it quickly and began shoving it into the water, sending ringlets of waves across the undisturbed stretch. The water became an even darker shade of brown, still concealing what lay below. Three steps into the ditch and pushing Chris ahead of me in the small boat as hurriedly as I could, the staleness wafted ungraciously upward, burning my eyes. The resulting tears ran freely down my cheeks. When the water reached my knees the soft creek bed underneath threatened my stability. The muck pulled and the uneven bottom became slick and unstable. I did not slow down. Taking longer, nearly impossible strides I pressed on—I had to get Chris out of that ditch.

As my feet gripped solid ground on the opposite bank, my right foot slipped in the mud, slamming my knee painfully into an embedded rock. I did not slow down. I hurled Chris and the pirogue roughly onto the bank, then scrambled up behind them. The bank was especially steep, and I clawed with my one available hand, frantic to get out and back into the light.

I glanced at Chris again. He was still happily sitting in the pirogue oblivious to what was going on. I heard quick breaths in rapid succession nearby and glanced around nervously. The panicked breathing was my own.

At the top of the embankment, I did not look back at the dreadful scene in our wake. I could not face whatever it was that had caused my terror. My racing heart began to slow, and the tightness in my chest slowly loosened its grip. My legs steadied. I closed my eyes and focused on breathing deeply. I was duck hunting with my son—something we enjoyed. Then it hit me.

A Harvest of Innocence

The grimy ditch I had just crossed in panic was as peaceful yet as terrifying as the watery tomb of Christopher Byers, Michael Moore, and Stevie Branch—their bodies lying just beneath the surface. My panic had been fear, dread that with each step I would graze the arm or leg of a dead young boy. Those past five minutes that day with Chris was my introduction to an intrusion that would visit me for years. It had sprung from the gruesome photographs of three mutilated little boys found in an Arkansas creek—crime scene photos I had examined thousands of times over the course of the trial.

I shifted my gaze again to the seven-year-old boy sitting happily in his pirogue. He was one year younger than the murdered children. I attempted a smile and then resumed our search for an area to hunt. Refusing to gaze behind us, I trudged forward with Chris still in the pirogue in the stifling September air.

With the leaves now blowing peacefully, my panic subsided. Chris was safe, but I would be carrying something else for years to come. More than 30 years to be exact.

40

In October 1995 Greg Crow left Stidham & Crow to open his own law practice, telling me he hoped to be working for the Arkansas Attorney General's Office in Little Rock in the months ahead. He agreed to continue to assist with Jessie's appeal and we began our preparations for oral arguments.

Finally, on December 18, 1995, a gloomy mist and coldness presaged our presentation before the Arkansas Supreme Court. We were tense. The Attorney General in his reply brief had been arguing that we had somehow failed to obtain a ruling on our key issue, the Rule 2.3 violation, a contention that surprised me since we obviously had. I had drafted the order on that specific point for Burnett's signature following the suppression hearing. It had clearly stated that Burnett had considered our amended motion and brief to suppress Jessie's confession on this issue.

During our oral arguments, all seven Justices seemed focused intently on this issue. After our presentation, I was upbeat, satisfied that our oral presentations had gone well. As we gathered our materials, packed our briefcases, and walked from the courtroom, Greg told me emphatically – "We either just won 4 to 3 or lost 3-4, but I feel like we may have just pulled it off."

Greg had worked as a clerk for a Supreme Court Judge in Missouri before joining me at the law firm in Paragould. During his time working in Missouri, Greg had developed an uncanny ability to "call" cases in the Missouri Supreme Court while watching oral arguments. He could read the faces and the body language of the judges. He told me once that he rarely failed to accurately predict the outcome of an appeal based on the questions that the justices asked the lawyers during their arguments. This he said, almost always revealed the way that they would vote on any particular case. Greg's comments as we were leaving the Arkansas Supreme Court that day would become perhaps the most foreboding of all the jarring moments in the case.

Jessie Misskelley, Jr. was having a rough time adjusting to prison. As he had been his entire life, he was an easy target. Being a convicted child killer did nothing to make his lot any smoother. He was a perfect prey, and there was an abundance of less-than-genteel men looking to make his life hell. In early January 1996 I walked into the office to find a frantic phone message relayed from Jessie.

"He said that it was an emergency. He said that they told him that they were going to kill him tonight."

I called the warden and diffused the situation, then got word to Jessie he was going to be all right. He would be placed in special protection. The situation only added to the tension as we waited for the Arkansas Supreme Court decision that would get Jessie Misskelley home again.

On Monday, February 19, 1996, the Arkansas Supreme Court affirmed Jessie Misskelley's conviction in a unanimous 7-0 decision. Greg and I were shocked. The most disturbing aspect of the Court's decision involved its ruling on the Rule 2.3 issue that should have prompted an automatic reversal of Misskelley's conviction. The Court concluded that we had not raised the Rule 2.3 issue in a timely fashion despite our Amended Motion and Brief on the issue. They further concluded that we had not obtained a ruling from Burnett on the issue. *Of course, we had done both things.* All this was a part of the official record in the case. *Why was the prosecutors' failure to respond to our amended motion and brief not a part of the consideration given by the Court?*

Back on December 18, 1995, when the Arkansas Supreme Court heard oral arguments in the Misskelley case it was apparent that at least some of the justices seemed to be swayed by our arguments on the Rule 2.3 issue. We seemed to have some votes. So, when the ruling came down that February morning, I was both devastated and disturbed by the 7-0 result.

Crow and I, in our callow minds, thought that this oversight would be corrected by simply pointing out this error on the part of the Court. Once we showed the Court exactly where in the official record of the case where we raised the issue and the Order Burnett signed denying the motion, justice would prevail. We immediately drafted a motion for rehearing and in the process, we pointed out to the Court the precise page numbers in the record on appeal where these documents appeared. We waited patiently for a response.

Appropriately perhaps, the Arkansas Supreme Court's decision on our motion for rehearing came down on April Fool's Day, 1996. When I read it, I felt like a fool, and I knew then, at least in my own mind, exactly what had happened. They merely said that the "Rule 2.3 issue would not be addressed again on rehearing." It is what they did not say that was so revealing. They never even mentioned the pages in the official record where we had pointed out their error. *Why were they pretending that something did not exist in the record when it was so easily verifiable?* It was not unlike a playground retort: "Because we said so, that's why."

Suddenly and quite publicly, it was entirely my fault that Jessie Misskelley was in prison for a crime he did not commit. My brilliant chess move was swept off the board as if it never even happened. Greg Crow did the best he could to console me, but I took it extremely hard. He had come over to the office to discuss our misfortune and that of Jessie Misskelley. At the end of that dismal chat, Greg turned and gave me something to hold on to, a glimmer of hope, something that had escaped me in my time of grief.

"You know what Dan; they can't have it both ways."

"What do you mean?"

"We either raised it or we didn't," he said. "They can't have it both ways."

Greg then elaborated by saying that if we had raised the issue properly, Jessie would have gone free. "They say we didn't raise it, but we both know we did," he continued, "that will be grounds for an automatic new trial based on irrefutable evidence that Misskelley received ineffective assistance of counsel. Either way, Jessie goes free. It's just a matter of time," Greg added.

I told Vicky that I would be out of the office for a few days. "I need time to take all this in," I told her. "I understand and don't worry about the office," she said as she embraced me. She had no idea the thoughts running through my head, or she would not have been so calm and collected. Or perhaps, she knew me better than I knew myself.

I spent the better part of the next three days seriously questioning if I wanted to be a lawyer anymore. Everything I believed in—everything that had compelled me to choose the law as my career and life—seemed like an elaborate hoax. I had gone to law school because I believed in the simple concept of a single word with all my being. That word was "justice." I did not want to be a part of something where "justice" was just a token and empty word.

Then I thought of my promise to Jessie that I would never give up. His impoverished family was without funds to move forward. I was, quite literally, his only hope. I had a commitment to my client and a commitment to my family, and despite the guilt associated with each commitment, I was suddenly focused like a laser beam on fixing this problem.

It was a huge problem, and the odds were stacked high against me. I had no idea how long it would take, but I knew from that day, April 1, 1996, that I would fight for as long as it took. It would be a guerrilla war, and I would have to pick my battles. Strike the enemy from the shadows. Sun Tzu's book, *The Art of War*, would become my blueprint. His quote, "In the midst of chaos, there is opportunity," became another of my mantras.

I took stock in what I had to work with. It was true that I had even less appellate experience than I had jury trial experience, but I had courage, and I sure as hell was not giving up or going away. It was true that I had just received a good solid kick in the teeth from the Arkansas Supreme Court. They had thrown me squarely under the bus, and I was not entertained by that notion. The chess game was back on, and I was ready to fight. And I never looked back again. I also wanted some redemption, a little bit for me, and a whole lot for Jessie Misskelley.

41

The next stage of the battle was to send off for my credentials to be admitted to practice before the U.S. Supreme Court. I would then file a *Writ of Certiorari* on behalf of Jessie Misskelley. Thousands of these Writs are filed with the Court each year from all around the country, and the odds of getting your case heard are quite slim. In 2017, the success rate for criminal case filings of Writs of Certiorari was 1.8%.

I was admitted to practice before the U.S. Supreme Court on May 26, 1996. When I called the U.S. Supreme Court Clerk's Office to ask for a continuance to file my Writ, I was told that the case had been assigned to Justice Clarence Thomas. The young clerk on the other end of the line seemed genuinely excited to hear from me and said that she and the other clerks had been waiting for me to file my *Writ of Certiorari*. Clearly, she and the other clerks had seen *Paradise Lost*. I could not help but think that this had to be a good sign and perhaps the odds were a little better than I thought.

Ten days later, I found myself on the cover of the *Arkansas Times* in a story entitled *John Grisham, meet Dan Stidham: Fiction pales against a Paragould Lawyer's real-life trial in a triple child slaying* authored by James Morgan. Once the article was put on-line, I started receiving cards, letters, and emails from all over the world applauding my efforts in the case. Reading John Grisham books was one of the ways I dealt with the problem of not having so much to do. I had become so accustomed to processing so much information on a daily basis since June 7, 1993, that I became a voracious reader in the aftermath of the direct appeal to the Arkansas Supreme Court. I did not need idle hands or an inactive mind. Just a few days after the cover story in the *Arkansas Times, Paradise Lost: The Child Murders at Robin Hood Hills* was released on HBO. The following morning, I had over a thousand emails in my inbox.

The year 1996 certainly had its share of dark moments, and it only got worse on the evening of August 8. It started when Arkansas Governor Jim Guy Tucker was convicted of financial misdeeds and forced to resign on July 16, 1996. Lieutenant Governor Mike Huckabee was then sworn in as the Governor of Arkansas. One of Huckabee's first acts as Governor was moving up, by a couple of weeks, the execution date of Frankie Parker, whose conversations in his dimly lit cell nine years earlier had helped forge my views of the law and its consequences.

The only logical rationale I could see for this move by the new governor was to thwart Mr. Parker's last-minute attempts at receiving a stay of execution. Calls and letters had poured into the governor's office from all over the world asking for clemency, including pleas from Mother Teresa, Pope John Paul II, and the Dalai Lama. Frankie Parker had found peace in Buddhism after a few years on Death Row and had been ordained as a Buddhist priest. He had been a model prisoner for many years after his conversion and had much left to contribute to society despite his crimes.

As the hours ticked by on August 8th, it became clear that there would be no stay issued. I called the Governor's mansion and asked to speak to Governor Huckabee. His chief of staff told me that would not be possible but said he would pass along my message. Because Huckabee was a Baptist minister, I held out hope until the very end that he would show mercy to a man I knew to be truly repentant. After more than 4,000 days on death row, William Frank Parker was executed by lethal injection at 9 p.m. on August 8, 1996. At 9:01 p.m. he was pronounced dead.

It was one of the darkest days of my life and even in the intervening years, it is still hard to find words adequate to explain what it's like to lose a client, even in a case I just worked on in law school. Frank Parker was guilty of the crimes he was convicted of. Frank Parker had helped to introduce Damien Echols to Buddhism on death row. I did not want the same thing to happen to Damien Echols, who unlike Frank Parker, was innocent. I had to get them out of prison, all of them.

Just as the torrid Arkansas summer was about to loosen its grip and let the cooler fall weather prevail, I received a letter on October 7, 1996, from the United States Supreme Court Clerk. It read:

> Dear Mr. Stidham,
> The court today entered the following order in the above-entitled case: the petition for writ of certiorari is denied.
> Sincerely,
> William K. Suter

I was disappointed, but not surprised. The odds had been stacked against us, yet again. The clock was now ticking on Jessie's Rule 37 petition. All my efforts to get an attorney in Arkansas to present an ineffective assistance of counsel claim on behalf of Jessie had failed. Things were really starting to look bleak. The year closed out with the Arkansas Supreme Court affirming the convictions of Damien Echols and Jason Baldwin two days before Christmas. It too would be a 7-0 decision.

42

Bruce Sinofsky and Joe Berlinger's documentaries, *Paradise Lost: The Child Murders at Robin Hood Hills* in 1996, and *Paradise Lost 2: Revelations* in 2000, would spark a startling crusade for justice. The documentaries created a growing and vocal court of public opinion across the country and the world. A movement to "Free the West Memphis Three" had launched soon after *Paradise Lost*. The sequel sent it into orbit. The day after its premiere in March of 2000 on HBO, I would get more than 5,000 emails from all around the world.

A sympathetic national audience was shocked after *Paradise Lost* was released. It would force the first small cracks in the case so carefully engineered by police, prosecutors, and the judge, who not surprisingly dismissed the film's assertions as heavily biased. They had thought, especially after the Arkansas Supreme Court's affirmation of the convictions of the West Memphis 3, that the whole thing could now be safely interred and forgotten. *Paradise Lost: Revelations* would shatter that misguided hope.

Both films would cast doubt on the convictions in a way I never could. They would be viewed in the parochial environs of Arkansas and the Mid-South as hatchet jobs, the type of skewed productions one would expect from liberal outsiders ignorant of the way things are done properly. *Revelations*, even more forcefully than *The Child Murders at Robin Hood Hills*, did not pull any punches. It was an advocacy film for the three defendants.

Locally, I began to see and hear signs that attitudes toward me and the case were changing. In 1998, I was chosen by the readers of the *Paragould Daily Press* as "Best Attorney." My pariah status began to wane, replaced with a grudging respect for what I had done and was still trying to do. I would soon be able to tell when either documentary was being shown without looking at a *TV Guide*. The emails and phone calls arrived in torrents.

One early morning around 2:00 am, I was startled awake by the ringing of my home phone. Climbing from bed, the caller ID revealed that the call was from New York. I picked it up expecting to hear Bruce Sinofsky's voice, but the voice I heard had a heavy *Tony Soprano* accent. The caller asked if I was the "Dan Stidham" who represented Jessie Misskelley from the HBO documentary. I grabbed the remote for the television and turned it on, *Paradise Lost 2: Revelations* was playing on HBO.

"Yes sir, I'm that Dan Stidham."

"Looks to me like your kid and the other two kids are innocent."

"Yes, sir, I agree 100 percent."

"It also looks to me that the crazy guy, you know, Byers, did the crime."

"Some people believe that, yes sir."

"You say the word, and I will have this Mark Byers guy whacked."

I could not believe what I was hearing. This guy was not kidding around.

"I think we are closing in on him fast and I would rather he get a lethal injection."

"I understand, but if you change your mind, you got my number."

I did not write the number down, and I erased it from my caller ID. Later, after the release of *West of Memphis*, I would recount this story to Mark Byers. He was not amused.

43

In August 1995, the *Arkansas Democrat-Gazette* reported the abduction and murder of Christopher Meyer just north up interstate 55 in Kankakee, Illinois. Meyer, 10 years old, vanished while riding his bike home from a boat ramp at a community park on August 7, 1995. The boy's bicycle was found on the opposite side of the Kankakee River from the boat ramp and his tennis shoes were found floating in the river. His body was found in a shallow grave a week later. He had been stabbed repeatedly and sexually mutilated, his penis and testicles were missing. His DNA was found in the trunk of a car owned by Timothy Buss, twenty-seven, who had been paroled in 1993 after killing a five-year-old year girl in 1981, and he was arrested.

I wondered what the odds were of such a coincidence. The child's name was unnervingly similar to one of the victims in the West Memphis 3 case, Christopher Byers, who had suffered the same type of sexual mutilation as the boy in Kankakee. Meyer, like Chris Byers, was last seen riding his bike.

I asked Ron Lax to investigate when exactly Buss was paroled in 1993. Lax quickly learned that Timothy Buss was still in prison on May 5, 1993, making it no more than just a strange and eerie coincidence.

A week later, I had lunch at the *Duck Inn* in Paragould with John Fogleman, who had by then been elected a Circuit judge and was conducting court in Greene County. On the short drive from the courthouse to the restaurant, Fogleman turned to me as I drove and said to me: "In my heart of hearts I believe that we got the right guys, but you need to check out the murder of a boy up the interstate in Kankakee."

I thanked him for the information but told him that we had already eliminated Timothy Buss as a suspect. He had not been paroled from prison until August of 1993. His comment prompted some curiosity on my part over just how sure he was about the convictions of Jessie Misskelley, Damien Echols, and Jason Baldwin, "heart of hearts" or not. In November of 1996, Circuit Judge John Fogleman was quoted in the *Phoenix Times* as saying that "There was a remarkable lack of physical evidence against anybody" in the West Memphis case.

Two years after the convictions, only Ron Lax and I were searching for the lost trails, missed leads, and unquestioned suspects left behind by the West Memphis Police. Over the years, as Damien Echols, Jessie Misskelley, and Jason Baldwin festered in Arkansas prisons, evidence grew that they had nothing to do with the murders. Almost from the outset, John Mark Byers, stepfather of Christopher Byers, and then later Terry Hobbs, stepfather of victim Stevie Branch, emerged as possibilities.

Neither Byers, Hobbs, nor their family members were strangers to the police or to trouble. The families of those murdered boys had tough lives, and what they were forced to live through, first the brutal murders, then living under an unrelenting public microscope, surely must have tortured them for years.

There was much violence in the lives of Mark Byers and Terry Hobbs, yet they were investigated only perfunctorily. And they were always let off the hook because they were "victims." After the murders sparked so much attention and fervor, and after Mark Byers had seemingly willed himself into the spotlight, the Federal Marshals

Service in Memphis confirmed he had been in their custody in 1992, a year before the murders.

He had been arrested by sheriff's deputies in Memphis on drug and weapons charges. He was also convicted in 1995 of contributing to the delinquency of a minor by forcing two kids to fight to settle an argument that left one teen seriously injured by a knife. The knife belonged to Byers, and he was holding a rifle while the two boys fought. Byers reacted to the cameras in the *Paradise Lost* trilogy like a seasoned performer, and whether he did so intentionally or not, his soliloquies raised many eyebrows.

Melissa and Mark Byers were both charged with burglary for allegedly stealing $20,000 of antiques from a neighbor's house in Cherokee Village, Arkansas, and trying to sell them at a pawn shop. Melissa was also charged later with aggravated assault for holding some carpet layers at gunpoint because she was not satisfied with their work. She died in 1996 under very suspicious circumstances. Her autopsy left more questions than it answered.

Mark Byers finally lost his status as "victim" when he attempted to sell drugs to an undercover informant and was sentenced to prison in the same Arkansas Department of Corrections that held Damien Echols, Jason Baldwin, and Jessie Misskelley. Terry Hobbs pled guilty in February 1995 for shooting Pam Hobbs' brother in the abdomen in November 1994. The brother-in-law reportedly had been confronting Hobbs over his alleged beating of Pam. Hobbs was able to avoid going to prison. Our investigators would later find other evidence of violence in Terry Hobbs' past.

"There was a cloud over all these people's lives before this happened," said Bruce Sinofsky, in a news article just prior to the release of *Paradise Lost 2*, "and it will continue till the day they die."

44

Not Long after *Paradise Lost* was released, three Californians who would become eminently helpful in spreading the word about the West Memphis 3 made a surprise visit to my office in Paragould. Kathy Bakken, Grove Pashley, and Burk Sauls had worked on the marketing material for the film and were about to start raising money for a defense fund. We spent a long evening together.

Each worked in the entertainment business in Los Angeles and knew people who might be willing to jump in and help. They planned to create a website and wanted to know more about the case, things that had not been revealed in the film. I had plenty to tell them. They were taken aback when I showed them evidence from the trial and the gruesome photos of the three victims. In a way, I was testing them to see if they would shy from the fight once they visualized what we were dealing with.

As part of the publicity for *Paradise Lost*, they had created a poster for the film that proclaimed *"It's frightening to think that they did it. Terrifying to think they didn't."* In the background was a photograph of a bicycle lying in the street. Most journalists and their producers, I told them, were afraid to stick their necks out too far because hanging over the case like a heavy cloud, was that one question, *what if they really did do it?*

I made it clear I was convinced of the innocence of the West Memphis 3. They did not need convincing, and I needed help. A fund-raising effort, using the new and emerging power of the Internet was not something I could do. I told them that right now the only people who care about this case are standing in this room.

In a later retrospective article on how the growth of the case had become a movement in *L.A. Weekly*, Bakken is described as an "intelligent woman with a generous smile and charming Kentucky twang." She would tell the *LA Weekly* reporter she recognized "everything I loathed about the South, the narrow-mindedness and religious bigotry." Burk Sauls, a writer, freelance movie prop technician, and an aspiring filmmaker, originally from Tallahassee, Florida, felt the same. Grove Pashley is a talented photographer, his work in high demand in Hollywood.

Within a year of our meeting, the three would have the website up and running. It would become instrumental in keeping the case in the public eye. As the Internet grew so did the amount of attention. Soon they would be joined by Lisa Fancher, owner of punk pioneer label *Frontier Records*. Fancher took over the marketing for the site, selling such things as the iconic black T-shirt emblazoned with the mug shots of Echols, Baldwin, and Misskelley, under which sat FREE THE WEST MEMPHIS 3 in white. Soon it became simply "Free the WM3." They were turning heads. Their efforts at securing justice for the WM3 was prominently portrayed in *Paradise Lost 2: Revelations.*

In 2003, the KGB, as they became known, organized a fund raiser at Los Angeles art gallery *Sixspace* called "Cruel and Unusual: An Exhibition to Benefit the West Memphis Three" hosted by Winona Ryder. At dinner the evening before the event, Ryder spoke passionately about the case to our small group that included Kathy, Burk, and Grove. Ryder asked me many questions about the case. I was impressed by her interest, and her willingness to host the event. I enjoyed meeting her. The exhibit drew a crowd of almost 5,000 Angelenos who lined up around the block just to get in.

The event was covered by national and international media, including the *BBC, USA Today, People magazine, Rolling Stone, Celebrity Justice*, and the *Associated Press*. Ryder also spoke, again quite passionately, about the case to the huge crowd that assembled. She then introduced me to the crowd for a few words about the case. It is still the largest crowd that I have ever spoken to. The event raised $20,000 for the defense fund.

45

The appeals process continued to ebb and flow, and with it, my moods and anxiety. I tried to take stock and move ahead. I justified the setbacks. After the Arkansas Supreme Court denial, I was bolstered by Greg Crow's comment that "they can't have it both ways." After the U.S. Supreme Court denial, I was running low on enthusiasm.

To many people in Paragould, I was the local madman, either the Arkansas version of *Don Quixote* or, less lofty, the village idiot, tilting at windmills no one else saw and talking nonsense that no one wanted to hear. People close to me, good friends, and family, would pat me on the back and tell me I should be happy with my efforts. Strangers would approach and offer vague consolations, saying I had done a great job. Jessie's life plus forty years sentence was not really that bad if you considered Damien Echols's death sentence, they would tell me. I felt patronized. Still, I talked about the case to anyone who would listen, and it did not take long to realize no one wanted to hear about it anymore—if they ever did in the first place.

People I was closest to, the people who loved me, would tell me to give it a rest. "Dan you gotta let this go," they would say. "You have to get on with your life." My own father warned me that the folks warming the stools at the local coffee shop were starting to talk. I knew that the talk could not be good if my own father was telling me to drop my obsession. My father was shocked when I told him that Jessie Misskelley was innocent. "Really," he replied. "Then do what you got to do," he told me.

Soon enough, I would have the responsibility to keep the case alive and moving ahead for not just one but two of the three defendants. While the thought of it was painful, "falling on my sword" was the only option left that seemed viable to me. In fact, I did not even give it a second thought. I had learned that Jason Baldwin's lawyers had abandoned him, and this deeply upset me. The clock was ticking on both Jason and Jessie's Rule 37 petitions. My efforts to get any attorney in Arkansas to present the ineffective assistance of counsel claim on behalf of Jessie had come up empty. No one would step up to the challenge.

With no attorney willing to assist me, I realized that I would have to do it myself. I kept hearing what Greg had said, "they can't have it both ways," but they would if the Rule 37 Petitions in Jessie and Jason's cases were not filed in time.

At the end of October 1996, a colleague in Little Rock sent forms to assist me in drafting Jessie Misskelley's *pro se* Rule 37 petition—that is, Jessie representing himself *against me.* That he could make a cogent argument on my failings as his attorney was not possible, but it would buy us some time to get a lawyer on board. I drafted one for Jason Baldwin to do the same, though I was not sure he would want to sign it or not. Somehow, I would have to talk him into it.

I was uncertain Jason would agree to see me, and I was even less certain he would agree to sign the pleading I had prepared. As I made the drive to the Arkansas Department of Corrections, I wondered what I would do if I were in his shoes. Seeing the lawyer for the kid who was responsible for him being arrested might be abhorrent to him.

When I arrived at the prison, I met with the assistant warden and explained that I had an important pleading I needed to get Jason Baldwin to sign. He said that he would ask Baldwin if he wanted to see me. A few moments later, the warden returned and said that Baldwin would speak with me. A guard led me through the secure area to a room the size of a basketball court. Off to one side was a room used as a computer lab. Jason sat just outside its door at a desk.

The guard left us, and after shaking hands I asked Jason if he had a lawyer working on his case. No, he said, adding that he had not seen his trial attorneys for some time. I knew then for sure they had abandoned him. I explained to Jason what a Rule 37 Petition was and how it impacted his case. I told him he needed to pursue this ineffective assistance of counsel claim because it could result in him getting a new trial. Jason understood, but I could see he was not completely comfortable with the idea of Jessie Misskelley's lawyer helping him. I told Jason I believed in his innocence, and that as soon as he signed the petition, I would do my best to make sure he had a lawyer to assist him.

He trusted me, for which I am entirely grateful. Not filing because of a procedural deadline would have been devastating to him. That afternoon, Jason Baldwin and I established a bond that has lasted until this day. I suspect it will last forever. I filed his Rule 37 Petition in Jonesboro on the way back to Paragould with a surge of relief.

I made the same trip to have Jessie Misskelley sign his Rule 37 petition. As always, he had a smile on his face that helped dilute the depression that always clung to me after a visit to the prison to see him. I felt I was abandoning my own child every time I left that vile place. He signed it and I filed it in Corning.

In his *pro se* petition, Misskelley asserted that Crow and I were ineffective as his counsel by failing to raise in a timely manner the Rule 2.3 issue—and this time the Arkansas Supreme Court had already stated so in their opinion affirming his conviction. This was our "they can't have it both ways" argument—and this time it would be checkmate, eventually.

A nuance in Arkansas law mandated that Judge Burnett would oversee the dispositions of both Jessie and Jason's Rule 37 Petitions. My biggest fear at that moment was that Burnett could invoke a provision in the law that would allow him to deny the Rule 37 motions summarily, without a hearing or even appointing a lawyer to represent either Jessie Misskelley or Jason Baldwin.

I held on to a sliver of hope. Rumors that Berlinger and Sinofsky were in the process of shooting another HBO documentary about the case were starting to blossom. I knew Burnett could not resist starring in another production, despite his usual complaints about publicity. He would want to preside over a hearing that would once again put him center stage.

46

The years between the releases of the two *Paradise Lost films* would challenge me emotionally, physically, and spiritually. The growing national and international base of supporters would become more strident and more organized in its calls for justice for the WM3.

I began to suffer nightmares about the case, and when I would wake in a cold sweat, I would see the three dead boys standing at the end of my bed, their wet, pale skin glowing eerily in the moonlight drifting in through the French doors leading to the deck outside. The specters were silent, staring, seeming to beckon me. I reached out to them thinking they would disappear. They continued to stare. I reached over to Kim, asking if she could see them. "Danny, there is nothing there," she told me. "Lie down and go back to sleep." The second time they appeared after a nightmare, I asked Kim again if anything was there, she was far from comforting in her response. After that, I kept the ghosts to myself and wrote it off as a side effect of the Ambien I had started taking to be able to sleep at all.

In July 1997, I felt a fluttering feeling in my chest. There was no pain, but I could feel an occasional skip in my heart beats. At Kim's insistence I had a battery of tests, including one that called for an injection of radioactive thallium before I was put on a treadmill while technicians did a CAT scan on my heart. Ultimately the tests revealed no problems. Not surprisingly, my doctor offered that I was suffering from stress and anxiety brought on by the murder case. He suggested anti-depressants and gave me a few samples. I flatly refused any prescription out of fear that people might think I was losing my mind. Paragould is a small town.

In the years ahead I would try meditation and yoga to calm myself. Each had a calming effect, but because they require a willingness to slow down, to breathe, to shutter outside distractions, they worked only if I made time to do it, if only for thirty minutes. It seemed that I had no down time, no openings to allow them to work. Instead, I immersed myself in building my law practice and working on Jessie's case.

When I could find some time to decompress, I was hitting a golf ball, shooting ducks, or fishing. In the years following the trials, I went bass fishing in Mexico at least once, sometimes twice a year. I spent as much time as I could with the kids, which always offered a calming balm. But soon they were off doing their own things like football, basketball, gymnastics, and piano lessons. My frequent trips to track down leads or find forensic experts began to conflict with the kids' activities. The kids did not seem to mind, but Kim did. They were growing up fast, too fast, and my marriage was slowly deteriorating.

My already fragile spirituality took a fatal blow after two young students, eleven and thirteen years old, shot and killed four classmates and a teacher at the Westside School in Jonesboro on March 24, 1998. By the time the carnage ended another ten students had been injured. The boys had armed themselves with weapons they had taken from the gun cabinet of one of the boy's grandparents. After pulling a fire alarm at the school and retreating to a nearby wooded area, they ambushed their victims as they filed out of the school buildings.

When I got home from the office that afternoon and learned of the massacre I was appalled, breathless. First, three dead eight-year-olds in West Memphis and now this. Why and how could this happen? *Had the world become so evil that children were not safe to ride bikes or attend school?*

For the second time in five years, the national media descended into northeast Arkansas to cover a tragedy involving children. The news stories about the shootings dominated everything. One local reporter did something that sickened me. At the school amid the chaos, the reporter asked parents of the murdered children why they thought their children had been killed while others had been spared. The grieving parents replied:

"It was just his time to go. He's with Jesus now."

"It was God's will."

When the same reporter questioned the survivors' parents the answer seemed the same to me.

"Jesus protected my child."

"An Angel swooped down and saved her."

I was stupefied. I walked the two blocks to the First United Methodist Church to see if the pastor was in. I found him in his study, knocked on the door and asked if I could come in. I stepped inside, shut the door behind me, and got straight to the point. How could a loving God let something like this happen to children? He gave me a copy of the sermon he had just written, a sermon I would never hear because I would not attend the service or set foot in any church for years after that day. Grasping for anything I could hold on to in something that I could not seem to rationalize, I asked my Pastor again, "Why would God let something like this happen to innocent children?" His only response to me was that I had to "have faith."

That was a commodity I lacked at that moment. I was completely and utterly devoid of faith, and it would be a long time before I would get it back. I walked home after the pastor's genuine but feeble response still searching for answers.

I knew that my anxiety was nothing compared with others stricken with the disease the WM3 case had become. I received a letter from Jason Baldwin, who I had begun writing after our meeting in prison.

Dan,

I just want to go home. Sometimes it seems to me that this mess is gone on forever and that it will never end, but I know it will. Someday I just want to do whatever it takes to speed up the process and bring Jessie, Damien and myself home and maybe even the real killer or killers to justice.

I think you can understand how I feel. During the first trial Paul Ford instructed me not to say anything to anyone and I didn't, and now I wonder if that was the right thing to do. Maybe I should have screamed out my innocence at every chance that I got, but really I don't know what to do. I am very thankful for all the help that I have received. You are right, I am very lucky in that regard. I just want you to know that I'm not going to ever give up or lose faith. I just wish that there was more that I can do for myself in this situation instead of having to rely on other people but I won't complain there.

Thank you Dan, for your help.

Jason Baldwin

There was that word again, "faith." My own self-pity and my misguided attempts to ease my own pain and suffering with alcohol seemed childish—petulant, by comparison.

47

I immersed myself in the activities of the Arkansas Trial Lawyers Association to help rebuild my law practice after the Misskelley trial and the direct appeal. In late August 1997, I attended an Arkansas Trial Lawyers event at the Winthrop Rockefeller Institute atop the Petit Jean Mountain near Morrilton, Arkansas. The institute was founded by philanthropist and former Arkansas Governor Winthrop Rockefeller. First elected in 1966, he was the first Republican governor of Arkansas since Reconstruction. The conference that year was much like any other conference until we adjourned for lunch the first day.

As we all made our way to the buffet line in the cafeteria, I noticed a man nervously approaching me from my right. He did not seem threatening, but he obviously wanted to engage me in a private conversation. When he was close enough, he asked me how Jessie Misskelley was doing. "About as well as can be expected I suppose, under the circumstances."

The man motioned me out of the lunch line toward a window in the corner, making sure we were out of earshot of anyone else. Then he dropped a bombshell.

"You know, you really didn't lose that case."

"What do you mean I didn't lose the case? It was a 7-0 decision."

"Actually, it wasn't. You won the case 4-3."

He explained that his sibling was a law clerk for one of the Arkansas Supreme Court Justices and was in the room when they voted.

"You won the case 4-3," he repeated.

I was incredulous, but at the same time a man I did not know was telling me that Crow's prediction had been accurate after all.

I asked the man what had happened to turn it into 7-0? "The justices got scared. They started discussing the inevitable backlash they'd get for letting Misskelley go free. They all became afraid of what would happen when they each had to run for re-election." I was too stunned to speak. He turned to me one last time.

"I just didn't want you to go through the rest of your life thinking that you had lost that case when you really didn't. If you ever repeat any of this, I will deny it. I can't get my sibling in trouble."

I could muster only a weak nod. He disappeared into the crowd, and I never saw him again. I stood there dumbfounded, trying to establish a motive for why this guy would tell me this if it was not true. I could find none, but it did corroborate Crow's prediction of the outcome after our oral arguments and explained a lot.

During the afternoon session of the conference, I could not focus on the speakers. I was in a deep trance trying to digest the meaning of this profound new information, wondering what, if anything, I could do with it.

My mind went back to what Judge Burnett had told me on the phone that morning when he said he would deny our motion to suppress, that our amended motion and brief were good but there was no way that he could "let this kid go." Burnett had even said that I would probably get him reversed on appeal. He was passing the buck, and now it seemed that the Arkansas Supreme Court had done the same thing.

In 2014, a member of that 1996 Arkansas Supreme Court would admit he had made a mistake in his ruling, a revelation I am still trying to digest. In frail health, seemingly overcome with the guilt that had weighed on him for years, he would admit that he was wrong. His admission, though welcomed at long last, could not change the fact that those young men had been left in prison and me jousting legal windmills for more than 18 years.

That afternoon at the Winthrop Rockefeller Institute, staring into nothingness, I knew that I had years of work and frustration ahead of me. At that moment I felt all alone. No one in the legal community seemed willing to go up against the establishment—except me. I could see no way that this information would benefit my client. In all the scenarios I played out in my head during that long afternoon, none resulted in any benefit to Jessie Misskelley.

After the conference was over, I rushed to a phone to call Greg Crow at the Attorney General's office to tell him about what the stranger had told me.

"I knew it," he said. "I knew it was 4-3."

Crow agreed that there was absolutely nothing we could do to help Jessie with this information. In the end, I was content to have the knowledge. I already knew that we had raised the issue properly and that the Court had blamed me so they could sidestep the Rule 2.3 issue without addressing it on its merits. But it did serve to motivate me. I was still in this for the long run. I continued to play the long game of chess with the State of Arkansas. In the years since the Alford Pleas, a second source, who would not go on the record, confirmed the same story of the 4-3 vote for the reversal of Jessie Misskelley's conviction. I offer this not for the truth of the matter asserted, but to add some corroboration to the story that the stranger had told me.

48

It would take a short West Coast trip in February of 1998 to reveal something so crucial that it would forever change the course of the case. First, I had to convince Kim I needed to go. I was always going somewhere. She did not seem to understand the importance of what I was trying to do, and it was driving a wedge into our marriage.

She resented the fact that I was still spending so much time on the case, not present even when I was home. I resented the fact that she was resentful.

"Can we afford it?"

"I'll only be there for two days."

The world's leading forensic experts were converging in San Francisco for a conference of the American Academy of Forensic Sciences, and I wanted to be there. I could not afford to miss what potentially could provide an enormous boost in my efforts to get help and shine new light into the dark corners of Jessie Misskelley's failed case—of my failed case. I had to go.

In San Francisco, it all seemed too good to be true. In a matter of three serendipitous hours, I moved the case forward more than it had moved since the trials. That San Francisco trip opened doors with alacrity and produced information that had been right before my eyes all along. I had not been able to see the forest for the trees. By the time I was heading home I had evidence that pushed the enormity of the flawed guilty verdicts against Jessie and Jason and Damien over the edge.

A little bit of stalking and a chance encounter in an elevator in San Francisco not only demonstrated the fatal flaws in Jessie's confession it also unequivocally revealed that the State's case had not been the first ever Satanic Ritualistic homicide on the planet. The hotel was swarming as the conference moved into full swing, with groups milling about in the lobby, chatting, and moving quickly from one presentation to another. The whole thing looked like an Oscar ceremony for all-star forensic scientists, there to seek help, and bask in the adulation of colleagues.

I sat in on a conference at which pathologists asked for help on troubling cases, looking for fresh eyes and new perspectives. Leaving the meeting, I spotted Dr. Michael Baden, one of the most respected forensic pathologists in the world. Jolted, but not shy, I ran over and asked Baden if I could speak to him about my case. He very politely told me that he was on his way to a meeting but might have time later that afternoon to talk.

Then I met Dr. Thomas David, a forensic odontologist who had agreed to consult with Damien's attorney, Ed Mallett, regarding a potential human bite mark discovered on the forehead of victim Stevie Branch. I also met Dr. Neal Haskell, a forensic entomologist, a scientist in a field I had always thought would be useful in providing answers to some troubling questions.

An hour later, I glanced up and saw Baden, Haskell, and David walking together, headed to the elevator. I could not believe my luck. I slid in behind them as the doors closed. I made an impassioned plea to the captive Baden as the elevator ascended, throwing in *Paradise Lost* and the growing interest it was sparking in the case. He rebuffed me, noting that his association with HBO could present a conflict of interest. I then asked the million-dollar question:

"Well would you at least take a quick look at what I have— and just give me fifteen minutes of your time? All my case materials are in my room on the seventeenth floor."

Suddenly, David and Haskell seemed interested. "Let's all go look at it," I said, and the next thing I knew we were all convened in my room as I spread out autopsy and crime scene photographs on the table. They were mesmerized.

Baden was the first to speak. What he said chilled me.

"I have conducted over 10,000 autopsies in my career, and these are the worst photographs I have ever seen."

David and Haskell agreed that the photos were the worst they had ever seen.

Baden picked up a photo showing victim Chris Byers with his genitals removed.

"This looks like animal predation to me."

Dr. Haskell then said that he agreed, and that the predation could be anything from crayfish to diving beetles or even turtles, depending on how long the bodies were in the water. A discussion ensued about the possibility that some of the wounds were scratch marks made by small animals, perhaps a dog or raccoon. This was an adult crime, they both said, not the work of three teenagers. They also said that the wounds were post-mortem, occurring after death.

Dr. Baden pulled a card from his jacket pocket and handed it to me. "Send me all the photographs and the autopsy reports and I'll at least give you my thoughts and perhaps a recommendation on whom you might consult with," he said. I thanked him profusely as he and David left the room.

Haskell and I moved our meeting down to the bar in the lobby. Over drinks he offered a quick lesson in forensic entomology. He revealed how quickly insects are drawn to a corpse. He had conducted experiments in the Antarctic where blowflies appeared within minutes and laid eggs on the body of a dead seal. We could, Haskell suggested, conduct an experiment in that same creek along the Interstate where the bodies were discovered with a dead pig. With that we could see what type of creatures might show up to feed. I was intrigued. The moment I got back to Arkansas, I sent an email dated

February 22, 1998, to Ed Mallett telling him of my encounter with Baden, David, and Haskell.

On March 10, 1998, because Arkansas is one of the last remaining states that has a prosecutor-controlled crime lab, I sent a letter to Brent Davis asking his permission to obtain all the autopsy photographs in the case. Davis' response was a condescending request for me to confirm that I still represented Misskelley and asking, "what information do you desire – for whom and for what purpose." I was livid and fired back a letter to Davis on March 18, 1998, advising him "that there has not been a moment since June of 1993 when I haven't been representing Mr. Misskelley. I, again, request copies of the autopsy photos of all three victims for all three defense teams so that we may further our appeals." I also told Davis that I was "puzzled at [his] apparent attempt to thwart our investigation and move forward with our appeals."

Davis' response was both predictable and typical. He had no objection to the Medical Examiner providing the photos but that I was not to share them with any other of the defense teams saying, "they will need to make their own requests." The cost of the photos was over $1,600 and this was at a time when there were not a lot of funds available to pay for them. The fact that Davis wanted us to have to pay for this three times infuriated me. Ed Mallett sent me a thousand dollars and I kicked in the rest. After I obtained the photos, we scanned them into a computer, and I shared them with Mallett. I also sent copies to Dr. Baden.

Damien Echols' Rule 37 hearing was about to begin. Of course, Burnett thought it would be endearing to set the first day of the hearing on May 5, 1998, the fifth anniversary of the homicides. Always the showman for the HBO cameras.

49

The year 1998 had brightness in other places as well. Bruce Sinofsky invited my son Chris and me to New York to see the Yankees play on the last day of the season. Chris was more excited than I had ever seen him. Baseball captivated America that year. Mark McGuire of the St. Louis Cardinals and Sammy Sosa of the Chicago Cubs were locked in an epic struggle to break Roger Maris' single-season home run record of 60. The Yankees had already won more games than any other team in the history of the American League. Chris was excited about going to Yankee Stadium.

We met Bruce and his son at a parking garage the day after we arrived, then took the subway to the Bronx, where Chris and I got our first look at the iconic Yankee Stadium, the original one. We got there early enough to visit Memorial Park, and I still have some great shots of Chris standing next to the plaques honoring some of the greatest Yankees who ever played the game, Babe Ruth, Lou Gehrig, Miller Huggins, Mickey Mantle, and Joe DiMaggio, who was being feted that day.

It might have been Joe DiMaggio Day at the Stadium, but for Chris and me, it was our day. We watched, awed, as DiMaggio was driven around the stadium in a convertible before the adoring crowd, then presented at home plate with replicas of all his World Series rings that were stolen from his hotel room back in 1960. The Yanks won and then we had dinner with the Sinofsky's. After dinner, Bruce showed me the Emmy award that he had won for *Paradise Lost*. New York energized me. It always does. The next morning, we were on our way back to Arkansas with memories that would last forever.

The year was capped off by another trip to California on December 4, this time to do the *Leeza Show*. Though the show cost more than $500,000 to produce, it never aired because producers deemed it too controversial. That always seemed to be the catch that prevented the case from being showcased. But this was about to change.

I would return to New York a year later. Joe and Bruce invited me to a private screening of *Paradise Lost II: Revelations*. They were making the final cuts and wanted my reaction. Naturally, I left the day before Kim's birthday. She was not impressed.

The rising sun caught the New York skyline and the stunning twin towers of the World Trade Center as the plane circled Manhattan. My eyes locked on the towers in the distance as the plane descended to La Guardia. My trip with Chris the year before seemed like yesterday.

That weekend jaunt presaged two things: the enormous national attention the case would attract after the release of *Revelations*, and the demise of my slowly crumbling marriage. The release of *Paradise Lost* three years earlier had begun to spread the word to people with influence. I had been told that actress Susan Sarandon, who had starred in the prison film *Dead Man Walking* and had won an Oscar for her efforts, had prevailed on musician Eddie Vedder, who had provided some of the music for *Dead Man Walking*, to "do something about this," giving him a VHS copy of *Paradise Lost*. Vedder, the front man for the band Pearl Jam, would later tell me he saw himself in Damien Echols. "I came from a pretty messed up childhood where the kids were smarter than the adults," Vedder would later tell me.

Vedder in turn would bring in influential San Francisco attorney John Philipsborn, asking him to review the entire case to see what could be done. Philipsborn, who specialized in criminal defense and international human rights cases, jumped in. He would in short order become the architect for both Jessie and Jason's cases. He first contacted me in December 1999 offering his assistance in the case of the WM3. *Revelations* would soon spark a firestorm of interest across the country—outrage outside Arkansas, and the predictable scoffing and tut-tutting from the usual crowd inside the State.

My New York preview was eminently satisfying. *Revelations* was hard hitting from beginning to end and had none of the unanswered questions of *Paradise Lost*. I knew immediately it would have a tremendous impact on focusing the ire of the growing number of people calling for justice. I left New York with a profound sense of optimism that the film's release seven months later in March 2000 would stir things up in the best possible way for the three young men still sitting in Arkansas prisons.

As the premiere of the new film approached, film critic Roger Ebert's review of *Revelations* came in early March:

"There is unlikely to be anything else on TV this week, or this month, more disturbing than this film. Watching it, you feel like an eyewitness to injustice."

I knew that Mike Allen, Brent Davis, and David Burnett would not enjoy being pilloried in *Revelations* any more than they did after the original film. They certainly would not share Roger Ebert's feelings. The headline of the *West Memphis Evening Times* after the Monday, March 13, 2000, premiere was terse but clear:

DETECTIVE, JUDGE IN MURDER CASE SAY HBO STORY SLANTED

"There is decency in journalism and HBO didn't show any," Mike Allen told the paper. "It's not fair to the families that live here." Allen said the new film offered nothing to show that the convicted men were innocent of the crimes. "They tend to leave out certain key elements of the trial," said Allen.

Judge David Burnett joined the circling wagons, astonishingly telling the paper that he had been "reluctant" to interview with HBO for either film. I found this to be hilarious. Burnett said the producers emphasized what they wanted.

"I thought they did a sorry job on both of them, putrid jobs. It made Arkansas and our community look like a trailer park."

If he had to do anything different in the case, the judge said, he would have left the television out of the courtroom altogether. "That won't happen again," said Burnett.

Revelations prompted a deluge of emails to then Arkansas Governor Mike Huckabee, asking him to step in to correct the injustice. The Governor's press secretary offered a canned response:

"The Governor has received your email and has asked me to respond. As the chief of the executive branch of government, the Governor has no investigative authority. He cannot re-open the case nor have any investigation done. I do want to assure you that DNA testing was done, and that a match was found among the men convicted. I am sure that you realize that *Paradise Lost* and its sequel are fictionalized accounts based upon a true story. These shows are not documentaries or news stories. The men convicted of murdering the three little boys are being given every opportunity to appeal in both state and federal courts. They are also receiving excellent legal representation. If you have further questions you might want to contact the Prosecuting Attorney who is handling the case."

Virtually everything in that press release was false, especially the DNA nonsense. The Governor never made any attempt to correct this statement or offer an apology. "Alternative Facts," it would be called today.

50

Paradise Lost and *Revelations* focused more than a few local eyes on what I had been up against and what I had been trying to do. In Paragould I had noticed a thawing of the icy regard in which people had once held me. Attitudes were changing. As the facts of the case slowly emerged, the moral panic subsided, and the murmuring and hard feelings softened. In a small town where I had lived virtually all my life, these things are easy to notice, and pleasantly so.

In early 2000, some folks began to encourage me to run for Greene County Municipal Court Judge, a part-time judicial position that would allow me to continue my work on the Misskelley case. I pondered the situation intensely for weeks. I asked my good friend Brad Broadaway if he would be ready to manage my campaign if I decided to run. As friends do, he said he would be happy to help and would do whatever was necessary. But there was a caveat. He told me I did not have a chance to win. Brad's warning had its intended effect. Running for office when only a few years before many people wanted to run me out of town would expose my neck. I went out talking and testing the waters, checking the temperature of the voters. It was palpable and folks wanted me to run. So, I threw my hat in the ring. That decision changed my life.

By March I had begun the requisite politicking. A very unscientific phone poll of likely Greene County voters showed I was leading by a 60-40 margin. I called Brad, who told me the results were unlikely, probably flawed.

I told Brad just a few days before election day in May, that I was planning to head to Seattle for a crucial meeting with Eddie Vedder an appointment that I had agreed to in April. "I wouldn't do that if I were you," Brad told me. "It would be a huge mistake to leave town now when you need that last week for a big push." Of course, Brad was right. That is what friends and campaign managers are for. Always careful to manage expectations and keep their candidate thinking they must work harder. To me, however, Jessie Misskelley came first, and I went to Seattle.

On May 23, 2000, I was elected Judge by the same 60 to 40 percent margin the earlier poll had projected. Two of my close friends, Dr. Mike and Lisa Jarman were two of my biggest supporters. One West Memphis 3 supporter left me a phone message on election night. "People are celebrating your victory all over the country."

A new chapter in my life had begun as I was sworn into office on January 1, 2001, by none other than Judge David Goodson.

51

When I received that call in April 2000 from John Philipsborn who asked if I could come to Seattle to meet with Eddie Vedder and some appellate lawyers about the case, I asked when, and he said Mother's Day, May 14—not a choice destined to add strength to my marriage or my campaign. I said simply, "I'll be there." Flying discreetly to Seattle, for the meeting with Eddie Vedder would be Philipsborn, attorney Steven Bright from the Southern Center for Human Rights, Damien Echols' lawyer Ed Mallett, and Michael Burt, an experienced appellate attorney and DNA expert.

I arrived in Seattle on the afternoon of the thirteenth, knowing I needed little time to prepare my presentation. I knew the case inside and out. I walked down from the Sorrento Hotel to the waterfront, where I found the Seattle Fish Market at Pike Place. I watched the vendors tossing fish about, bought some T-shirts and hats for the kids, then made my way down to the docks, surrounded by the alluring smell of smoked salmon.

I skipped breakfast the next morning, Mother's Day, opting for more sightseeing. I ate an early lunch at a Chinese restaurant just down the hill and then walked back up to the hotel. Sitting at a fountain outside, I saw a man who I knew had to be John Philipsborn. As I approached, he stood up to shake my hand and said "Hi Dan." We chatted for a few minutes, then decided to head to the meeting.

I was planning to head to the airport immediately after, so I grabbed an elevator to my room to gather my stuff from the sixth floor, including my case files. Halfway up, the elevator stopped, and a man and a woman stepped on. The man had longer dark hair and was wearing green army fatigues and combat boots. Our eyes met briefly, then we both looked away without a word.

I gathered my belongings from my hotel room and headed up to the meeting. As I walked into the Sorrento Room on the top floor of the hotel, the man in green fatigues stood from his chair and said, "I'm Eddie Vedder. I thought that was you in the elevator." We both laughed and I said, "I thought that was you too." The others soon started arriving as well. Vedder's publicist Nicole Vandenberg and Lori Davis Echols rounded out the meeting.

Everyone exchanged pleasantries and introduced themselves, and when we finally sat down for the meeting, Eddie Vedder explained briefly why he had become interested in the case. He spoke a little about his childhood and how he felt a connection to the case because of it.

When it was my turn to speak, I felt like an advertising executive trying to pitch a new ad campaign to his clients. Looking at my notes from the meeting, I had outlined a status report for each defendant including my own client, and then I answered questions. As the discussion progressed, I began to feel for the first time a sense of "we" instead of "me." I hoped I had done enough to sell the idea.

The final confirmation came when Vedder turned to his publicist and said "give them what they need" to get this done. I was elated. Ms. Vandenberg immediately responded with "what about saving the whales and our support for the homeless; we are committed to these issues." Eddie looked at her and said:

"It's only money, we'll make more. We will have another concert, whatever it takes."

This was not braggadocio on his part. Eddie Vedder had spoken from his heart; money was not an issue to him. It was clear to me he was committed to both justice and the WM3.

As the meeting disbanded, Eddie came over as I gathered my things and sat next to me at the conference table. We started a wide-ranging conversation about everything from the WM3 to music. I took the liberty of asking him for a couple of autographs for Daniel and Chris. We found some Sorrento Hotel stationery that was laying on the table. He wrote: "To Daniel: Hope you are well...I appreciate and respect your dad. He should get you a guitar!" The other read "Hey to Christopher, I will see you when we come to your town. Until then, be good."

Vedder then asked his publicist to make sure that I had four tickets and backstage passes for the upcoming concert in Memphis later that summer. Soon everyone was gone but Vedder, me, and Ed Mallett.

"Hey," Vedder asked me, "when does your plane leave?" "I have a few hours," I replied. He turned to Mallet and asked him if he wanted to join us for a few beers in the bar downstairs. So off we went downstairs to the bar, the three of us. We drank beer and talked a little about the case. Soon Mallett had to leave to catch his plane to Houston, and we bid him farewell. Eddie and I talked about politics, his friendship with Sean Penn, and myriad other issues.

Our long chat was down to earth, remarkably informal, and easy. People would walk by and do a double take looking at Eddie, but no one approached him. Finally, much to my dismay, it was time for me to go and catch my plane. We stood and as I reached out to shake his hand and thank him, he instead gave me a warm embrace. I was leaving with a new friend and ally. It could only be a matter of time until justice arrived. I could feel it.

Back home a few days later, Brad Broadaway faxed me a blog that Eddie Vedder had participated in the day after our meeting in Seattle. In the blog, "Sigmagirl" asked: "What is the West Memphis 3? Vedder replied:

"There was an interesting case concerning the death penalty that took place in West Memphis, Arkansas...Basically it comes down to three teenagers who are accused, perhaps falsely, of a tragic crime against some younger kids. What is interesting about it is it seems the teenagers were chosen from the town because of their dress and the fact that they were the only three in town that wore T-shirts with rock bands on them, like Metallica. In New York they would not be picked out of the crowd but they stood out in West Memphis."

"In New York they would not be picked out of a crowd" were my own words to him over the beers we had shared at the Sorrento.

52

A month or so after my return from Seattle, I was sitting in my den eating a TV dinner. I clicked on the remote for the TV and the MTV Music Awards came on. As I was debating changing the channel, South Park Co-Creator Trey Parker, accepting an award, suddenly yells "Free the West Memphis Three" as he exits the stage. I nearly choked.

Over the course of the next three days, thanks to Eddie Vedder and John Philipsborn, I would meet criminalist and forensic expert Marc Taylor, who invented a blood test used to locate blood in O.J. Simpson's infamous white Bronco. He and I would later review all the physical evidence in the WM3 case at the West Memphis Police Department—with the anxious consent of prosecutor Brent Davis.

Officer Regina Meeks, the police officer who refused to go inside Bojangles on the night of May 5, 1993, was assigned the task of monitoring our actions. She called Brent Davis when Taylor began to run a presumptive test on the knife that Mark Byers had given to the HBO cameraman in December 1993. Davis told me over the phone to file a motion for re-testing and let the Court rule on it before any kind of testing could be performed.

On the conference table at the West Memphis Police station that day, along with all the other evidence from the case, was a photograph of Detective Mike Allen discovering the first young victim's body in the muddy creek. This photograph had always puzzled me because Allen's pants were not wet, meaning of course, that he had not yet entered the water. *How did he know that the bodies were in the creek?*

My curiosity propelled me to ask Officer Meeks about this photo, with the hope I might receive a logical explanation. Her response began with, "I probably shouldn't tell you this…"

It seems that in 1993 the police department had just acquired a new 35 mm camera and an officer was playing around with it while they were searching for the missing boys. Allen saw a child's shoe floating in the creek and the cops bet that he could not retrieve it without getting wet. The photograph I saw on the table was taken as he attempted to win the bet, just before he fell into the creek and bumped into the first of three young bodies. It was all by chance, over a bet, that the bodies were discovered. Clearly, the WMPD didn't want this to be the narrative of them finding the first body before or during the trials. It made me wonder what else they might be concealing.

In the Fall of 2000, I received an email from one of the appellate lawyers from our Seattle meeting who had reviewed the Misskelley trial transcript. It read:

"I admire the courage and forthrightness with which you defended your client. The reality, however, as you forewarned me, was that a combination of the judge's attitude toward the case, the symbolic meaning of the case in your community, and a lack of experience within the defense camp produced less than a desirable trial."

Adding to this assessment was an undated note in my file from another of the attorneys who had reviewed the trial transcripts that read, "Burnett was the best lawyer in the Courtroom."

On November 4, 2000, John Philipsborn came to Arkansas. He and I, again with the nervous consent of Brent Davis, reviewed the physical evidence to prepare a list of items that needed to be retested. On November 17, with more than a little help from my new friends, I filed a motion to Preserve Evidence and Access to Evidence for Testing on behalf of Jessie Misskelley. It felt great to not be in the fight alone.

On February 8, 2001, I filed an Amended pro se Rule 37 Petition on behalf of Jessie Misskelley. I would file the same motion in Jason Baldwin's case as well. Because no Arkansas lawyers had entered the case. I was a ninja.

On Valentine's Day 2001, Pam Hobbs emailed me a note expressing her heartbreak and grief over the loss of her son and acknowledging the trial was "hard on everyone involved with everything you had to see..." With all the trauma she had been through, it seemed improbable that she would recognize mine. She said she wanted to talk further about the case. In small steps, she would soon become an important ally.

On October 1st, 2001, I received a phone message from a lady in Florida that stated that she needed to give me "some information." On October 9th, 2001, I returned the call. She told me she was distantly related to Judge Burnett and that four months before the trials of the WM3 began "David made what [she] thought was a statement that showed prejudice."

"I'm gonna burn them," she reported he had said.

The national attention ignited by the HBO films would also draw another kind of correspondence. In late October 2001, I received a thick envelope postmarked from an Oregon Correctional Facility. Inside was a letter from Keith Hunter Jesperson, who called himself the "Happy Face Killer." His signature was accompanied by a small happy face, an eerie juxtaposition.

In a long hand-written letter Jesperson, in meticulous detail that included crude maps where he had hidden the bodies, outlined the murders of eight women he had committed. As I continued to read, I realized the intent of his letter. I was a mere conduit. He asked if I would be so kind as to get in touch with Joe Berlinger and Bruce Sinofsky to see if they might be interested in doing a movie about his crimes. I forwarded the letter to Bruce Sinofsky. They declined his offer.

In November 2004, I received a package from Hawaii. Inside was a pastel seascape, sent from a gallery in Maui. Whomever painted it was talented. I was puzzled until I found a letter in the package and immediately recognized the handwriting of the "Happy Face Killer." He had written to the gallery asking for "photographs of cascading waves-beaches-birds of Hawaii. Lagoons with boats, you name it..."As you can tell from the return address, I'm in Oregon's maximum-security prison in Salem," he told the gallery in his pitch.

"I made some very stupid mistakes that landed me here for the rest of my life. Because of who I am, I'm not allowed to sell my art to anyone other than friends and family. What a waste. Another starving artist. I survive off donations sent to me by pen pals worldwide. Because of who I am, you may just decide I'm not worth the bother to help me. So be it. I understand. But I do hope you can look past it and help me out. Enjoy the art."

Then it became clear to me why the gallery had forwarded the art to me. Jesperson had written "PS: If you don't want the art I sent, instead of destroying it, please send it to Daniel Stidham PO Box 856, Paragould, AR 72451."

53

The year 2002 proved to be a huge one for the case, and a year of transition for me personally. My role in the case would change rather dramatically and I would, yet again, be forced to confront my own spirituality.

Mara Leveritt, an unrelenting investigative journalist, would publish her book *Devil's Knot* in 2002. It, just like the *Paradise Lost* films, would have a huge impact on the case. Mara, in an incredibly detailed fashion complete with extensive footnotes, chronicled the case from its inception in 1993 up until 2001. I always referred to Mara as "my hero" because she was the only journalist in Arkansas who had the courage to cover the story, and like me, she never gave up.

She would later sell the rights to her book, and it was adapted into a feature film with the same title. Actor Michael Gladis, perhaps best known for his portrayal of the character Paul Kinsey in the first three seasons of the television series "Mad Men," played me in the film. Gladis reached out to me about *Devil's Knot* to get a feel for the cadence of my voice and prepare himself for the role. His devotion to his craft impressed me. We discovered that we shared many interests and stayed in touch for a while even after the film was released. Just as production started with the film, Gladis called and asked me what the brand name of the glasses I wore during the trial. I told him that I still had them in a drawer somewhere and ended up sending him the actual glasses themselves. He wore them in the film.

My vow to Jessie that I would get him out of prison never waned. Jessie, ironically, was thriving in prison, living for the first time in his life with a structure and regularity that he had never had at home. Somehow this gave me some small measure of comfort, but he did not deserve to be there. We had formed a tight bond. There would come a time, however, when my role in this process would change.

In 2002, Jessie Misskelley and Jason Baldwin would finally have experienced appellate lawyers in place to push forward with their appeals. John Philipsborn would represent Jason Baldwin and Michael Burt would become Jessie Misskelley's lead counsel. Each was supported by Arkansas counsel, two well-known and highly regarded Little Rock attorneys, Jeff Rosenzweig for Jessie's team and Blake Hendrix for Baldwin's. Both John Philipsborn and Michael Burt would bring vast knowledge and experience into the case.

By the time John Philipsborn and I met, he had tried many capital cases, and been involved in a significant number of capital case post-conviction litigation. He had served as a litigator for the largest group of criminal defense lawyers in California and had written dozens of amicus briefs for cases that ended up before the United States Supreme Court, Federal Circuit Courts, and State Courts of all kinds. He had co-counseled San Francisco's last capital case to go to trial and taught at a local law school. He had also done a lot of continuing legal education writing and lecturing in various parts of the country on mental health issues, becoming well known for his work involving forensic mental health. His law firm was the first to have used "diminished capacity" as a defense in a criminal trial. John also worked on human rights cases all around the globe.

Michael Burt's work in the arena of DNA had lawyers from around the country interested in getting him involved in cases and resulted in his involvement in many forensic science issues before he worked on the WM3 case. While on the WM3 case, he was one of the first Federal

Death Penalty Resource Counsel named in the U.S., and as a result, he has worked on death cases around the country, often specifically dealing with forensic science issues. John and Michael met in 1984 and they collaborated on several cases, had written some articles together, and lectured at various capital case seminars by the time we started our work together after our meeting in Seattle. I was ecstatic to be working with these lawyers on the case. That feeling of being all alone in the case had quickly subsided and I was more than grateful.

I wrote a letter to Jessie in October 2002 whereby I broke the news that Jeff Rosenzweig—Frankie Parker's lawyer—and Michael Burt would be his new lawyers and would be shepherding the various motions still afloat through the courts, including the ineffective assistance of counsel claim. It ripped me up because I knew the subtleties were beyond Jessie's level of understanding. No matter how I phrased the letter, or how much positive light I focused on the transition, Jessie would read and understand only one thing. I was abandoning him.

On its most practical level, the letter was meant to allow Jessie to recognize Jeff and Michael when they got in touch to start the new round of legal maneuvering. In the letter, I assured Jesse, in emphatic terms he would understand, that getting these two new lawyers was the best thing that had happened to him. Not wanting to undermine his childlike fragility about good and bad, friends and enemies, I told him I would still be there, working as I always had been to get him out of prison and back home to his father. But the fact was, he was still in prison and would remain there for nine more arduous years. A single day in prison is an ugly, violent existence, even for someone as immune to such things as Jessie.

Soon after *Devil's Knot* was published, I received a frantic phone call one evening from a young woman who told me that she was literally about to commit suicide. She had read Mara's book and had watched the *Paradise Lost* films and could not help the feelings of depression and despair she was experiencing. She told me that she identified, quite acutely, with the same teen angst and struggles in life that the WM3 had also experienced and that there was simply no reason for her to live.

I had nothing substantive at that moment to offer this young lady, so I started with all the cliches you hear about preventing suicide. I asked her if there was anyone, a friend, or a family member, that she could call? Her answer was that she had no one. My next move was to try to distract her. I told her that there must be something to live for and that I was glad that she had reached out to me. She said that she just wanted to thank me for working so hard on the case before she died. I continued to try desperately to talk her out of killing herself and was failing miserably. I wondered why the good Lord had placed this enormous task at my feet.

Suddenly, and without thinking about what I was saying, I told her that she just had to have faith that God had a plan for her and that her life did have meaning and purpose. I told her that without faith, there would have been no way that I could have maintained my fight for the WM3 for so long and that it would require this faith to sustain me for the rest of the battles ahead.

I seemed to have reached her somehow. I told her that I would stay on the phone with her for however long it took to make sure that she was fine. Soon, she told me that I had talked her off the ledge. I asked her to please call me back the next day so that I would know that she was okay.

Only after she called the next day to tell me that she was fine, did I realize that I had given her the same advice my Pastor had given me years earlier when I was struggling. There was that word again—"faith." If I had helped this young lady in some way, it could not have exceeded how much she had helped me. Without her, I could not have restored my faith.

54

The headline read "Ten Years After a Nightmare: Local Lawyer Still Believes in His Client's Innocence." On July 26, 2003, the *Paragould Daily Press* ran a front-page feature, complete with a three-column photo of me standing in front of the iconic bicycle poster for *Paradise Lost*. In the interview, I spared no details, reciting the numerous irregularities and steamroller tactics used by police in the case. "We are hopeful that we can get another opportunity." I told the reporter. "I think if we had the opportunity, the results of the case would be dramatically different."

One interested reader disagreed. Sometimes the spotlight can bear down too brightly. On his judicial stationary, Judge David Burnett wrote to James A. Badami, head of the Arkansas Judicial Discipline and Disability Commission:

> Dear Jim: Enclosed is a copy of an article that recently appeared in the Paragould Daily Press. I believe comments made by District Court Judge Dan Stidham in this article are in violation of the canon of ethics for the following reasons:
>
> 1) a presiding District Court judge should not make deroga-

tory comments about the Arkansas Supreme Court in a trial court;

    2) Judge Stidham is still representing one of the defendants and murder case; and

    3) the case is still active in my court. Please read the enclosed article and let me know what opinion as to whether or not these comments by a presiding judge are a violation of the canons of ethics."

    Sincerely David Burnett

I would not have ever known about the complaint that Burnett had filed against me had it not been for the carbon copy of the letter from the Arkansas Judicial Discipline and Disability Commission advising Burnett that his complaint was being dismissed.

The late Dr. Robert A. Leflar of the University of Arkansas School of Law was one of the nation's leading legal scholars and he had a quite different perspective of justice than did Judge David Burnett. Leflar's primary expertise was in the field of conflict of laws. He taught that course at the law school in Fayetteville, Arkansas, that now bears his name, for more than 60 years. He also taught at NYU and directed the Annual Survey of American Law at New York University for 30 years. This seminar attracted appellate judges from across the country. As Dean of the law school at the University of Arkansas, he orchestrated the desegregation, without litigation, of the school of law in 1948—making the University of Arkansas the first major Southern public university to open its doors to African Americans.

Not only did Professor Leflar write *the* book on conflicts law, but he also wrote a text called *Appellate Judicial Opinions,* published in 1974 with a Foreword by none other than Warren E. Burger, Chief Justice of the U.S. Supreme Court. I had Professor Leflar autograph my copy of his text on Conflict Law while I was in law school, but I found my copy of Leflar's *Appellate Judicial Opinions* on Amazon. When I received the book in the mail, I opened it up and was surprised to see a familiar name written inside the cover. Steele Hays, a respected

Arkansas jurist who retired from the Arkansas Supreme Court in 1995, just prior to the *Misskelley* decision, was the original owner of the book. He had written under his name "Annual Survey of American Law NYU Law School, denoting that he had attended one of the NYU seminars by Professor Leflar.

Inside the book, on page 153, Justice Hays drew a bracket around one paragraph following Leflar's description about how the "peculiar American separation of the trial judge from the appellate judge has tended to make the latter more and more of a legal monk:"

"One more and a deeper cause there certainly is for this trait — the substantial loss (temporarily, let us hope) of the *conception of justice*, in contrast to the rule of law, as an element in every case."

Justice Hays even underlined "conception of justice" and placed a blue star in the right margin to further signify its importance. It was almost as if I was back in law school again, listening to a lecture from two of Arkansas' most preeminent jurists. There were other notations made in the back cover of the book. Steele Hays had inserted a quote from Justice Harry Blackmun of the U.S. Supreme Court that appears on page 203:

"It is much easier to write a biting dissent than a constructive majority opinion."

This was so important to Justice Hays that he underlined the quote in the text on page 203 as well. This makes me wonder if Justice Hays had still been on the court in 1996 would he have written a "biting dissent" or applied the "conception of justice" in the Misskelley decision? In my mind, at least, the answer is clear.

Justice Hays died on June 23, 2011. In an article about his life and death, the *Arkansas Times* said that Justice Hayes "was a lifelong opponent of the death penalty, although he set those views aside in considering death cases on the Supreme Court. His rulings on the Supreme Court were motivated by justice as well as the law."

A few pages later in *Appellate Judicial Opinions*, Dr. Leflar tells the story of a Little Rock lawyer named George Rose Smith who wrote an article for the *Arkansas Law Review* in 1947, under the heading: A Suggestion:

"It will be useful to every appellate court in America if some competent lawyer undertakes an independent and impartial analysis of the current opinions of the court...The independence of such an analysis may annoy some members of a court, because the conclusions in the analysis will not be complementary to every judge. That may be one of the major values of the analysis. At any rate, such an analysis, if made by a fearless and competent critic, can have value both to the court itself and to the bar of the state, by enabling them to understand better how the court functions, or fails to function, as a good appellate court should."

The members of the Arkansas Bar and the citizens of the state of Arkansas did not seem to mind George Rose Smith's criticisms of the Arkansas Appellate courts' decisions. He was elected to the Arkansas Supreme Court two years later in 1949.

Judge David Burnett does not like criticism of any kind. He especially did not like the criticisms I offered about the *Misskelley* case in 2003. In fact, he disliked it so much that he not only filed the complaint against me with the Arkansas Judicial Discipline Commission, but he also began openly looking for an opponent for me in my judicial seat. He failed, but the timing of this was most unusual, just months ahead of my testimony in the Misskelley Rule 37 proceedings, where Judge Burnett would be given the task of determining my "effectiveness" at trial in 1994. *Would Judge Burnett and others engage in the same task of drumming up an opponent for me eight years later in 2016?*

55

Peter Jackson, of *Lord of the Rings* fame, and his partner Fran Walsh, produced the documentary film *West of Memphis* to give the WM3 the trial that they never had with all the new evidence that had been discovered since their original trials. When the film was released in 2012, Jackson said that he abhors injustice of any kind.

In the wake of *West of Memphis,* Terry Hobbs remains a lightning rod for the case. In many minds, he murdered those three boys. There is much circumstantial evidence that continues to point to him, including some less than conclusive DNA evidence of his hair found in a knot used to tie one of the victims, which he has always deflected by noting the three boys often played in his house.

And there are the witnesses who claim to have seen him that night with the three boys, which he adamantly denies. Terry Hobbs has over the years maintained a steady if disingenuous defense. One thing is for certain, there is more evidence pointing to him than there ever was against the WM3. There was absolutely no forensic, or physical evidence, ever found linking any of the West Memphis Three to the murders.

I found out about the DNA results and their implications for

Terry Hobbs in a phone call from Pam Hobbs. This was followed by a letter from Damien Echols:

> ...I don't know if you have heard the news yet or not, but the results of the DNA tests are back, and Brent Davis has a copy. There is nothing vague, open-ended, or left to interpretation—the summary says blatantly that me, Jason, and Jessie are all excluded...there is no way Davis or Burnett can try to twist, manipulate, or interpret the results in any other way...when I think of it I can hardly breathe. I've been in this box for 14 years now, but that time may very soon be coming to a close. I can hardly believe it. I'm trying not to get my hopes up, but this is huge. I hope you are well. I'm sending good vibes your way, and perhaps soon we can talk with no glass between us or guards around us. Take care.
> Yours,
> Damien

Terry Hobbs has done little to step into the shadows. He would sue Dixie Chicks singer Natalie Maines for defamation, a huge mistake on his part. Not only would Hobbs lose the highly publicized case, but by filing the suit, he was subjected to hours of videotaped depositions that brought out things he probably would have wished to have kept hidden. For his efforts, he was ordered by the judge to pay Maines's legal fees of $17,590. I seriously doubt he has paid. I have always wanted to conduct some depositions regarding this case. The fact that Hobbs didn't see that coming because of his lawsuit against Natalie, still has me scratching my head.

Hobbs continues to point to Damien Echols, Jason Baldwin, and Jessie Misskelley as the culprits, and in 2019, he wrote a book about his travails, of which he has had many. Hobbs described what it was like the day Damien Echols, Jason Baldwin, and Jessie Misskelley walked free after the Alford Plea in 2011.

"It's like ripping a Band-Aid off a wound. It hurt all over again," he said. "I still believe in my heart that Jessie, Jason, and Damion Echols are responsible for what happened to our children."

Pam Hobbs, once so vocal in her hatred of Damien, Jessie, and Jason, began to have her doubts. She along with Mark Byers, who would be killed in a car accident in June 2020, became two of the biggest advocates for the WM3. And both seemed to conclude that Terry Hobbs had killed the three eight-year-olds in 1993.

In 2003, Pam told me that she no longer trusted either the West Memphis Police or the prosecutor, Brent Davis. She claimed to have evidence that could implicate Terry Hobbs in the murders, including several knives and a partial dental plate. One of the knives belonged to Stevie, she said, and would have been in Stevie's pocket the day of the murders since he carried it with him all the time. Terry had hidden the items in what she called a "strong box."

She described how she had obtained this strong box. The story itself, like many other things in the case, is suffused with violence. She had been living with Terry Hobbs across the river in Memphis when they got into a violent argument over a trip to a casino in Tunica, Mississippi. Terry had accused Pam of "looking at other men."

After they returned home to Memphis, according to Pam, he threatened to kill her, then took a knife and cut up all her clothes, slicing out the crotches of several pairs of her underwear. Pam had called her sister for help and as they fled Memphis, they brought with them Terry's strong box, which they had pulled from its hiding place. They pried open the box and discovered the knives and the partial denture. Pam told me that she believed that the items in the box were tied to the murders, and to Terry's involvement in them.

The story of the box and Pam Hobbs' explanation to me provides another glimpse at the unsettled life of Terry and Pam Hobbs. Watching Terry cut up her clothes in Memphis reminded Pam that he was capable of spontaneous and irrational violence, that jealousy might have made it possible for Terry Hobbs to have harmed young Stevie. She added another twist. When Terry Hobbs had shot Pam's brother when he confronted Hobbs over the abuse of his sister, Pam told me that Terry, to avoid prison, sought sympathy by telling prosecutors in the case that "I was the father of one of those boys killed in West Memphis in 1993."

Pam, through her sister, turned everything over to me. With a detective from the Paragould Police Department, I met Pam's sister at a café in Steele, Missouri. After donning gloves, the Detective and I photographed everything. We then placed everything into evidence bags, which I then put in a large paper sack, and finally sealed into a cardboard box. The detective and I sealed, dated, and initialed everything. I did not expect to see my daughter Kathryn and her mother sitting on the couch in the Den when I carried that box inside my home to place it in my concrete vault. Kathryn was transfixed on the box. She soon would be asking questions that eleven-year-olds shouldn't be concerned with, questions that would vex her, and eventually her little brother Michael, for years.

I emailed a memorandum to John Philipsborn and Michael Burt about Pam Hobbs' box and sent them copies of the photographs. If nothing else, I wrote, I felt it was important that a victim's parent had reached out to me and appeared to no longer believe in the prosecution's case. It seemed like a milestone at the time. I had no idea just how important it could become later.

It seems I was not the only one who was haunted by images of the dead kids. That virus spread to my family. Kathryn had become so intrigued by that box that somehow, she convinced Kim to tell her, at least in general terms, what was in it. That knowledge frightened Kathryn very much. According to Kathryn's journal, which she has shared with me for the first time only recently, she talks about why she was terrified:

"I remember very vividly the summer the knives came to us. I saw Daddy enter the house after a long day's work. He did not say a word and walked straight down the hall and down to the basement where his vault was in his office– carrying a mysterious box.

Now, the last time I saw him carrying a box, it contained my beloved Siamese kitten that I had gotten just the Christmas before. So naturally, I thought he was hiding a present of some sort. I started asking Momma questions and eventually found out that it was not a present at all. It was a potential murder weapon. A potential murder weapon involved in the deaths of three little boys just ninety miles down the road, and it was being kept in the vault."

From that point on, the little kids never slept in their bedrooms in the basement again. They would either fall asleep on each end of the couch or they would sleep on a pallet in the living room, sometimes ending up in my bed. Kathryn describes what it was like for her back then:

"We would try to get our parents to let us sleep with them, but our ploys often came up empty handed. Since it was summer, our bedtimes were nonexistent. Therefore, we could disguise our fear of sleeping in the basement as simply falling asleep on the couches upstairs while watching TV. That did not last long though because our parents wanted us to sleep in our own beds. When I finally told my mom how scared I was, she understood and was sympathetic. She let me and Mikey make pallets and sleep on the floor in the formal living room, just on the other side of her and Daddy's room. Well, she told Daddy what we had discussed, and he came in and sat with us in the formal living room. He told us that we had nothing to fear because he was going to protect us. I always felt safe with him around, but if he went out of town, there was no question about it; we were sleeping with our mom."

Mikey did not understand what it was that he was supposed to be afraid of, but he was scared, nonetheless. He is 28 years old now, and I am not certain he has ever watched any of the *Paradise Lost* films or *West of Memphis*. He has never expressed much interest in the case, and that is fine with me.

56

In a 1969 ruling, *Holt vs. Sarver*, a federal judge declared the entire Arkansas prison system unconstitutional. Conditions were so poor that merely being a prisoner in Arkansas constituted cruel and unusual punishment, the judge wrote. The opinion in *Holt vs. Sarver*, was the inspiration for the 1980 film *Brubaker*, starring Robert Redford.

I had made dozens of trips down to the Arkansas Department of Corrections to visit Jessie. Without fail, each time I turned off Highway 65 into the prison complex, what I saw unsettled me. There were still shotgun-wielding men on horseback watching over the "hoe squads" of prisoners as they worked in the fields. In the searing heat of late summer, the inmates' white uniforms provided little contrast with the white cotton fields stretching as far as the eye could see. From the outside nothing appeared to have changed in forty years, and prison reforms across the country since the 1960s had little or no effect on the way prisons were run in Arkansas. I had no idea what it was like on the inside, though. When I visited Jessie, I never ventured farther than the safety of the warden's conference room.

My visits followed predictable, cautious steps. I would drive up to the front gate separated by guard towers protected by ominous rolls of razor wire. I would park my truck and walk slowly, arms raised, through the metal detector. I'd be patted down, and my briefcase would be opened and inspected. Then a guard would escort me into the safe and clean main lobby of the prison and into the warden's well-lit, air-conditioned, and comfortable conference room to visit with Jessie. After Jason Baldwin was transferred to the Varner Unit, I would visit him there as well. These visits, disturbing in many ways for many reasons, nonetheless gave the illusion of order—of controlled, managed safety.

That insulation and illusion was stripped away in 2003 when I drove down to see Jessie and have him sign some pleadings for his new appellate lawyers. The warden's conference room was being used, so I was told that I could use the prison law library, which was deep inside the bowels of the prison. The plan seemed benign enough to me, and I was looking forward to finally seeing what it was like past the comfort of the lobby of the warden's office. That feeling was about to change.

A guard arrived to escort me back to the law library. As we walked down the hall, we passed a large, fluorescent-bathed room reserved for visits, the unease abated a bit. It seemed almost pleasant. There were a few prisoners chatting across tables with wives and brothers and parents. Children were smiling as they skittered about, seemingly unaware of their surroundings or the watchful eyes of guards stationed strategically throughout the room.

Farther into the prison, we stopped at a set of bars controlled by a guard inside a glass control pod. My breathing picked up a notch. A loud warning signal erupted as the gates of bars separated and rolled away to the right. We stepped though and walked ten yards to a second set of bars in front of a Y-shaped hallway. Suddenly we were passing into the glass-lined barracks, and the illusions of safety and order and benign control dissolved quickly. I hoped that the glass was thick and unbreakable. As the doors behind us clanged shut again, my stomach began to churn. There was a finality to the sound that put me on edge.

This was the world where Jessie and Jason lived. On my left, along a corridor, were three tiers of bunk beds stacked to the ceiling—each barrack from Dante's lowest level of Hell reserved for men with little or no hope. As we passed through, I could not stop staring at the wild-eyed inmates who were staring right back at me—an outsider entering the violent and angry innards of the prison for the first time.

Along the corridor I noticed a painted yellow line not unlike a highway stripe. It ran uniformly only two feet right of the glass separating the hall from the barracks. I instinctively moved to the right just in case the glass was to give way somehow.

In the windows of the barracks, prisoners had assembled to watch me walk though their world. I was a vulnerable visitor now, with only a seemingly fragile thickness of glass separating me from chaos. As we passed each tier of barracks, the inmates began what appeared to be a ritualistic expletive-filled rush to the glass. I noticed with an averted glance a dripping glob of spittle sliding down the glass. I investigated the face of the guard escorting me down the hall, hoping for some sort of assurance that this was somehow a normal situation —that I had not stepped into a newly rising riot. I wanted the guard's assurance that things were not about to go very wrong. He was unmoved, his face blank. He said nothing until we arrived at what I hoped would be the safety of the law library.

The walls of the law library, like the barracks, were made of steel and glass. I was a small fish in a giant and transparent aquarium, still vulnerable to the manic stares and hollering of the inmates in the cells directly across the hall. This did little to nothing to ease my anxiety.

As the guard went to retrieve Jessie, I tried to gather my thoughts and to know that every expression, every tentative move I made, would be under those hateful gazes of the prisoners across the hall.

As the guard shut the door behind me, the cacophony rising from the inmates became muffled, but never stopped. After Jessie was led into the library, even with the door closed, the noise rose, as if the main show had just begun. I took some small relief knowing the guard had taken up station outside the door. I wanted nothing more than to get the hell out of there as quickly as I could.

When Jessie came in, I extended my right hand, a masculine gesture, rather than embracing him as we were accustomed to. "Is this normal?" I asked, with a quick turn of my head, to the screaming prisoners behind us. "Yeah, they do this any time fresh meat comes back here."

Suddenly, I was "fresh meat," not a category that I thought I would ever be placed in. I got down to business immediately, skipping the usual pleasantries we normally exchanged during a typical visit, immediately pulling the documents I needed him to sign from my briefcase. After he signed them, I looked up to see if the commotion outside had subsided any. It had not.

I glanced over at Jessie. He seemed completely unconcerned about the threat of violence just twenty-five feet away from us, separated only by the glass walls. I made up some story about how I needed to get back home and get the papers filed, thinking it would be best for both of us if I left sooner rather than later. The thought of him being interrogated about our visit by the screeching inmates he had to live with weighed heavily on my mind. I did not want my presence in the barracks that day to cause any problem for him, so I kept the visit as short as possible. I knocked on the glass for the guard. He retrieved Jessie and me at the same time, and as we left, Jessie took a right and the guard and I went back down the hallway to the left.

In the safety of my truck in the prison parking lot, I felt my heart rate begin to drop for the first time, and the near nauseating feeling in my stomach begin to ease. Before I turned the ignition, I resolved to never go back to that law library again.

57

A short, unexpected phone call from an attorney in Fayetteville in March 2004 would stir the case awake. All those years of sitting on a guilty conscience had finally gotten to Vicki Hutcheson. And the year had already started off well.

A slight ray of hope broke in the early days of 2004, a small indication that the growing number of people calling attention to the case, myself included, were beginning to make progress. I was invited in February to speak at my alma mater, the University of Arkansas School of Law in Fayetteville in March, at what they were ambitiously calling "*Innocence Lost: A Symposium on Wrongful Convictions.*" Was this a sign my efforts were finally taking hold in my home state? By then, of course, the case had sparked outrage in many areas of the country, and around the world, but to have its perfidies and ill-mannered intrigues called attention to at home meant a lot to me.

To me the upcoming March symposium on wrongful convictions was like a jolt of adrenaline. Finally, a decade after the convictions, someone in Arkansas was willing to admit that the West Memphis 3 had been railroaded. Even though it was a law student group that sponsored the event, my old law school was nothing short of bold in this endeavor.

The symposium was powerful and reassuring, with one speaker recounting a New Orleans case of prosecutorial misconduct that made it explosively clear how unscrupulous prosecutors could easily manipulate a case if they valued convictions more than justice. I sat rapt as I listened, hearing reaffirming accounts of how patience and determination will often win out. It was what I had needed to hear. By the time it was my turn to speak about the WM3 case there were few left in attendance. The one notable exception was the Philadelphia attorney, J. Gordon Cooney, Jr., who had presented the New Orleans case. After my presentation, he walked up and told me to never give up. Someday, he said, you will get that break you need.

I took heart from the day's activities, and I stood, stretched, and tightened myself for the long drive back to Paragould. I felt good as I left the Robert A. Leflar Law Center. It had been a day of hope. The drive from Fayetteville to Paragould is long and arduous. I had made that trip dozens of times as a law student. The meandering route almost due east across the northern part of the state to Paragould is tiresome and takes close to five hours if you are lucky. I was worn out by the time I arrived back home that night. I had just reached up and hit the button on the garage door opener when my cell phone rang. The attorney from Philadelphia was right. Someday I was going to get that break I needed. I just never imagined it would be the very same day.

I looked down quickly at my phone and saw that the number was from the Fayetteville area, but I had no idea who it was. I answered, expecting to hear someone from the law school telling me I had left something behind. Instead, the person on the other end told me she was a lawyer from Fayetteville who at that very moment had Victoria Hutcheson in her office ready and willing to recant her trial testimony in the Misskelley case.

"Under oath?" I asked.

"Well, not under oath but I think you are going to want to hear this. How soon can you get to Fayetteville?"

"I just left there! I spoke at the law school this morning."

I sat in my truck almost paralyzed by the implications of that call.

Ten years after her mumbling, dazed and highly questionable testimony had helped seal Jessie's fate, Vicki Hutcheson was willing to recant. Her testimony was part of the charade contrived by police and prosecutors to successfully build up the Satanic angle. It was the only evidence that they produced that even came close to corroborating Jessie's ridiculous confession.

Now, ten years later, her admission that her trial testimony was false was both exhilarating and frustrating. It provided a slim ray of hope, but unless she recanted under oath, it would do us no good. I had known for ten years she had lied during Jessie's trial. And now as I sat in my truck, the good fortune that phone call meant was settling in. This was huge. I told Hutcheson's lawyer that I would be in her office in Fayetteville the next afternoon at 2:00 p.m. I quickly thought of how I might avoid repeating that numbing ride back and forth across the state.

I decided to charter a plane. Within an hour, I had found both a pilot and a plane for the excursion back to Fayetteville. I retrieved my video camera and a tripod, and a trip to Walmart yielded some blank 8mm cassettes. This time her recantation would be videotaped. I did not want to wait another ten years or risk the chance that she would change her mind.

Later that evening, I did some research on perjury and concluded that Vicki Hutcheson could not be successfully prosecuted for recanting – the statute of limitations had expired. I hoped that she and her lawyer would agree with my assessment. Knowing that would thaw her long-held reluctance to come clean, I hoped.

The next morning, I met the pilot at Paragould's Kirk Field, and we lifted off for Fayetteville. The entire trip took an hour and a half. An assistant from the lawyer's office picked me up at Drake Field in Fayetteville and drove me the short distance back to the law office where I would come face to face again with Victoria Hutcheson, whom I had not seen in ten years.

Vicki seemed glad to see me, and it was apparent that what she was about to tell me was weighing heavily on her conscience. I was eager to hear her story. As we sat down in the lawyer's comfortable office, the tension gradually ebbing, I stressed how I was convinced Vicki could not be charged with perjury because the statute of limitations had passed. I was relieved that they seemed to agree.

The camera and recorder running, I placed Vicki under oath. It was solid, recorded, and videotaped gold. She recanted her fabulist story of the so-called "esbat," or witches meeting, and the ride in Damien's non-existent car with Jessie. It was what I had been waiting for and had expected. She expanded the story into something I had not expected—and this was no small task, since the underhanded and oily manner of the prosecution had by that time been firmly embedded in my mind. With the camera running, she went on to say that every word of her trial testimony in 1994 was a lie.

First, and not entirely surprising to me, she said she had been self-medicating with Valium and morphine during her testimony. At one point she described Brent Davis coming into a witness room during the Misskelley trial to make sure that she had enough meds to be able to testify. This was troubling, but there was more trouble to come.

There never was any esbat, she said. And she had not even been anywhere near Damien and Jessie that night. She had made the entire bizarre episode up. She had been scared out of her wits by the West Memphis police and feared losing custody of her son. As she spoke, I could clearly see she had been coerced by the police to take part in the fable they were weaving about the Satanic ritualistic murders, just as they had done to squeeze out Jessie's confession.

As the tape rolled, she described how the West Memphis police took her and her son Aaron across the river into Memphis, across state lines, so that neither she, nor her son Aaron, could be subpoenaed by the defense lawyers in the Echols and Baldwin trial. Someone, she said, either the police or prosecutors, had actually paid for the motel room and their food for the entire length of the second trial, even moving her and Aaron on one occasion to another motel because they feared Ron Lax was closing in on her location. She said by the time she was brought back home; Jason Baldwin had been sentenced to life in prison without parole and Damien Echols was sitting in prison with the death penalty over his head.

That day in Fayetteville it was noticeably clear that those dark consequences had weighed heavily on Vicki Hutcheson over the years. She was tense and sobbing occasionally as she relieved herself of the burden of such heavy lies. Vicki Hutcheson's story fits cleanly into other patterns in the case. First, the way she had been coerced into creating the fiction of the esbat. But second, that the police, whose conduct was imputed to the prosecutors, were very much at ease with the idea of hiding witnesses.

Suddenly my mind slipped back to a phone conversation that I had with Joyce Cureton back on March 2, 1998. She was the head matron of the Craighead County Juvenile Detention facility, and she had evidence that Jason Baldwin was innocent. She told me that she was ordered by the Sheriff of Craighead County to leave town so that the lawyers for Echols and Baldwin could not locate her to serve her with a subpoena for the trial.

In the film *West of Memphis*, Cureton states that the Sheriff told her "Joyce, this is simple. Crittenden County fucked up and now we have to clean up." *Who directed the Sheriff of Craighead County to "clean up" what Crittenden County had, to put it more mildly, messed up?* Just like Jessie's "police car confession," it is hard to imagine a scenario where the Sheriff would have conceived such an idea on his own without some intervention by a prosecutor. Afraid of losing her job, Cureton said that she hid out in Jackson County, Arkansas, with a county-issued car and county credit card, where she and her husband stayed in a motel until the Echols and Baldwin trial was over. Indeed, a familiar pattern had emerged.

As we taxied down the runway for the flight back home to Paragould, the sun was beginning to slip behind the last mountain behind us to the west. As the last rays of sunshine faded, I looked out the window to the east into the darkness, waiting for the next small town or city to light up the night with its streetlights and the lights of homes and businesses. Each would begin with a small glow and then erupt into a brilliance gauged only by the size of the hamlet just below the plane.

I started to imagine the impact of what I had now secured in my briefcase. I knew it would not immediately spring the prison doors open for my client and his co-defendants, but I knew the cumulative effect of this and the other evidence that the defense was slowly uncovering would help begin the dismantling of the prosecution's entire case against our clients. I walked through the door at home and went directly to the kitchen to make a sandwich. I had not eaten all day. Then I went to my home office and wrote a memo to John Philipsborn and Michael Burt:

Ms. Hutcheson stated "that her trial testimony was completely false; that she had consumed approximately 10 valiums and a morphine tablet just prior to her testimony at the Misskelley trial; that prosecutors knew she was taking all of this medication; that police threatened to implicate her in the crime, and to remove her son from her custody if she didn't testify the way they wanted her to at trial; she said that the police also advised her that they could make her criminal charges that were then pending against her at the time of the trial go away; that Jerry Driver suggested to her the story of the "esbat" that she testified to at trial. She now states that she never went to any such witches meeting with Damien and Jessie."

The next day I got a return email from both Philipsborn and Burt. Both felt Vicki's recantation was a tremendous break in the case. A week or so later, after they had watched copies of the video that I had sent them, John called to remind me that I was no longer an attorney of record in the case, and that perhaps I should have called and let an investigator go and take the statement. I had not given it a second thought. I had simply fallen back into my familiar role as attorney for Jessie. John acknowledged that it was clear that Hutcheson wanted to talk to me personally, and that it was important to get the statement before she changed her mind. But his response was a stark reminder that my role in the case had now changed dramatically. I needed to remember that in the future.

Unfortunately, the future was not looking bright for my failing marriage. Kim's resentment toward me and the amount of time I was away working on the case and at the office made matters even worse. I think we both knew it was over, but neither one of us wanted to hurt the kids. We started a pattern of co-existence that ended in 2007. We were able to keep things afloat until March 2008, when after nearly twenty-four years of marriage we were divorced on my forty-fifth birthday.

58

In 1994 the science and dynamics of false confessions were just emerging. Today the concept of a false confession is universally accepted, and we can now identify the factors that can lead to such an injustice. Despite this, there are still people today who refuse to believe that anyone would confess to a crime they did not commit. They think that they, or anyone else, could withstand the rigors of a long and brutal police interrogation. Studies have shown that after four to six hours of intense interrogation even a person of reasonably high intelligence will begin to break down psychologically. This includes military personnel who are trained to withstand such psychological pressure. With such training someone might be able to withstand the pressure for a while, but only if they understand the rules of what I call an interrogation—something the police more tenderly call an interview.

Jessie Misskelley, 17 years old, intellectually challenged, with no parent present to offer advice, and with absolutely no concept of his Miranda rights, his right to remain silent, his right to counsel, and his right to walk out the door at any time, did not have a chance.

False confessions occur more often than they should, even today. According to the Innocence Project, 375 people have been completely exonerated since 1989 using DNA testing, including 21 people on Death Row. Of those 375 people, nearly a third of them gave false confessions to the police. These are frightening statistics. We can now, statistically, demonstrate that innocent people have been executed for crimes they did not commit. Damien Echols could have easily been among them.

Jessie Misskelley had no idea of the significance of what he had told police as they badgered him throughout the day on June 3, 1993. He sat through approximately 12 hours of grilling—agreeing, changing, dodging—until those 12 hours fit neatly onto a thirty-four-minute audio tape, followed by a twelve-minute audio tape to clarify the first. Apparently when Deputy Prosecutor Fogleman arrived at the WMPD to listen to the first audio tape, he was concerned about something that Gitchell and Ridge were not—the time of the murders that Misskelley gave them. Fogleman knew that the murders had not occurred at noon as Misskelley had stated on the tape and that the three victims and Jason Baldwin had not skipped school that day. In addition, the three kids were seen riding two bicycles on the service road at 6:30 p.m. Gitchell went back in to fix these problematic issues. He immediately and quite vigorously suggested to Jessie Misskelley that the murders had occurred sometime after 7:00 or 8:00 p.m. and Jessie was happy to oblige.

Jessie Misskelley was no match for the police who knew, after some encouragement from John Fogleman, what they needed and exactly how to get it. Today, every credible expert who has reviewed Jessie Misskelley's confession has concluded it was both false and coerced.

There are several ways to demonstrate that it is a false confession. The entire concept of the police and prosecution's main assertion—that the murders were part of a Satanic ritual—have been completely debunked for years. Even if you were the type of person who still wanted to engage in the fiction of Satanic Ritualistic Homicide, six of the world's leading forensic pathologists have now unequivocally testified, or given Affidavits, that the wounds on those three young boys in West Memphis once thought to be associated with a "Satanic Ritualistic Homicide," were caused by animal predation.

We know also that Jessie's confession was false because he never told the police anything in the confession that they did not already know or had assumed was correct. So, factually, it does not hold water. Woefully, it did not hold water back in 1993 either. But such is the inherent power of a social and moral panic and the horrific result it can bring.

False confessions are real, and there is a prodigious amount of scientific research to back that. I have had the great pleasure and honor of working with, in one way or another, some of the leading experts in the field of false confessions. Dr. Richard Ofshe, Dr. Richard Leo of the University of San Francisco School of Law, and Steven Drizin and Laura Nirider co-founders of the Center on Wrongful Convictions of Youth at the Northwestern Pritzker School of Law in Chicago. Experts now understand there are three types of false confessions.

The first, "voluntary false confessions," arise when innocent people come forward to police voluntarily because they are seeking attention. Think of John Mark Karr in the JonBenét Ramsey case who confessed to the murder just for his 15 minutes of fame. The second is what Dr. Richard Leo calls "persuaded false confessions." These are people convinced by their interrogators that they committed the crime when they did not. The final category, and the one at the heart of Jessie Misskelley's confession—one that Richard Ofshe was ready to demonstrate to the jury back in 1994 in great detail—is a false "compliant" confession.

In false compliant confessions the suspect is psychologically coerced by interrogators to confess even while believing he is innocent. The suspect confesses "to escape a stressful situation, avoid punishment, or gain a promised or implied reward." In a false compliant confession, the suspect realizes, often incorrectly, that the short-term benefits of the false confession "outweigh the long-term costs."

For Jessie Misskelley, confessing he had witnessed the murders was more palatable than continuing to absorb the hostility of his interrogators. He was tired. He wanted to go home. At some point during the unrecorded part of the interrogation, Jessie concluded that he wanted out of that stressful situation and the enormous anxiety it was causing. The only way out, he wrongfully concluded, was to tell the police what they made abundantly clear they wanted him to say. Jessie had assumed, incorrectly, he could fix it later. Also, he did not understand that he could just get up and leave anytime he chose.

The courts have long given police carte blanche to use any tactics shy of physical abuse, or extreme psychological torture, in the interrogation room. This was certainly true of the way police conducted Jessie Misskelley's confession. They threatened him with execution in the electric chair, something Jessie Misskelley could understand even with his limited world view. He was given a polygraph test, and then told that he was "lying his ass off," when he in fact he had passed. They showed him a horrible crime scene photograph of one of the victims to frighten him and produce a statement, a fact that Detective Bryn Ridge eagerly admitted in his testimony during the trial.

Jessie Misskelley's confession is a mix of ideas created by the police, then offered to him as a narrative saturated in religious and social superstition—that he had taken part in a Satanic ritual. For the police and for many in the community, there was no other way to explain the brutality of the murders. The police and the public needed to get rid of the evil that had come upon them. The West Memphis Police had their "Satanic" motive, and they provided Jessie Misskelley with the script. The only problem was that their patsy was incapable of performing that script because he was, and remains, too intellectually challenged.

The United States Supreme Court addressed this very issue in the case of *Haley vs. Ohio* in 1948. A 15-year-old boy was arrested for his role as a lookout in a robbery in which a confectionary store owner was shot and killed. He was brought to police headquarters at midnight and interrogated without the presence of an adult or an attorney for five straight hours by five or six officers in relays of one or two officers at a time. At 5:00 a.m., after being falsely told that two other boys had implicated him, he confessed. He was convicted of first-degree murder in state court; the conviction was affirmed by a State appellate court and then the State supreme court. In the U.S. Supreme Court, Justice William Douglas wrote that:

"A 15-year-old lad, questioned through the dead of night by relays of police, is a ready victim of the inquisition. Mature men possibly might stand the ordeal from midnight to 5 a.m. But we cannot believe that a lad of tender years is a match for the police in such a contest. He needs counsel and support if he is not to become the victim first of fear, then of panic. He needs someone on whom to lean lest the overpowering presence of the law, as he knows it, may not crush him...When the police are so unmindful of these basic standards of conduct in their public dealings, their secret treatment of a 15-year-old boy behind closed doors in the dead of night becomes darkly suspicious."

In my mind, Jessie Misskelley's warm up for his false confession behind closed doors was "darkly suspicious." One cannot help but wonder what Justice Douglas would have thought of the interrogation of Jessie Misskelley. In *Haley,* the interrogation lasted only five hours; Jessie Misskelley's was twelve hours. Steve Drizen would sum it up succinctly by stating that "Jessie was not convicted on the basis of Jessie Misskelley's statement, and neither was Damien or Jason. They were convicted on the basis of Gary Gitchell's confession. All they had to do was get Jessie to agree to it."

59

Jessie Misskelley's world is an alien landscape he has never understood and has never learned to navigate successfully. The one constant for him is a steady stream of people seeking to take advantage of him, an easy, if malicious pastime. It has been that way since he was a bullied young boy starting out in school. Never sure how to react to these assaults, his responses were often inappropriate.

I would learn a lot from an examination of Jessie Misskelley in 2004 by a leading forensic psychologist. I learned that ninety-five to ninety-eight percent of the people Jessie Misskelley encounters in life are intellectually superior to him. This includes every grade schooler, police officer, prosecutor and judge he meets. I note this not to demean him, because I love him. He is a charming, charismatic, and loving man. I had been trying to get inside Jessie Misskelley's head for years, to understand how he views the world, how he deals with daily challenges, and most importantly, why he confessed.

After they announced Jessie Misskelley's confession, the mood at the West Memphis Police Department was described in newspaper reports as "jubilant." Officers Gary Gitchell and Bryn Ridge would both later admit they thought Jessie Misskelley was mentally challenged. Ridge described him as a "little slow." Gitchell would say duplicitously that Jessie Misskelley had simply been "confused."

The malleability of Jessie Misskelley's mind, how he perceived the world, eased the way for Gitchell and Ridge to craft the confession. An easy target, Jessie had been persecuted for much of his life. In response, he developed ways to cope. That day and night in the West Memphis Police Department was no different.

San Francisco forensic psychologist, Dr. Tim Derning, would examine Jessie Misskelley over two days at the Varner Unit of the Arkansas Department of Corrections in 2004. He would produce a clear and unambiguous assessment of Jessie Misskelley's mental capabilities that clarified my understanding of how Jessie Misskelley perceived the world around him.

Jessie Misskelley, Dr. Derning found, "is cognitively impaired and as a result is quite susceptible to having his will overborne through confusion, stress, intimidation, coercion, or deception." As police kept up the pressure the day and night of the confession, Derning said that Jessie Misskelley, "was quite susceptible to agree to something he did not understand, ultimately leading to an involuntary confession." Under the enormous stress of the interrogation, he dealt with the pressure the only way that he could by attempting to please his interrogators. The term for this instinct, Dr. Derning said, is "cheating to lose" – a survival mechanism Jessie uses to mask his very real cognitive and intellectual incapacities. He does not understand the world and its nuances but hides that fact to avoid embarrassment.

In his report after the examination, Derning wrote that Jessie Misskelley "seeks to appear competent and intelligent, as though he understands more than he does." In a life where his disability made him the target of ridicule, Jessie Misskelley learned exceedingly early to pretend he understands what someone is talking about. He agrees with anything someone tells him. While this gives him some sense of fitting in, it also makes him especially vulnerable to authority figures.

Dr. Derning's assessment also provided a stunning revelation that was lacking before the trial in 1994. It would have been a game-changer had we been blessed with it back then. It would prove to be invaluable as the defense team worked its way through the Rule 37 hearings. *Jessie Misskelley was not competent to stand trial back in 1994.*

Dr. Derning's examination disclosed that Jessie Misskelley did not adequately understand the nature of the criminal proceedings against him and was not able to consult meaningfully with Greg Crow or me, or to assist us in preparing his defense. He lacked adequate decision-making processes to help us.

I already knew that Jessie Misskelley thought that I was a police officer back in 1993, but Dr. Derning's report outlined how Jessie Misskelley Jr. did not have the ability to comprehend what a lawyer was—nor did he understand the role of the judge, the prosecutor, or the jury. Jessie did not understand the basic concept of a jury trial and had, at best, only a superficial understanding of his Miranda rights. Likewise, he could not comprehend the consequences of waiving those rights.

He would tell Dr. Derning that the right to remain silent meant, "You don't have to talk to nobody." He did not associate the right to remain silent in the legal context of protecting himself. He was not able to explain why he did not have an attorney during questioning by the police in 1993. In fact, he did not know an attorney could protect his legal rights.

Dr. Derning remarked that he had in 2004 expected to find a different Jessie Misskelley than the 17-year-old convicted by the State of Arkansas in 1994. Based on his experience, Dr. Derning noted, the longer people are exposed to the criminal justice system and incarceration, the better their mastery of their constitutional rights, the nature of criminal proceedings, the roles of the participants in the system, and the nature of the criminal charges against them. For Jessie Misskelley this was not the case. He still did not understand what had happened, nor had he developed a more sophisticated sense of his situation, even after ten years in prison and countless appeals.

I recall a prison visit where Bruce Sinofsky and Joe Berlinger worked on *Paradise Lost: Revelations*. In a scene from the film, Jessie is asked how he is faring in prison. Jessie's incongruent response was:

"It just keeps getting better and better by the day."

An inmate with even an average intellectual capacity would have described prison life much differently. In prison, Jessie Misskelley had a structure and routine that was good for someone with his mental challenges. He had a job, a place to sleep and food to eat. He had it better in prison than he did back home at the trailer park in the dire poverty he lived in. He did not grow intellectually, and he still did not understand the legal system that put him there.

According to Dr. Derning, there was something else that was particularly intriguing about the way that Jessie Misskelley interprets the legal system and how it operates both then and now. Jessie believed that he had an absolute obligation to tell the truth in the courtroom. In his mind, that obligation took precedence over any other rights or obligations he had as a criminal defendant. This is exactly what Jessie described each time he was confronted with the issue of testifying against Echols and Baldwin in an exchange for a more lenient sentence, "I can't lie on them no more." This is remarkable because it explains how Jessie could lie to police officers, to prosecutors, and even me, but once he entered a courtroom, he simply was incapable of doing so. Even more telling is that this explains how he can lie with his hand on a Bible, something I have personally seen happen more than once.

In the 2012 case of *Miller vs. Alabama*, a case consolidated with another one from Arkansas, the U.S. Supreme Court ruled that "mandatory life without parole for those under the age of 18 at the time of their crime violates the 8th Amendment's prohibition on cruel and unusual punishments." The Court went on to say that "mandatory life without parole for a juvenile precludes consideration of his chronological age and its hallmark failure to appreciate risks and consequences."

Two years later in 2014, twenty years after my stab at having the death penalty removed from Jessie Misskelley's trial because of his limited intellectual abilities, the United States Supreme Court issued a ruling that would have shattered Judge Burnett's jaw-dropping "street smarts" decision had it been in effect in 1994. The high court adopted a rule that says state courts must consider more than just raw I.Q. scores in determining if someone is, to use the 1994 lingo, "mentally retarded." The high court also said that someone who fits this definition should not face the death penalty. I take some small measure of pride in having argued this issue twenty years earlier before it would be embraced by the U.S. Supreme Court. The wheels of justice turn slowly.

In that same year, I exchanged some emails with Dr. Derning, trying to get an even more passionate understanding about the enigmatic Jessie Misskelley. Derning told me that Jessie possesses a "concrete" level of thinking. Concrete thinking does not have any depth. It refers to thinking literally, or in the periphery of any given moment or situation. Abstract thinking, on the other hand, goes beyond the periphery and delves below the surface of a given situation allowing that person not just the ability to evaluate the task or problem at hand, but the circumstances and later consequences of that decision. Jessie's inability to think abstractly explains a lot.

To Jessie Misskelley, a courtroom is a place where you cannot tell a lie. It is open to the public, and thanks to Judge Burnett's self-admiration, no one could prey upon him inside there without the world and the HBO cameras recording it. But perhaps he understands one thing better than those men who preyed upon him during this case, that the courtroom is sacred, a place where you *must* tell the truth no matter what.

60

The day I had anxiously anticipated for over fourteen years was fast approaching. Knowing I would have to subject myself to the rigors of an ineffective assistance of counsel claim had been like eating glass. Knowing that it would help generate a new trial for Jessie Misskelley helped me ignore the indigestion. A couple of months before the hearing, the Office of the Arkansas Attorney General sent me a letter advising me I would face jail time for contempt of court if I discussed my testimony with anyone. I called Crow, and without discussing the case, I asked him if he had received the same letter from the Attorney General. He had. *I wondered what the attorney general was afraid of?*

Judge Burnett would take similar action to stifle attention. I do not think that his choice to conduct the hearings in perhaps the smallest courtroom in Craighead County, barely large enough for all the lawyers let alone the media, was a coincidence. Burnett also issued a "gag order" that prevented the lawyers and witnesses from talking to the media about the case. The one person the attorney general and Judge Burnett could not "gag" was Lonnie Soury, the media consultant hired by the Echols defense team. Soury was neither a lawyer nor a witness, but he was a master of his profession. The State of Arkansas seemed to be very afraid of the truth I was about to tell at the hearings.

My wait for the Rule 37 hearings was difficult. Consequences were strewn everywhere and had been for years. The year before the hearing proved to be tough and was getting tougher. The reality of my divorce and how it would affect the kids soon sunk in. My daughter Kathryn was fifteen and she was not coping well with the divorce. I did not know it at the time, but she was constantly asked for details of the WM3 case by students and teachers at Paragould High School. She never mentioned this to me until recently. Michael had just turned thirteen. In middle school, he had not been subjected to being grilled about the case.

In those final days before the hearing, I sat them down and tried to explain what was about to happen. I told them the court would be conducting a hearing to determine whether I had been a good enough lawyer for Jessie Misskelley during his trial back in 1994. It was a stark reminder of how much and for how long the case had wrapped around our family. Kathryn was eighteen months old when the Misskelley trial began in Corning. Michael had not yet been born. It seemed the more I tried to explain what was happening, the deeper their confusion. In the end, I told them that it was likely that some people on television might say some bad things about me and how inexperienced I had been back in 1994. "Don't worry about what you might hear," I said. "Just tell them that your dad did his job." I thought my efforts to prepare them for what was about to happen had failed miserably, but mercifully folks did not intrude.

The afternoon before my testimony, I presided over court in Paragould. It did little to distract me from the task of falling on my sword the next day. After calling the docket, I retreated to my chambers and was hanging up my robe when one of my clerks knocked on the door and came in.

"Tomorrow's the big day I guess," she said.

"Yes, it is, the big day."

"You'll be fine. You know that don't you?"

"I know. All I have to do is tell the truth."

"Everything will be fine here. Don't worry about a thing."

"I won't and thank you so much."

She may not have known it, but her words did much to comfort me.

61

Walking into that cramped hearing room in Jonesboro on September 30, 2008, ready to expose my sensitive skin to the cudgel in the hands of Michael Burt, I was not sure if I had slept at all the night before. When I arrived at the Craighead County courthouse I was immediately swarmed by reporters. I warmly reminded them of the gag order imposed by Judge Burnett, but they still seemed disappointed that I had no comment. They had grown used to my frequent comments after my role as advocate for Jessie Misskelley had morphed into being head cheerleader for the WM3.

A bailiff waiting for me at the glass doors brought me up the back stairs and deposited me into a small jury room sparsely decorated with two shaded windows, a small conference table and a closet-sized restroom. I had brought some notes along, but not much else. Fourteen years of memories would have to serve me. I counted my breaths to keep calm as I waited. Fifteen minutes later, the bailiff returned.

"Your Honor, they are ready for you," he said.

I nodded and followed him into a tiny windowless courtroom. Burnett sat on the bench to my right. At a table for the defense were Michael Burt and Jeff Rosezweig, representing Jessie Misskelley Jr., and John Philipsborn and Blake Hendrix representing Jason Baldwin.

Brent Davis and a couple of lawyers from the attorney general's offices sat at a table across from them. Jessie Misskelley, neatly dressed in a new suit, sat beside Burt and Rosezweig, looking attentive.

I inhaled deeply, stepped up into the witness stand, and was sworn in. The Rule 37 hearing would be emotionally painful. I knew I would be exposing myself, and that the process would be unsettling. But my many sleepless nights worrying about it could have been better spent. I had hoped to at least take my beating quickly, move ahead, and in some way heal. If I had known that I would be on and off the witness stand over the course of the next two years, I would have been more selective choosing which nights I had spent staring at my bedroom ceiling.

On that first day, Burt would ask me questions that we both already knew the answers to. My testimony was bookended by two especially important issues. First was my lack of experience as a young lawyer, followed by the Rule 2.3 issue that had been set in stone by the Arkansas Supreme Court in 1996. Not many lawyers ever get to watch their inexperience in a criminal trial unfold on HBO as I had. I would do penance for my sins, real or not, and I would be set free knowing that I had done all I could to get Jessie Misskelley out of prison. My reputation could be rebuilt, but a life wasted in prison could not.

Michael Burt asked me to recount Judge Burnett's bizarre intrusion into the jury room during the Misskelley trial. I testified that right before lunch on the second day of deliberations under the pretense of ordering them food I explained that Burnett then knocked on the jury room door and told the jury members inside that he was going to order food and asked what they would like to eat. The foreman explained that they did not need lunch since they were almost finished. Then I recounted what Burnett's admonition was to them —That he was going to send out for food anyway because they would still have to come back after lunch for sentencing. The jury foreman then asked Burnett "What if we find him not guilty? Will we still have to stay?"

My story was met first with gasps and then stony silence in the Rule 37 hearing room. After the hearing, a local television reporter followed Burnett out to his car in the parking lot and asked him point blank if my telling of his jury room behavior in the Misskelley trial was true. For all to see, at five, six and at ten, was Burnett's skillful and agile reply.

"It could have taken place, I guess, but I don't really recall," he said.

Anything Burnett did revolved around his own sun, focused on putting himself and his reputation in the best possible light. He knew damn well what he had done.

As day one of my testimony ended, a debate emerged over whether Judge Burnett would allow any of the forensic experts that had been assembled by the defense team to testify at the Rule 37 hearings. "Well, I don't want to re-try the case," Burnett proclaimed. "That's not the purpose of this hearing." Burnett then, for the second time that day, forecast his ruling in the Rule 37 hearings by saying that "the record is going to be so voluminous" it would take the Arkansas Supreme Court ten years to read the transcript.

After each of the four defense attorneys—Philipsborn, Burt, Hendrix and Rosezweig— argued to the court that this evidence was both relevant and proper for the court's consideration of the *Strickland* standard, Judge Burnett asked Brent Davis for his position. Davis said that he thought that the *"far-reaching scientific evidence stuff"* should not be something that should come into the Rule 37 hearings. It was clear that neither Davis nor Burnett wanted to hear any testimony that might suggest the actual innocence of the West Memphis Three. They had good reason to fear that "far-reaching scientific stuff." It would be devastating to them and their case.

As I started gathering my things to leave, Brent Davis urgently reminded Burnett to admonish me that I was still under the "rule." Burnett looked at me, and as if to scold a young child, and said "Yeah, that means you can't discuss your testimony with anyone until you're finally released."

I would not testify again until November 19th, when it was Brent

Davis' turn to begin his cross-examination. We spent most of that day with Davis putting into the record all the reasons he believed Jessie Misskelley, along with Echols and Baldwin, were guilty of the first ever Satanic Ritualistic Homicide recorded on the planet. This, of course, included transcripts and testimony regarding all the so-called confessions Jessie had made post-conviction. It seemed important for him to get this into the record so the Arkansas Supreme Court would know about it, an effort that would later backfire.

November 20th was more of the same. Davis would ask me about my efforts on behalf of Misskelley in the nearly fifteen years since his conviction, as if that would somehow mitigate my lack of experience in 1993 and 1994. Davis seemed more interested in getting the year 2008 over with so he could wash his hands of the whole sordid affair by assuming the soon-to-be-retiring Burnett's Circuit Judge seat on January 1, 2009. Burnett seemed to sense this and noted that he would like to finish up with the hearings before December 31st. "But if we don't, then I guess I'll just have to work some next year," Burnett announced. My heart sank. It was clear that Burnett had already arranged to continue to hear the case into the next year.

I would not have to appear again to testify until April 2, 2009. The Rule 37 hearings became for me a prolonged flogging interrupted frequently by petty sniping, objections, and an abundance of condescension from state attorneys. In the end, I expected that Judge Burnett would proclaim that I was the greatest lawyer the world had ever seen— not because he believed it to be true but because my deftness and skill as an attorney were necessary for him to prevail. I could only imagine how difficult a task that would be for him.

As my testimony in the Rule 37 hearings closed, Michael Burt would email me:

"As always, thanks for your thoughtful attention to the case. I agree with you that all the issues were covered, so no need for your return. I know I speak for everybody when I thank you sincerely for all the hard work you have put into this case over the years. Jesse has a good shot at this point largely because of all you have done for him and your courageous testimony at the Rule 37 hearing. Needless to say, we will not win in front of Burnett. But somewhere, somehow, justice will prevail."

That was the whole point of it all—"somewhere, somehow, justice will prevail." But like a penitent sinner, I was exhausted, bloody, and stained by the end of my testimony. Still, I felt the elation of grace, of knowing I had told the truth and laid it all out there. Fortunately, my kids had been spared what I had expected would be disparaging press for me, especially by the local media. Instead, my testimony and truthfulness earned me accolades and respect from all around the world.

62

Jessie Misskelley does not like snakes. Detective Bryn Ridge at the Rule 37 hearings testified that he was genuinely concerned about snakes when he was searching the ditch after the bodies of the three boys had been removed. This prompted a startled Misskelley to lean over to Michael Burt at counsel table and say, "There would have been snakes in that ditch and that proves I'm not guilty because I don't like snakes."

Dr. Tim Derning began his compelling testimony on November 21st, 2008, the day after I testified. His 2004 assessment, he said, revealed that Jessie Misskelley has "mental retardation," or "MR," and that it is "static, chronic and essentially unchanging."

Derning clearly established that at the time of Jessie's arrest in 1993 and during his trial in 1994, he was *not* competent to stand trial, completely incapable of assisting us in his own defense and incapable of making a knowing and intelligent waiver of his *Miranda* rights. In addition, Derning testified unequivocally that Jessie's statements were not voluntary— that they were not knowingly and intelligently made because he was incapable of understanding the implications of making those statements.

Derning was referring to all of Jessie's so-called confessions, including both of his June 3rd, 1993, statements to police, the "police car" statement on his way to prison, the infamous "Bible confession" at the prison, and the one obtained by Brent Davis just ahead of the trial for Echols and Baldwin. Derning would have a lot to say about these "statements."

He testified that our trial psychologist's conclusions were wrong on virtually every count. Our expert had failed to accurately diagnose Jessie Misskelley's "mental retardation," and incorrectly found him to be competent to stand trial. He added that it was "difficult sometimes to testify" about our trial psychologist's evaluation or even try and understand it because it was "so irrational" and "just bizarre." This, of course, magnified my key mistake of failing to retain a competent trial psychologist or properly vet the one we had after I could find no one else.

At one point during Michael Burt's direct examination of Dr. Derning, Judge Burnett interrupted to try and jam a stick in the spokes of that diagnosis, just as he had been doing for years as a prosecutor and judge. Once again Burnett tried casually to bring up his "street smarts" argument that had worked so well for him in the past in determining such trivial things as whether someone was eligible for the death penalty.

Burnett asked Dr. Derning if he had taken "street smarts" into consideration in reaching his conclusion about Jessie's mental retardation (MR) diagnosis. Dr. Derning unequivocally said "no," and then proceeded to explain exactly how he had reached his conclusions.

Dr. Derning, just as the U.S. Supreme Court would eventually decree six years later, stressed the importance of broadening the definition of MR beyond an I.Q. score. To get an accurate representation of Jessie Misskelley, Derning said, you must look beyond his I.Q. scores and examine his daily life, his level of functioning, what people said about him, and what he was able to do. He went on to explain that societal stereotypes and the myths of MR make this process difficult for people to understand. They expect someone who has MR to look or dress a certain way, he said. "All this creates a misunderstanding about what people with MR are like," he added.

"Jessie is typical of somebody, especially in forensic cases, where you don't pick it up right away," said Derning. "You don't look at him and say 'Gee, that guy is 'mentally retarded' the way you would with somebody else." "Does that answer your question about 'street smarts'?" Derning asked Judge Burnett. "I think so," was Burnett's reply.

Dr. Derning then proceeded to explain that people with MR can do a lot of things we might not necessarily expect them to be able to do, like taking the subway, driving a car, having a girlfriend, or having a job. Derning stated he knew people with MR who had become accomplished artists. In other words, people with MR have strengths that may co-exist with their weaknesses, though they will always have the deficits. Jessie Misskelley's deficits included impaired socialization skills, impaired reading ability, problems with language and extremely poor school performance, Derning stated.

In response to further questions from Michael Burt, Derning pointed out that Jessie's MR meant that he was more likely to be susceptible to coercion and pressure from others, including situations where leading questions were used against him. "Imagine a lifetime of being the least capable person in the room, who knows the least, who can't explain things, who is being told how to do things, maybe scolded for that. Then being teased and ridiculed and made fun of," explained Derning.

When their intelligence is being tested, or they are pressured, people with MR are "very susceptible to manipulation, and coercion," Derning said, "in response they make things up to mask their mental deficits because they are embarrassed. They will pretend that they know something when they do not because they are trying to figure out what's what, and what is it that you want from them, what's the right answer without really considering what the implications are." The results can be disastrous when a police officer exerts pressure on someone like Jessie Misskelley, Dr. Derning asserted.

Burt asked Derning about Jessie Misskelley's ability to read and understand the waiver of rights form before his interrogation by police on June 3, 1993. "Jessie never demonstrated any ability that would come close to being able to read something that long, that complicated and respond to it, understand it with comprehension."

Burt moved on to specific portions of the trial transcript where there were interactions between Jessie Misskelley and Judge Burnett:

"THE COURT: Let the record reflect that this is out of the presence of the jury, which hasn't been sworn at this time. Mr. Misskelley, I need to ask you some questions. First of all, today is Wednesday the 26th and we are ready to proceed to jury trial. And as soon as we get out there the clerk will swear the jury. Do you understand that?
MR. MISSKELLEY: "Uh, tell the truth? Is that what you mean?"
THE COURT: No, I'm asking you do you understand we're about to start your trial?
MR. MISSKELLEY: "Oh, yea, I understand."

"Well, it gives us another example of his confusion," explained Derning. "It's very typical of people like Mr. Misskelley to isolate on one word or one sentence. He heard the word swear, swear in the jury, but he didn't get the larger context." That also demonstrated Jessie's inability to understand the nature of the proceedings and his inability to assist his defense at the time of his trial, Derning pointed out.

When he interviewed Jessie in 2004, Derning asked Jessie, "If you plead guilty, can you still try and convince the judge that you are innocent?" "I guess, yes, I guess you can," Jessie responded. Derning said that this response surprised him. After years of being in the system around his lawyers, the trial, locked in prison with jailhouse lawyers, Jessie should have had a better grasp of the question. He should have been able to understand. Yet he did not.

Dr. Derning was in the courtroom the day before and had heard both my testimony and the audiotape of Jessie Misskelley's "Bible Confession." His testimony regarding both, lost in thousands of pages of transcript, put a dagger into the heart of the prosecution's case. Reading the transcripts in 2020, I found it difficult to breathe.

Brent Davis thought it would be prudent, mistakenly as it turned out, to ask Dr. Derning his opinion of Jessie's post-trial statements. Had Mr. Misskelley's mental deficits changed? Davis asked. Mr. Davis did not get the answer he was looking for.

"I don't know if there was anything there that is going to be any different or change my opinion—not because I'm stubborn, but because after hearing what I heard yesterday, it just seems like more of the same. I got an understanding yesterday of events of Mr. Misskelley overriding his attorney and trying to make a deal with your office. I wasn't aware of any," Derning replied. "I just found it confirming to my opinion that he doesn't really understand what's going on."

Davis, wobbling from Derning's response said, "Well, I am lost in some respect. Did you say, 'trying to override his attorney' what do you mean?" "Mr. Stidham testified yesterday that against his objections—objections and warnings—he made it clear that he was not okay with Mr. Misskelley giving statements and meeting with you," Derning replied.

Davis quickly pivoted to the "Bible confession." "If the facts of that confession occurred *without any law enforcement officers requesting that* or being present in the room…would that affect your viewpoint or the value that you had placed on his ability to communicate with his attorney in that statement?" he asked Derning.

Davis was disingenuous in his wording of that question, which is important in terms of Derning's response. First, I was at the prison the day of the Bible confession because two law enforcement officers had ignored my instructions and warnings that they were not to talk to Jessie under any circumstances on the way to prison, the so-called "police car statement." Second, I was there only because Davis had asked me to talk to Misskelley about testifying against Echols and Baldwin, which was my obligation to my client no matter how much it irritated me.

Derning responded. "Well, Mr. Davis, to be honest with you, when I listened to that tape, I heard more of the same, which was Mr. Stidham constantly structuring, asking questions, having to probe, Mr. Misskelley—rarely spontaneously saying anything. Mr. Stidham had to hope that he was asking the right questions, pertinent questions, important questions to unlock something from Mr. Misskelley."

When Davis failed to get Dr. Derning to change his opinion, Judge Burnett decided it was his turn to try. Burnett told Derning that it "puzzled" him that someone with limitations on his abstract thinking, his inability to remember details, or to conceive an idea, could come up with the story Misskelley did. "How can that come about?" asked Burnett. Jessie's story was not "convincing and doesn't hold together in the long run," Derning replied, adding that Jessie's new story provided no corroborating information. "I listened to it," Derning said, "and I didn't find anything different at the end of the day."

Burnett persisted. After surprisingly admitting that he might be interrupting Davis' cross-examination, Burnett raised the issue of Jessie's whiskey bottle statement, I suppose, just in case Davis had forgotten. How could someone who "functions at such a low level" come up with a story like that?" Burnett asked. Derning told Burnett, as he had before, that Jessie's story "wasn't very well conceived," adding that "We heard Mr. Stidham having difficulty believing it."

Dr. Derning further cemented his diagnosis of Jessie Misskelley's intellectual capabilities when Michael Burt asked him how much of the Rule 37 proceedings Jessie Misskelley understood. Derning responded that Jessie did not understand why I was on the witness stand, nor did he have any idea what Rule 37 was. In fact, Jessie had expressed anger at how I was being treated on the witness stand by both counsel for the state as well as the defense.

Not contented that Derning was emphatic about Jessie Misskelley's lack of understanding, Brent Davis decided to run right back into the street without looking both ways. Was Jessie Misskelley's prison conversation with Mr. Stidham an attempt to "get himself out of trouble?" he asked. Would that not require "mental functioning and mental processes which you previously said he's not capable of?"

"No, I never said that" Derning replied. If Jessie understood the nature of his perilous situation, he would have said to Mr. Stidham,

"Look I want to cut a deal with the DA and I am going to provide a confession or a statement to them that they can use." Jessie would have presented a consistent story, and would not change it, Derning said. "You [Davis] didn't have him testify at those trials. Frankly, I think that was probably very smart because I think he just could not hold it together and give a cohesive story that would have assisted you," Derning said. Davis, clearly stunned, told Derning:

"...it wasn't that I didn't have him testify at trial. I didn't have any control over that—do you understand that?"

"Sure," Derning replied. "But I'm just saying that you wouldn't put him on the stand. He couldn't help; that's all. That's all I mean."

And that is when it happened. It jumped from the pages on the record, Davis replied:

"Okay. And you understand that a prosecutor can't, at his whim, meet, discuss, and go over testimony with the defendant to see if he is —what his story is and what he's capable of as far as relating the facts to the jury, right?"

Somehow, in the intervening 15 years Davis had forgotten that this was precisely what he had done— "meet" with my client behind my back, and over my strong objections, to "discuss and go over his anticipated "testimony" at the Echols and Baldwin trial with Burnett's explicit permission and approval. Derning knew what Davis never seemed to quite figure out. Now we have something that we can refer to as the "Davis confession."

63

Between April and October 2009, the state's efforts during the Rule 37 hearings for Misskelley and Baldwin had more unintended consequences. The state had set out to finally close the door on the case and move on. Instead, they opened themselves to scrutiny they could not overcome. Throughout the year of intermittent hearings, the defense teams would pick apart the state's case with that "far-reaching scientific evidence stuff" that Brent Davis and Judge Burnett did not want anyone to hear about.

After my final testimony on April 3rd, the hearings were postponed again until August 10th. As they resumed, Rosenzweig and Philipsborn asked Judge Burnett, again, to recuse himself from the case because he was running for the Arkansas Senate. Again, Burnett refused to let go of the case. This was a clear ethical violation on Burnett's part.

I was excluded from the courtroom after my testimony and never had the opportunity to listen to what the other defense witnesses said. For most, reading the voluminous transcript of the Rule 37 hearings today would be about as exciting as settling down in a favorite armchair and pouring over the New York City phone book. For me, hidden within the more than 2,900 pages are revelations that would become a throat punch to the state's case, revelations that were later obscured by the Alford pleas.

Later, when I read the transcripts, I would be surprised, shocked, and at times amused. Over the course of the hearings, the defense teams led by Burt and Philipsborn offered testimonies from four of the best forensic pathologists in the world, and affidavits from others, most notably Dr. Vincent Di Maio. Each expert testified that wounds on the three victims were caused by animal predation. Specifically, each defense pathologist testified that the wounds to Christopher Byers' genital area were due to animal predation. This would expose the state's case for what it really was, a complete and utter work of fiction.

Dr. Werner Spitz would be the first to testify. Asked by John Philipsborn if the mechanism of injuries to the three boys were "fists" and "sticks" as described by Jessie Misskelley in his confession, Dr. Spitz' response was that there was "not evidence of being beaten with sticks. There is not evidence of being punched with fists. There is evidence of animal predation." When asked if he saw any injuries to the boys' bodies indicative of knife wounds, Dr. Spitz replied that he had performed at least sixty thousand autopsies in his career and seen every conceivable kind of knife and cutting wound. There were no knife wounds to these children, he said.

Next to take the stand was Dr. Michael Baden, who testified that he had performed at least 20,000 autopsies during his forty-plus year career, twice as many as he had completed since our first discussion about the case. He recalled meeting with me in San Francisco in 1998 and discussing the issue of animal predation. Baden stated that he agreed with Dr. Spitz. Burt asked if this was a conclusion that jumps out immediately, or one that requires careful study. "It was like looking at my grandmother. You know it's your grandmother—it's either your grandmother or it's not," Dr. Baden replied. "After I reviewed the materials," said Dr. Baden, "I was concerned that a mistake had been made in attaching guilt to the three people who were convicted. The testimony about cults, particularly what was testified to as to the cutting off of the penis and scrotum or cutting the penis and removing the testes by a human, was just wrong."

On August 12th, Dr. Richard Souviron, a forensic odontologist, testified that the wounds on the children were "more likely than not, turtles, or a combination of "turtle, a coon or a dog." The scratch marks on the bodies were "not made by a knife. That I am positive of," he said. Souviron noted that he did an overlay of the "Rambo" knife found in the lake behind Jason Baldwin's trailer and compared it to the scrapings on the bodies. This absolutely eliminated the knife from having made the marks. So much for the Grapefruit demonstration by Fogleman in the second trial.

The last of the defense pathologists to testify, on August 13, was Dr. Janice Ophovon, a forensic pathologist who specializes in pediatric pathology. When asked by John Philipsborn if a knife was used to remove the scrotal sac, testes and deglove the penis of Christopher Byers, Dr. Ophovon was emphatic. "There is no question. This is not a close scientific question at all. It was not a sharp tool." "Basic pathology," she said, "showed the wound was caused by "small animal predation."

The cumulative effect of these testimonies from the defense was devastating for the state of Arkansas. In fact, it completely obliterated the case against the WM3. The defense team's steady series of clean and effective jabs in the end proved too much for the prosecution to withstand. But like the fighter who continues to think he can shake it off, the state plodded ahead.

The state had been aware of most of these defense experts' conclusions since May 2007 when members of the defense teams and some of the experts themselves met with Dr. Frank Peretti and Brent Davis at the Arkansas State Crime Lab. The State had told Burnett that it planned to call their own forensic pathologists to rebut these findings. By October 2nd, the last day of the Rule 37 hearings, no outside forensic pathologists were available to testify that Arkansas Pathologist Frank Peretti's findings were even remotely accurate or correct. I submit that they could not find anyone willing to refute the testimony of the best forensic pathologists in the country, if not the world. Instead, the State of Arkansas did what it had always done—used smoke and mirrors. Assistant Attorney General Ken Holt, in a tragic attempt to establish that there was no aquatic or animal life in the ditch where the three boys' bodies were found, called Mike Allen and Bryn Ridge. Each said there was none. On cross-examination each former detective crumbled and ultimately admitted that they had seen turtles in the same area before. The defense teams then called John Mark Byers to the stand. He would say that his stepson Chris and friends would often bring home large turtles after visits to Robin Hood Hills and put them in his pool. With nothing left in the arsenal, Kent Holt called Dr. Frank Peretti to the stand to rebut the defense forensic pathology experts.

Describing himself as an animal lover who had bred turtles and tortoises as an avocation, Perretti stated that he was certain that there were no turtle bites on the victims and that there was no animal predation on the bodies. When asked to explain how the defense experts had all agreed that there was animal predation, Peretti said simply that they were wrong, even though he admitted that animal hairs had been found on the bodies. All of this, of course, was to be expected. What was not expected was an almost offhand comment from the beleaguered medical examiner after dogged cross-examination by Michael Burt. It would catch my full attention reading the transcript of Peretti's testimony in 2020. Michael Burt's undressing of Perretti had completely flustered the medical examiner whose testimony the state had relied so heavily on at the trials — and now as their last line of defense in the Rule 37 hearings for Misskelley and Baldwin. Burt pointed to Perretti's lack of credentials, his repeated failures to pass his National Board certification test before giving up completely, his motives, mistakes, and most importantly, his changing testimony between Jessie Misskelley Jr.'s trial and that of Damien Echols and Jason Baldwin. Perretti had become both agitated and defensive on the stand. Driving home my long-held belief that the West Memphis Police had misinterpreted the data provided in Dr. Peretti's official autopsy reports to create evidence that the victims had been sexually abused, Burt's masterful cross-examination had clearly gotten under Perretti's skin. It was that misinterpretation of Peretti's autopsy reports that prompted police to lead Jessie Misskelley down that chosen path in the first place as they coached his confession. Dr. Peretti was the only one who could fix that misinterpretation at both trials in 1994. He was now attempting to do it again. Peretti stated that he did not know what he could have done to correct a prosecutor's misimpression about the lack of medical evidence regarding sodomy or forced oral sex.

That is when he said it. His words screaming out at me from the transcript, left me dazed. Badgered by Burt about why the lake knife was not introduced as evidence in the Misskelley trial but used in the Echols and Baldwin case a few weeks later, Dr. Perretti's blurted response would inadvertently and emphatically summarize the state's entire case against the West Memphis Three:

"Prosecutors can make you testify to things. You know what I am saying?"

This was a landmine comment, buried just beneath the surface in a very lengthy transcript, that had just exploded like a nuclear blast. A casual observer might easily overlook it, write it off as a testy rejoinder to Burt's pinpoint drilling. But I understood its meaning. To a lawyer and, more importantly, to an appeals court judge, it was a stunning admission. Peretti had clearly insinuated that he had modified his testimony in the Echols and Baldwin case at the request of the prosecution—"they can make you testify to things. You know what I am saying?" The floodgates had opened.

Over the course of the Rule 37 hearings, the defense team, with surgical precision, revealed the absurdity of the original prosecution theory of the case. *Why couldn't these men just admit that they were wrong?*

64

The theory of Satanic Ritualistic Homicide has long been discredited. Retired FBI profiler Ken Lanning conducted an exhaustive study in the late 1980's on the topic and concluded there was no such thing. He could not document a single case, anywhere on the planet. His conclusions were replicated by studies in the United Kingdom.

Peter Jackson and Fran Walsh retained perhaps the most famous of all FBI Profilers, John Douglas, to work on the West Memphis Three case. Douglas's work on the case was depicted in the film *West of Memphis*. Soon after the Alford Pleas, Douglas himself wrote a book entitled *Law & Disorder: The Legendary FBI Profiler's Relentless Pursuit of Justice*. Douglas and his co-author devote several chapters in the book to his work on the WM3 case. Douglas wrote that when he first came to West Memphis, he was "surprised" to learn that the West Memphis PD had contacted his unit at Quantico at the time of the murders in 1993. Douglas said that he was the unit's chief at the time but didn't remember the WMPD reaching out. According to Douglas, "in this case the police talked to two other agents in the unit, who gave them advice about what kind of questions to ask during door-to-door canvassing." Douglas added that "there was no record of any follow-up at the time."

Then he mentions a chance encounter he had with Ken Lanning. This piqued my curiosity. Douglas wrote the following about that exchange with Lanning:

"When I returned home from this trip [from West Memphis], I happened to get a call on another matter from Ken Lanning. Ken had offered advice in the JonBenét Ramsey case while he was still in the FBI that the prosecution team hadn't liked and was subsequently shut out of the investigation. I asked Ken if he'd ever had anything to do with the West Memphis murders before he retired. Oh, yeah, he replied. Someone from the prosecutor's office called me based on the guide I had written, described the case and told me that they were pursuing it as a satanic murder."

When asked by Douglas what he told the prosecutor, Lanning's reply was "I said I thought they were letting the theory drive the investigation." Lanning also told the prosecutor, who had to have been either Brent Davis or John Fogleman, that if he were to "bring up that this is a satanic murder, they'll laugh you right out of court." Douglas asked Lanning what happened next. Lanning said "Nothing. They never called me back. Next thing I know I am reading about it in the papers—and the motive is satanic ritual."

Douglas then wrote in *Law & Disorder* that during his years at Quantico, he had learned to never "dismiss anything that Ken Lanning had to say—a lesson lost on at least these two prosecution teams."

Douglas then summed it all up by stating that the "only thing that Ken was wrong about, as it turned out, was that the West Memphis district attorneys were *not* laughed out of court, and that is precisely where the tragedy of murder was compounded with the tragedy of miscarried justice." I couldn't agree more. I had the honor of meeting John Douglas at the Sundance Film Festival in 2012 for the screening of *West of Memphis*. At the post-screening event the film's producers started handing out movie posters and everyone was getting them signed by others at the gathering. Peter Jackson, Fran Walsh, Amy Berg, Steve Drizen and Laura Nirider, and others, all graciously autographed my movie poster and offered kind things to say about my work on the case. John Douglas simply wrote: "To understand the artist, *look* at the artwork."

65

The steamy Arkansas afternoon was winding down on August 18, 2011, when my cellphone rang around 5:30. The workday was ending and I did not particularly want to jump into something new, so I glanced quickly at the caller ID. It was newly elected prosecutor Scott Ellington on the other end. I answered. What he told me, abruptly and without preamble, astonished me.

"Your boy is getting out tomorrow."

"My boy? What are you talking about?"

"Misskelley," he said, as if we were talking casually about a football game.

"How?"

"He's taking an Alford Plea. And just so you know, the other lawyers were more than happy to leave your boy in prison, but I told them it was all three or none. I knew you would hate me for the rest of your life if I left Misskelley behind."

"That is good to know."

"Be in Craighead County Circuit Court in the morning around 9:30 a.m.—and remember this is top secret."

I am quite certain I was the last phone call Ellington made that day to those of us whose lives had become so entangled in this nightmare. I was stupefied. Hearing that the other lawyers had considered leaving Jessie Misskelley in prison was infuriating, but I was unsure where to direct my anger. *Who wanted him left behind?*

After my call from Ellington, I immediately called John Philipsborn in San Francisco. All he could tell me was, "Yes, it is happening," adding quickly that he found the situation "nauseating." John had that afternoon concluded a death penalty case in California and was waiting for the jury to complete its deliberations. He had little time to elaborate, and to add insult to injury, the trial judge in California refused to allow John to contact Jason Baldwin and discuss the Alford plea. Before he hung up, he told me that Jeff Rosenzweig and Blake Hendrix would be in Jonesboro the next morning on behalf of Jessie Misskelley and Jason Baldwin. Bewildered, I put down my phone and told Lea Ann what had just happened. She was ecstatic.

Ellington's phone call was the first of many surprises that would reveal themselves over the next decade as I struggled to make sense of it all. Ellington's "top secret" admonition lasted about an hour. CNN began reporting that a "mysterious hearing" would be taking place the next morning for the West Memphis Three in Jonesboro. I called my ex-wife Kim and told her the news. "Congratulations," she said. "You finally got him out of prison, just as you promised him you would."

The irony of the situation would later plague me. I had worked so hard to free Jessie Misskelley but I had nothing to do with the Alford Plea—and it seemed I was the last person to know about it. Ellington might just as well have tased me. I was still skeptical. I had gotten my hopes up many times over the years only to have them crushed. Getting your teeth kicked in for almost two decades makes you feel that way. *What had happened?*

For one thing, David Burnett, who had been elected to the Arkansas Senate, had finally been exorcised from the case. Judge David Burnett, who had made one last attempt to close the door to the case and sweep everything back into a dark corner where it would not ever see the light of day again had failed. Burnett had left for the more ambiguous world of politics, where his talents would serve him ably.

On November 4, 2010, the Arkansas Supreme Court reversed rulings by Burnett in 2008 that had denied motions for new trials for Damien Echols, and separately, for Jessie Misskelley and Jason Baldwin. In its ruling, the Supreme Court remanded the cases back to the circuit courts, ordering evidentiary hearings to consider new evidence. On November 30, 2010, Judge David Laser was assigned the task of conducting these hearings, which he scheduled to begin in December 2011.

But something had been cooking that I had not gotten a whiff of. I had been working to see Jessie Misskelley walk free for over eighteen years. I had dreamed of it, obsessed with it, had run the scene though my mind so many times—a new trial. Never in my wildest dreams had I conjured thoughts about what played itself out in Jonesboro the next day on August 19, 2011.

Still confused, I arrived at the Craighead County Courthouse early with Lea Ann. Judge Laser was in the courtroom conducting a "closed hearing" with Damien Echols, Jessie Misskelley and Jason Baldwin, their appellate lawyers, and prosecutors. Not unexpectedly, I had not been invited to attend. When it concluded the three were moved to the small jury room directly behind the same courtroom where in 2008 and 2009, I had testified in the Rule 37 proceedings. I had wanted to speak with Jessie Misskelley before the main hearing, to see how he was holding up.

As I approached the door to the jury room, I was stopped by a court security officer who told me I couldn't enter. He said, "I'm sorry, your Honor, but not without Judge Laser's permission." I thought that this was odd. I walked the short distance to Judge Laser's Chambers to seek permission to visit with my client. "Dan, I don't have a problem with it," Judge Laser said, "if Rosenzweig doesn't. Get his permission." As I turned to walk out of Judge Laser's chambers, he leaned across his desk and said:

"Dan, you're not going to try and derail this train, are you?"

"Why would I do that? My client is going home today."

He seemed relieved, which puzzled me even more. Based on the information I had at that moment, the release of the West Memphis Three seemed like a win, despite John Philipsborn's misgivings. I wish I would have known then what I know now. It would take some time, but later I would share the same misgivings about the Alford plea as John.

Leaving Judge Laser's chambers, I was still in the dark about how all this had unfolded. But there were a few things I knew to be absolute. The odds of getting a wrongfully convicted client out of prison are almost zero. Defense lawyers are sometimes required to define "winning" in a way that may seem unclear to everyone but their client. Jessie Misskelley was walking out of prison on August 19, 2011, and at that time it seemed like a huge victory to me.

I found Jeff Rosenzweig in the hall outside a conference room where the lawyers were still putting the fine details into the plea documents. I told him Laser wanted me to ask his permission to see Jessie. As I expected, he said he did not have a problem with it. As I turned to walk away, Jeff said, "Dan, we would have gotten a new trial simply based on Burnett's refusal to recuse from the case after he announced his intent to run for the Senate." I nodded in agreement, but Rosenzweig's comment only added to my growing confusion. I could not help wondering, why the Alford plea if we were going to get a new trial? Even though I had yet to read the Rule 37 transcripts, I too thought that we had completely destroyed the State's case, and nothing could resurrect it. Everyone seemed to agree that Judge Laser was going to grant us a new trial.

Upon gaining entry, I was horrified by the scene in the small jury room. It was teeming with security officers, certainly more than were required to guard three young men who were about to be released from prison. Sitting in eerie silence, almost catatonic, along the east wall were Damien Echols, Jessie Misskelley, and Jason Baldwin. Three kids, now in their 30s, the best years of their lives stolen by what some might say were morally bankrupt men and a morally bankrupt judicial system.

Shackled by handcuffs and leg irons and connected to one

another like a chain gang about to go out and hoe cotton in the fields, each instead wore a suit and tie. The only rational, though illogical explanation for the large number of guards was that they were somehow afraid that these young men might try to escape before the State of Arkansas could set them free.

"I am glad you are getting out today," I told them as they looked up at me blankly, "but this is a cowardly way out for the State of Arkansas." I made sure that I had said it loud enough for all the guards to hear me. I reached out my hand to Damien. The hand he offered in return was cold. I do not believe I had ever seen anyone so pale who was still alive. He was so fragile looking, that I recall hoping he would survive long enough to walk off Arkansas' infamous Death Row in the minutes ahead. More than I, Damien was still skeptical whether this was actually going to happen, more so because he was the one in shackles. I feigned confidence, thinking that it might improve his outlook and mine.

Next, I turned to Jessie and shook his hand. He smiled as he always did and said "Hey Dan." At the end of this odd chain gang was Jason Baldwin. I extended my hand to him and we greeted each other with a firm handshake. In doing so, we pulled all three men's hands and the chains attached to them in unison. The chains rattled, adding to the idiocy of it all.

"Dan, am I doing the right thing?" Jason asked indecisively. I was taken aback by his question, but again, based on the limited information I had at that precise moment, I said "Sure kid, you are going to see your momma tonight." I would feel some measure of guilt about this later when I learned he was the last holdout in accepting the Alford plea.

Jason and I have stayed close over the years. We've discussed the Alford Plea on several occasions, and he has repeated that he holds no animosity toward anyone regarding the Alford plea—even though we both now know that he had the most to lose and the least to gain from it.

I left the jury room to seek out a friend and ally I had not seen in some time. Eddie Vedder had been secreted in another room down the hall that was as highly guarded as the one I had just left. When I entered the courtroom everyone's eyes turned to me as if I would be the messenger announcing the "mysterious" hearing was about to begin.

When I saw Eddie, he smiled and rose from his seat to greet me with a warm embrace. I thanked him for all his help in getting us to where we had arrived that day. He introduced me to Natalie Maines of the Dixie Chicks. I thanked her as well. Terry Hobbs' foolish lawsuit against her for slander was a gift from above. It allowed the defense team to conduct his deposition under oath about his past, and more importantly his movements back on the day of the murders, including how his DNA may have been found in the ligatures that had bound Michael Moore.

Finally meeting Natalie, I could feel that she shared the same sense of uncertainty over whether the day's promise would unfold. Then the real messenger arrived. We all made our way into the courtroom where the public hearing would take place. The burden I thought was about to be lifted from my shoulders took another twist.

As I was introducing my fiancé' Lea Ann Vanaman to Eddie and Natalie in the courtroom, a deputy sheriff approached me and asked if I wanted to speak to Mark Byers. I stood and walked over to the other side of the courtroom and as Byers shook my hand, he leaned down and whispered in my ear.

"Promise me," he said, "that you will find the real killer. We both know who it is."

Then Pam Hobbs stepped from behind Byer's towering bulk. We embraced, and she too asked for the same promise. I said yes to both. *How could I do anything else?*

The hearing itself was brief, stripped of drama, free of emotion but for a short outburst from Stevie Branch's biological father. Nor was there any sense of catharsis. Judge Laser vacated the convictions of the three men who had become known as the West Memphis Three. Then, one by one, all three pleaded guilty to three murders while maintaining their innocence—pursuant to the procedure outlined in *North Carolina vs. Alford*. As Jason Baldwin would say at the press conference after the plea, it took a false confession to put them into prison and another false confession to get out.

As the courtroom emptied, a strange sense of controlled chaos emerged. Lea Ann took a picture of Jessie and me with her cell phone outside the courtroom while the prosecutors began their press conference downstairs in the basement. Then Lea Ann and I quickly jumped in the elevator to the basement to find a good spot to watch the ensuing defense team press conference. We emerged to find ourselves unexpectedly standing behind Ellington, and his two deputies, as Ellington was addressing a sizable gathering of local, state, and national media. I tried to fade into the background, pushing myself in a corner, wishing I were not there at all.

As I stood there, trying to be invisible, a reporter asked Ellington, "If you think they are guilty, why are you letting them go?" Surely, I thought, he had prepared himself for this inevitable question. It became clear that he had not.

"Well," he said, "I hope that they have rehabilitated themselves."

I cringed.

As the prosecutors filed out toward the elevator, Lonnie Soury, the fiery New Yorker, and media relations manager retained by the Echols defense team, looked at me and said, "Hey Judge, would you like to take a few questions before we get started with the next press conference?" I looked out at the sea of reporters. "Thanks, Lonnie, but no thanks. I'll take a pass." He smiled and said, "I get it."

The West Memphis Three and the appellate lawyers began emerging in waves from the elevator into the tight space in front of the cameras. I was still standing in the corner with Lea Ann as space grew claustrophobic. As the mass pressed in, I found myself standing directly behind Eddie Vedder and Natalie Maines. As the second press conference was about to begin, Natalie Maines' bodyguard who was standing to her right in the last spot on the front row, turned to me and insisted that I switch places with him. "You've played a big part in this judge," he said. "You should be standing up here not me." I did what I was told.

When the press conferences were completed, I walked Jessie

Misskelley out of the courthouse, his lone bodyguard, and quickly deposited him into the battered sedan where his father was waiting. A huge crowd had assembled outside but no one bothered us. As he got into the car headed back to the same trailer park that he had left on June 3, 1993, Jessie asked me if I was going to the "big party" over in Memphis later. "No," I told him, "I wasn't invited."

Even if I had been, I would not have gone. I told Jessie that my son Chris was having his twenty-fourth birthday party tonight. Jessie grinned back at me and said, "I ain't going either." As they pulled away, father and son reunited for the first time in almost two decades, I was washed with a sense of pride in what had been accomplished by so many people working together for justice. *But I was still confused about how it went down.*

My attention was diverted, and as I looked up, I saw Mark Byers surrounded by a large group of reporters. As I drew near, I heard him say that "This is not right and the people of Arkansas need to stand up and raise hell because three innocent men are going to have to claim today that they are guilty to a crime they didn't know, and that is bullshit...this is wrong what the State of Arkansas is doing to cover their ass and I am sick of it."

There were hundreds of folks standing around cheering the release of the West Memphis Three. Suddenly, my mind raced back to the scene outside the West Memphis Police Department and later the Crittenden County Courthouse when those then young men were arrested and arraigned. There were no cheers for them in 1993. I liked this crowd in 2011 much better.

Lea Ann and I left for the birthday party back home in Paragould. Chris told me that the release of the WM3 was the best birthday gift ever. Early the next morning, Lea Ann and I left for the Ozark Mountains of north central Arkansas, where we had hurriedly reserved a cabin and a pontoon boat to avoid the media for a couple of days. I was not ready to speak about something publicly that I did not yet understand completely. Cell phone coverage there was sketchy at best. We rested, undisturbed.

66

Only one man in the State of Arkansas directly involved in this case has ever expressed any remorse. In June 2014, in an interview for an oral history project for the Arkansas Supreme Court, Justice Donald L. Corbin mentioned his role in the WM3 case. I admire both his courage and his candor. These are his own words:

"I keep thinking, surely there was something that I could have done. I should have asked more questions, you know. I guess in fairness to me there wasn't really anything else I could do. I worked really hard on that case."

"I'm saddened by it. Three boys' lives were ruined because of something I had a hand in. I couldn't protect them because I didn't know any better. I judged that case on the evidence that I had the first time, and then I totally changed my position when this new evidence started coming in. But it took eighteen years for them to do that. I still feel badly about it, that I had a hand in it, that they used me, that the State used me to convict kids who didn't do it."

I always liked Donnie Corbin. I still have fond memories of him coming to some of the Greene-Clay Counties Bar Association fish fries that I hosted long ago at my cabin on the Black River. I did not know him outside these few brief encounters, but the few times I was around him, I recall that he was a captivating storyteller.

I wish I could have discussed his 2014 interview with him prior to his passing in 2016. If I had, I would have asked him to elaborate on some of the things in his interview, most notably what he meant when he said, "that they used me, that the State used me to convict kids who didn't do it."

Who did he mean by "they?" When he referred to the "State" using him to convict kids that were innocent, did he mean the original prosecutors? Judge Burnett? Of course, I will never know the answers to these questions. I am happy to find solace in his words that were not ambiguous at all.

His contrition came far too late to prevent the malevolent harvest of innocence of the best years of the lives of those "kids who didn't do it." Nevertheless, it is still a remarkable and powerful admission that validates the work of the defense teams in bringing the state's malfeasance to light. Justice Corbin said that he was "sad" that he "had a hand in it." I believe him.

67

My father always taught me that a man is only as good as his word, and John Fogleman always kept his word with me. Shortly after the Misskelley trial in 1994, when Fogleman ran for circuit judge, I worked as hard as I could for his opponent because I thought he would be a reincarnation of Judge David Burnett, complete with Burnett's legendary bias towards the prosecution in every criminal case. I was wrong about that. He was fair as a Circuit Judge. He suppressed evidence when it was illegally obtained. He followed the law. After both trials, Fogleman quickly took the circuit bench and played no further role in the WM3 case. He did not work tirelessly like David Burnett and Brent Davis to ensure that the wrongful convictions of the WM3 remained intact even after it became crystal clear to everyone else that they were innocent.

On August 28, 2008, Fogleman sent me a letter asking me for my support in his race for the Arkansas Supreme Court. At the bottom of the typed letter, he wrote in his own handwriting, "Maintain your passion for the law and causes." It may surprise some people, but I supported him wholeheartedly.

Shortly after the Alford Pleas in the Fall of 2011, I looked down the long back hall behind the courtrooms at the Greene County Courthouse in Paragould and saw John Fogleman. We were both about to take the bench at opposite ends of the hall. Instinctively, I waived to him, and he waived back. I could not help but wonder how he felt about the Alford Pleas, but I never gave it much thought as the day went on. After court, I was standing in the parking lot next to my truck engaged in conversation with my prosecutor Allen Warmath and my oldest son Daniel when I looked up and saw Fogleman walking to his vehicle with his robe in one hand and his briefcase in the other. I waved to him again. After he placed his things in his car, he walked over to us. As we shook hands, he looked at me and said "I don't really know how to say this other than just to say congratulations. This would not have ever happened but for your perseverance. I just wish they would have gotten new trials instead of it happening the way that it did." I thanked him for his kind words and told him that I would have preferred new trials as well. To this day, he is the only person involved in the case who has ever had the honor to say what he said. He did not have to say it, but he did, and it meant a lot to me.

68

Shortly before Christmas 2020, sitting quietly in the comfortable and subdued light of my study, I began to mull over something someone had told me years before. I had set it aside but as I sat there the comment began to press on to my peace. Shortly before the Echols and Baldwin trials began, this person had told me, Brent Davis had offered Jason Baldwin a plea deal of just five years if he would testify against Damien Echols. I knew how desperate Davis had been in his pursuit of Jessie Misskelley's testimony ahead of the same trial.

I decided to go straight to someone who would know the truth. I sent a text message to Jason Baldwin asking him if this was true. It was late and I did not expect a reply from Jason until the next day.

Not one to stop worrying once I had started, something else began to nag at me. During the Echols-Baldwin trial, Michael Carson, a former inmate at the same juvenile detention facility where Jason had been held, testified that Jason had admitted his guilt to him when they shared a cell together—which they never had. Carson has since emphatically recanted his testimony, but of course the damage had been done. Whether Baldwin and Carson ever shared a cell could have been easily checked out by the prosecution–but of course

Davis did not seem much interested in the facts. The pattern of prosecutorial duplicity had been set long before Michael Carson testified.

If Brent Davis had offered Jason Baldwin a plea deal of five years before the trial began, how confident was Davis in Carson's testimony? Was it the "fifty-fifty" kind of confidence that he and John Fogleman had expressed to the murdered boys' parents in that famous scene from *Paradise Lost*? The thought is frightening when you consider that the five years offered to Jason would have essentially been "time served." He would have been free soon after the trial if he had testified against Echols. I was having trouble wrapping my mind around it. If it was true, had Davis gone to the victim's parents a second time to get their approval? If so, did he tell them about Michael Carson?

The answer came to me the next morning in an exchange of text messages from Jason Baldwin. "Good morning," Jason texted. "You are correct: the first offer was 20 and the second offer was down to five with an emphasis on jail time credit and good time, meaning go home soon." My response was a simple: "Wow."

This was a stunning confirmation to me, even after so many other jaw-dropping revelations. Jason pointed out that the prosecution would have been compelled to "craft a different believable story" that would minimize his "fictional role" to secure a conviction against Damien Echols. Jason told his attorneys that he would not be a part of anything that involved lies and condemning an innocent person. I told Jason that most people would not have been able to reject a time served offer like that. And I told him that I admired him for what he did.

There was no way he could have testified against Damien Echols, he said. I already knew that because I know the type of man Jason Baldwin was—and is. The last thing he told me in our stream of texts was that "I guess you could say, I dismissed their offers with extreme prejudice."

He was right. When I thought of all the beatings Jason endured in those first years in prison, including broken bones and a fractured skull, I could not help but admire Jason Baldwin even more than I already had before he confirmed that extraordinary plea offer. Jason refused to "sell out" his best friend. At age sixteen, he displayed more courage than most men could muster in a lifetime.

Jason and I have a relationship based on mutual admiration and respect. In the time since our texting, I thought about an email he had sent me back in 2017 in which he wrote, "Hey Dan! Check this out! You're my hero!" He attached a link to a podcast interview that he had done just hours earlier. I went back and listened to the podcast that day in December 2020 after Jason confirmed Davis's five-year offer.

In it he spoke about how he had spent 18 years in prison for a crime he did not commit and that he had emerged from prison a better person despite all that he had been through. He also spoke of his work now in helping others who have been wrongfully accused and convicted. When the moderator of the podcast asked him to talk about the steps that led to his release, he said it was a monumental effort by lots of people and then he had this to say about me:

"Jessie's trial attorney, Dan Stidham, after our direct appeals were over with, he was the only attorney that would still do anything for us, right. The other attorneys moved on...but I remember him sending me a pro se, which means on your own, Rule 37. He was like, you know, if you don't file this within 30 days, you're going to be what's called procedurally barred...It was a stroke of genius on his part and just showed how, what, a great person he was, and it really was so lucky for us, nobody else did that...by Dan Stidham filing that...that saved our cases, all of our cases, and that was an amazing thing to do."

Then Jason spoke about the Alford Plea. "Honestly," he said "I refused the Alford plea when it was first offered to me. I was like, no way." Then he added, "We had won an evidentiary hearing. We have a new judge, Judge Laser, from all intents and purposes a reasonable judge, not like Judge Burnett, the guy that, who was on our trials, on our appeals for so many years. That guy is not reasonable, and I believe he is a crook. And so, I had hope."

Jason had hope but because he is the outstanding young man that he is, he understood that Damien's life in prison was different than his own. Damien lived in what Jason described as a "concrete coffin" on death row not knowing when his last day on Earth would be. Jason also described how bad Jessie had it with his disabilities and the fact that around the time of the Alford plea, Big Jessie had stopped his weekly visits—which had been like clockwork for all those years—because his health had deteriorated. By the time 2011 had rolled around, Jason's situation in prison had changed dramatically. Instead of being beaten and treated with contempt, he had begun to be treated with respect by both the inmates and guards. "Everybody was my friend," Jason said. "The guards respected me, and they cared for me." Some of the guards told him that they were praying for him, that their wives and grandmothers were praying for him. They all wanted him to be exonerated someday. One guard told Jason that he had been to a Megadeth concert and that they had told the crowd to "Free the West Memphis Three!"

To be clear, Jason said he did not want to be in prison—he wanted to go home to his family—and he knew that he did not deserve to be in prison, but his life in prison had grown to have some "meaning." He was working in the prison school teaching other prisoners GED classes, and he felt as if he was making a difference. "It really wasn't hard for me to keep fighting even for another 18 years," he said in the podcast, "but I couldn't make that decision for Damien, or for Jessie."

In the end, the offer was contingent on all three men taking the deal, not one or even two. Jason's moral compass guided him to help Damien and Jessie by agreeing to the Alford Plea. This act of selflessness brought him to a decision that was not necessarily in his own best interests. I understand, very much, his willingness to keep up the fight for his exoneration. I wanted the same thing for Jessie, and I too would have been willing to fight for another 18 years.

69

Part of my endeavors to understand the Alford pleas included a review of the state of the evidence after the completion of the Rule 37 hearings. I had concluded from reading the transcripts of the hearings that it was crystal clear that the wheels of the prosecution's case had completely fallen off. They simply could not prevail in a new trial.

By the end of 2007, and certainly by 2008, both Jessie Misskelley and Jason Baldwin each had two causes of action pending. The first was an appeal pending before the Arkansas Supreme Court of denial of habeas corpus relief. Simultaneously, under Arkansas' Rule 37, Jason Baldwin and Jessie Misskelley were pursuing post-conviction remedies by introducing evidence mainly centered on their contentions that they had been ineffectively represented by their counsel during the original trials. The appellate lawyers submitted that a wealth of information that had been available at the time of the original trials that had either not at all been investigated or had inadequately and ineffectively been reviewed, assessed, and acted upon by the trial level defense teams an assertion that I have never disputed.

Damien Echols' Rule 37 Petition had already been adjudicated, and thus the legal framework set out by the lawyers who were representing Damien at the time was much different from that set out by Jason Baldwin's and Jessie Misskelley's post-conviction lawyers. One issue that was unique to Jessie's case was, of course, the Rule 2.3 issue. That seed that I had planted back during the suppression hearing in January 1994 had grown solid roots by the time of the hearings and as Greg Crow had so aptly stated, "they can't have it both ways." On this issue alone, at least in my opinion, Jessie should have, and would have, been granted a new trial.

While the initial post-conviction hearings placed before Judge Burnett had involved the Echols defense team for a short period of time, the fact that Damien was not involved in those hearings meant a few things that turned out to be of great importance. First, much of the post-conviction publicity that attended the cases focused on Damien, who was the only one of the three who had been sentenced to death. Like Jason's lawyer, John Philipsborn and Jessie's lawyer, Michael Burt, Damien was also represented during post-conviction litigation, at least in part, by a San Francisco based lawyer named Dennis Riordan. Dennis was a highly visible and quite successful appellate lawyer who had achieved remarkable results in several nationally noticed cases. He, along with others among Damien's lawyers and defense team, made sure that most aspects of the post-conviction developments brought out in the Misskelley and Baldwin Rule 37 hearings were conveyed to the attention of the press – which turned out to be quite beneficial to all three defense teams because Judge Burnett had issued his gag order.

But there was one main difference that distinguished Damien's "West Coast" defense team and the new "East Coast" defense team working on Echols' behalf. Counsel for Jason and Jessie were all very accomplished trial lawyers *in addition* to having accumulated a tremendous amount of post-conviction litigation experience. Michael Burt and John Philipsborn were highly noted for their handling of complex cases involving cutting edge forensic science issues. With few exceptions, they were the attorneys who had selected the laboratories and experts who would be employed to review the physical evidence in the WM3 case, and where possible, to do retesting and reexamination.

Michael Burt, by the time of the post-conviction hearings in Jonesboro started, had achieved national recognition for his work on cases involving DNA evidence – and he had been the first lawyer in the United States to actually secure a judge's ruling excluding DNA evidence from a case that had been prepared with what had then been a relatively new platform due to some of the inaccuracies that could crop out through use of that technology.

Having been involved in the case for decades and encountering many lawyers who came and went along the way, I was surprised that the post-conviction lawyers for Misskelley and Baldwin did nothing to call attention to themselves, or their work, during the Rule 37 hearings. I have tremendous respect and admiration for them because they did their work quietly, some of which would be referenced by the lawyers who were then working on the Echols defense team. The attorneys for Baldwin and Misskelley were contending, among other things, that errors by the original defense lawyers deprived them of a full and fair opportunity to demonstrate their innocence.

In my testimony at the hearings, I explained the prejudice that I felt Jessie had suffered because of my relative inexperience in cases as complex as his. I was also able to make references to aspects of the unfairness of the proceedings – one of the first times that I was in that situation in the presence of both Judge Burnett and Brent Davis who had been instrumental in getting what I had been contending for years was a completely erroneous conviction in Jessie's case.

Paul Ford, the lead trial lawyer for Jason, also testified. The Rule 37 hearings gave him the same opportunity as I had, under questioning by John Philipsborn, to explain decisions that he had made during the original trial. He also failed to acknowledge concerns that had arisen given information that had been surfacing about the problems with the evidence that had been presented, mostly without effective responses. The record of the post-conviction hearings also helped explain where Jason Baldwin's evidence could and should have been presented in such a way as to demonstrate that Jason could not have been involved in the murders. This evidence included both his school records and the memories of teachers and classmates that he had been at school, had actually worked on a specific art project during that period of time, and did not manifest any behavior, injuries, or outward signs indicative of his having spent a long night in a wooded area near water involved in the killing and tying up of three young boys. Ford made no attempt to put on an alibi defense for Jason though there were many witnesses available. In other words, Ford, just like Echols' trial lawyers at Echols' Rule 37 hearing, refused, for the most part, to accept any responsibility for any misgivings at the original trial of Echols and Baldwin. In fact, Ron Lax told me after Echols' Rule 37 hearing, that he was furious with Echols' original trial lawyers because they, as he stated to me, seemed to be working in concert with Davis's assertions that they were quite effective at trial.

The experts that Philipsborn and Burt brought to the case to testify in the Rule 37 hearings combined to explain, in detail, that the statements that had been attributed to Jessie Misskelley could easily be shown to not be true, or even possible. The serrated survival knife that was said to have been found in the lake behind Jason Baldwin's home had been carefully examined at the time of the original trials by the Arkansas Crime lab. In addition, tracings of the shape of the knife had been made. By the time of the post-conviction hearings, it was determined that those tracings had been lost – an important point, since the tracings had originally been put together to allegedly demonstrate that the grooves in the survival knife fit with the patterns found on the young victims.

The post-conviction hearings were also a platform at which the post-conviction lawyers demonstrated that the State's DNA evidence at the time of trial was proverbial junk science, an analysis conducted by a would-be expert who had neither the training nor understanding sufficient to stand behind the findings that he allegedly made. The post-conviction lawyers had highly experienced, well qualified forensic scientists from several laboratories review, and in some instances reanalyze, the evidence demonstrating that not only was there no evidence linking Damien, Jason, or Jesse to the scene, but that there had been other evidence, including some hair evidence and other items that had been uncovered during the post-conviction investigation and reanalysis of evidence, indicating that other individuals had left signs of their presence in one of the ligatures that had tied up one of the boys and elsewhere.

By the time of the hearings, the post-conviction lawyers had followed some of the advice that I had given them about what seemed to be the blatant unreliability–and fiction–of the notion of the killings having had the 'trappings of the occult.' And during the years leading up to the post-conviction hearings, various individuals who had worked on the post-conviction case had obtained interviews and recordings of the various individuals who had claimed to have heard of meetings that had involved interest in the occult that had supposedly taken place in the West Memphis area. These various theories by juvenile probation officers, alleged local 'experts' on ritual killings and the occult, and other speculations turned out to be uncorroborated rumors and, in some cases, pure fabrications. By the time of the evidentiary hearings, the post-conviction lawyers and I had approached notable alumni of the FBI's criminal profiling section known as the Behavioral Analysis Unit or BAU. These profilers' careful analyses demonstrated why the original theories of the 'occult' involvement were uncorroborated and unsupported. I met with two retired FBI profilers from the *Academy Group,* including Mike Napier, at the crime scene and they both felt that the proximity of the scene to the busy interstate, and truck stop, likely meant that we could be looking for a very mobile serial killer, potentially a long-haul truck driver. As I am now aware, after having spent a 35-year career as both a lawyer and as a judge, standards of practice that apply to the preparation of the defense of a case like the West Memphis Three cases require extensive preparation and investigation and proper funding.

It was clear to me once I finally had the opportunity to speak at length with John Philipsborn, Michael Burt, Blake Hendrix, and Jeff Rosenzweig after the Rule 37 hearings and the quite sudden deployment of the Alford pleas, things had not happened as I had once perceived. I was even told that these hearings had made somewhat of an impression both on Judge Burnett – who actually asked Dr. Souviron to lecture to one of his classes as a result of the hearings – as well as the State's lawyers, including those members of the Attorney General's Office who were helping litigate the post-conviction hearings.

By the time of the end of the hearings, fiber evidence had been reviewed at a leading university's laboratories, allegedly human hairs had been reviewed by forensic veterinarians and determined to have been non-human hairs, but animal hairs of various kinds. Other work by Philipsborn and Burt were going on that would have continued into further hearings, or up to the time of a retrial of the cases had such a retrial been ordered. All of us on behalf of Misskelley and Baldwin felt certain that a new trial would have been ordered by Judge Laser after he was assigned the case.

But as we all know, negotiations that resulted in an agreement for the Alford pleas, foreclosed the need–or occurrence–of new trials. I now know from having spoken with the post-conviction lawyers who represented Jason and Jesse were highly disappointed in not having been able to have had a full opportunity to finish litigating the cases, including to retry them if necessary. I, too, was highly disappointed once I was able to understand the complete circumstances of the Alford pleas.

The point is that since the Alford pleas were reached in 2011, matters that were raised or litigated during the Misskelley and Baldwin Rule 37 hearings were never discussed or reported about in the media. Regrettably, since a lot of the publicity of the case revolved around DNA retesting or the possibilities of alternate suspects, little public notice was given to everything that came out during the many days of post-conviction hearings that occurred. The hearings involved many different witnesses, including a few of the prosecution's witnesses during the initial proceedings and included many different witnesses who could, should, and would have testified in a full and fair trial of the cases.

I know that some of the critics of the outcome of the West Memphis Three negotiations–and some of the persons who profess to believe that Jesse, Jason, and Damien were clearly guilty of the crimes–have no knowledge of, or familiarity with, the post-conviction Baldwin and Misskelley Rule 37 hearings. In all the discussions about further hearings, the possibility of pardons, the state of the evidence and the like, I have never heard anyone refer to the hearings or to their contents. Because of this book, all that is about to change.

Fortunately, those hearings are matters of record. Too little attention was paid to them, and it is highly regrettable, in my view, that the post-conviction discussions and negotiations for the Alford pleas did not focus on those hearings. I know from my many conversations with John Philipsborn over the years that in part because he was a participant in the preparation and litigation of the hearings that he is of the view that much more could have been made of the evidence that was produced at those hearings and that one of the problems that resulted from the changes of lawyers for Damien Echols in the runup to the final negotiations was that the lawyers who took over Damien's representation did not have the scope of knowledge of the details of the case that Michael Burt, Jeff Rosenzweig, Blake Hendrix, and John Philipsborn had by the time of the conclusion of those hearings. Indeed, the State's lawyers who were involved in the hearings have never been asked to comment on the extent to which their views about the evidence in the West Memphis Three case may have been changed because of having participated in those hearings. Of this, I am certain, no reasonable jury would have found any of the West Memphis Three guilty given the state of the new evidence had they been given new trials and the Alford pleas had not been entered.

70

Back in August 2015, Tom McCarthy and I had just finished the first draft of *A Harvest of Innocence*, but the brilliant light of the Alford Pleas still blinded me. The following month I would be blindsided yet again by some old familiar foes from the WM3 case. I would have an opponent for re-election for the first time ever in 2016.

It would take five more years before I would completely unravel the mystery of the Alford plea before it came close to unraveling me. In August of 2011, watching those young men head off to new lives knowing I had fulfilled my promise to Jessie Misskelley to get him back home seemed to be the culmination of all I had fought for. At first, reflecting on the long struggle, it seemed like a gift from above, an answer to my prayer, a means to an end. The light that day had cast shadows I did not see immediately. In my confusion over what had happened behind closed doors to get those young men out, I had thought that the Alford Pleas were a victory.

It soon proved pyrrhic. The West Memphis 3 were free but still guilty in the eyes of the law, and more grievously, the way I saw it, in the eyes of the State of Arkansas. The State had washed its hands of the entire affair with backroom bargaining that dismissed the case and erased its culpability with a brief stroke of a pen. My efforts to try in some way to justify it, to understand it, soon began to gnaw slowly at the brief sense of peace I felt in 2011. It eroded my gratitude and transformed it to anger, and at times, a deep penetrating bitterness.

In my speaking engagements that followed the Alford Pleas, I sometimes struggled with the task of explaining —or trying to explain— what an Alford Plea was. The younger the audience, the more difficult the task. The concept of an Alford plea is at its very core is both illogical and ambiguous. One of my colleagues, the late Dennis Riordan, at the time of the plea described it as "oxymoronic."

I discovered an article published by the *Thomas Jefferson School of Law* in San Diego in which Steven Braga, the newest member of the Echols Defense team and Scott Ellington, the two key architects of the Alford plea, discussed the circumstances surrounding it. The article, *"The West Memphis Three and their Alford Plea,"* seemed precisely what I had been looking for.

According to Braga, "the Alford plea was the only compromise we could come up with to try to bridge the gap between the State's absolute refusal to drop the charges and the Three's absolute demand to maintain their innocence of crimes they did not commit." Ellington said he "recognized the opportunity to put a nearly 20-year-old case to rest." Rejecting the unfathomable possibility of facing a trial within the next few months, he invited defense counsel to come back with an offer to resolve the entire case.

According to the article, Ellington recognized that this compromise was "less than ideal, but effectual. It certainly was not a perfect resolution to the case for the State, but it was much better than having three trials, trying to convince thirty-six jurors of the defendants' guilt using old evidence, failed memories, changed minds, dead witnesses, and the parents of two of the victims who now say they believe the defendants are innocent of the crimes." Reading that article was revealing. I realized that I had been looking at the Alford plea through a different prism than both Braga and Ellington. According to the article, "Since both attorneys came into the West Memphis Three case in January 2011, Braga and Ellington were relatively free of the emotional ties the original attorneys had to the much-disputed case. It appears that their fresh perspective helped them obtain a model legal compromise wherein all parties left feeling not quite 100% victorious."

I wanted no part of this "not quite 100% victorious" analysis. I needed something more. What I longed for was redemption. *But would I ever find it?*

In 2016, Senator David Burnett and I both had opponents. Only one of us would be re-elected.

71

Perhaps the most precise commentary about the Alford Plea came in an article written by Sean Flynn for *GQ* magazine on December 7, 2011. Reading it again ten years later, I discovered some nuances I had overlooked:

"On August 19, they pleaded guilty to murders they swear they did not commit, and, in exchange, a judge sent them home. Their release had nothing to do with right or wrong, with guilt or innocence, and least of all with who killed those boys more than eighteen years ago. It was an act of legal expediency, a way to let three innocent men out of prison without the bother and embarrassment of actually exonerating them...It's called an Alford plea, which is rare, a seeming paradox and, maybe just this once, an ugly way out of an uglier situation."

Flynn came into his reporting having virtually no knowledge about the case. But he was a quick study, and his conclusions were both accurate and quite telling. Flynn's reporting reveals much about the men who would not be "bothered" or "embarrassed" by this "Legal expediency," and their motives for doing so.

Senator David Burnett, in his interview with Flynn, played the role of victim in this "ugly way out." People wanted to "vilify" him regarding the Alford Plea, Burnett told Flynn. "I didn't find them guilty. Two juries did." Burnett may not have found them guilty, but his preposterous rulings and antics reflected an indelibly strong bias for the prosecution. He even admitted this in a cut from one of the first *Paradise Lost* movies bonus sections that didn't appear in the film. Look no further than his exclusion of Dr. Richard Ofshe's testimony versus the inclusion of Dr. Dale Griffis' testimony —and their credentials or lack thereof.

One prosecutor would speak only off the record, but in a clever bit of reporting, Flynn spoke of his "observations" surrounding that interview that are quite revealing. The chief prosecutor, Brent Davis, was never mentioned in the *GQ* article but Gary Gitchell and Mike Allen were. Flynn wanted to speak to Gitchell because the retired lead investigator in the case had been quoted in *Paradise Lost Three: Purgatory* as saying that he would love to sit down and tell everyone what "really happened." Gitchell apparently was not all that interested in telling Flynn, or anyone else, about "what really happened" after the Alford pleas because he would not return Flynn's phone call for an interview. Mike Allen, now the Sheriff of Crittenden County, did not want to talk to Flynn either. At least he had the decency to call Flynn back to tell him.

Scott Ellington spoke to Flynn quite candidly. "I had one shot." Ellington said. "One lucky shot, and that was to get rid of the whole case. That Alford plea was a gift. A gift to *me*." Ellington then drove this point home when he famously made the analogy that "If you gotta eat a maggot sandwich, you don't nibble it. You just get it over with." In the same breath, Ellington admitted to Flynn that at a new trial "certainly the Satanic-witchcraft angle, that would not sell."

The Alford Plea allowed the police investigators, the trial judge, the old prosecutors and the new one who inherited the case to jump in a lifeboat and safely get off a sinking ship. And the men who were responsible for the catastrophe in the first place got a free pass. Any remaining skeletons could remain aboard that sinking ship and disappear.

Reputations could remain untarnished, and reparations would

not have to be paid to the wrongfully convicted. These men had their cake, and they ate it. They could say that they believed that Damien, Jason, and Jessie murdered the three children and hide behind their assertions forever. But as Sean Flynn pointed out so eloquently: "…such pronouncements are to be expected from the men who sent three teenagers to prison on little more than a well-told campfire story."

There was still just one nagging detail that was left unresolved for me. How could Ellington have accomplished that "one lucky shot" to rid himself of the entire WM3 case without the consent, or at least the acquiescence of, those men who had fought so hard not only to promote that "well told campfire story," but to maintain it as their regime of truth for nearly two decades.

Part of the answer was contained in an article from the *Arkansas Democrat-Gazette* published the day after the Alford plea that I had not read until 2020 because I had been hiding out in the Ozark mountains from the press when it was published. The article quotes Ellington, who said that he had "made the rounds and talked to the former prosecutors Brent Davis and John Fogleman." Ellington elaborated by saying that "Everybody was saying that it looked like Laser would give us a new trial." *Does this mean everyone thought we would get new trials?*

Were the former prosecutors afraid of a new trial and what it would reveal to the world? Logic dictates that Ellington, by saying this to the reporter, was obviously looking for some measure of cover for himself. As you read further, Ellington said that he had contacted former Circuit Judge and then Sen. David Burnett "to notify him of the plea." The reporters had contacted Burnett themselves to get his response to the Alford Plea. Burnett, not known for his ability to shy away from reporters told them that he "still thinks the three men killed the boys." No surprise there. Burnett added that he was "satisfied that justice was done." *But was he really?*

I wanted to know more about these revelations, but even a decade later, nobody seemed to want to resurrect that "ugly way out of an uglier situation." They were happy to let this thing rest for good, simply fade away. *I was not.*

From my digging deeper, it seems that neither Brent Davis nor John Fogleman tried to oppose the Alford Plea—something one would have expected them to do stridently. If either man had confidence in their work, if they felt without reservation that the West Memphis 3 belonged in prison, Damien Echols perhaps executed, wouldn't they have strenuously objected to the Alford Plea? Wouldn't Burnett do the same?

I continued to drill even deeper. A source unwilling to be on the record told me that Brent Davis had advised Ellington that "if you can get it done, get it done." "It," of course refers to the Alford pleas. If this is true, this is a far cry from Davis's well documented efforts and ferocious fight to maintain that "well-told campfire story." I cannot find a single comment attributed to Brent Davis in any news article, documentary, or story about the Alford plea or the WM3 case since August 19, 2011. It seems that the entire sordid affair is something he would prefer to simply forget. *Not me.*

I recently discovered the transcript of the "closed hearing" held by Judge Laser just prior to the public hearing on August 19, 2011. It stirred my emotions even more than a decade later. According to the transcript, Stephen Braga told Judge Laser that:

"It's been a war for 18 years. The Alford plea is a unique kind of plea, rarely used, but there specifically for the best interest of the defendant, the interest of justice and judicial efficiency when you have this kind of war. How do we stop this war? They're forced to fight for 18 more years. Alford plea says no. The defendants get to maintain their innocence, the prosecution gets a guilty plea, finality is reached."

This was easy for Braga to say all that because he did not fight in the "war" for over 18 years like I did. There are not pieces of him left scattered on the battlefield. He does not bear the wounds or scars of this war like I do.

The Alford Plea had robbed me of a victory that I had always dreamed would take place in the courtroom in the form of a new trial and an acquittal for Jessie Misskelley and his co-defendants. In the decade following the Alford plea, as I learned its origins and contortions, it increasingly gnawed at my soul. My own personal trauma was not only the "war" itself, but the void it left in me after the Alford pleas. All those kicks in the teeth, being thrown under the bus, and then falling on my own sword seemed trivial matters to those who were promoting the Alford pleas. What disturbed me the most was that the Alford pleas meant there would be no inquiry into the atrocities of the "war," no war crimes tribunal, no consequences, and no reparations. Ultimately, these feelings of darkness served themselves up as my own personal demons, and they still haunt me from time to time, especially on anniversaries like May 5 each year.

I was compelled to find the right balance between the darkness and the light of the Alford pleas, a middle path. I had to navigate through them in a way that would allow the storm to pass over me without my getting lost in its debris. I could have easily let all this anger and bitterness destroy me. Instead, in the end, I chose to embrace it, pick it up, and examine it more closely. When I did, I was surprised at what I discovered. Truth and justice are sometimes elusive creatures, and prayers to find them often go unanswered for decades. As my pastor once told me, you must have "faith." I take refuge where I can.

In an email on Thursday, September 7, 2011, John Philipsborn wrote:

> Dan,
> One of our co-counsel kindly forwarded an interview you did recently in which you indicated that you were going to write a book about your experiences with the case—a task that I hope you accomplish. You also said some very kind things, which I thank you for. I continue to maintain that without your keeping the case alive, and without your great assistance, we could not have set up the basis for relief. Meanwhile, I hope you are well, and that you take satisfaction in paving the way. I look forward to catching up. Thank you for the kind words,

John

So, in the end, I discovered that I did not really need the redemption that I thought I could only get with a new trial. I will settle, instead, for being one of the first lawyers to present a "False Confession" defense to a jury, writing this book and telling the world what really happened in this case and being a relatively good chess player. I also take satisfaction in my perseverance, always getting back up when I get knocked down. And now I know why Judge Laser asked me that question over a decade ago: "Dan you are not going to try and derail this train, are you?" It made no sense to me at the time, but it does now. Judge Laser knew that knocking trains off the tracks is what I do best.

Recently, a new friend told me that my calling was that of a "rescuer." It had a tremendous impact on me. She was vaguely familiar with my work in the case, and she said that she saw me as a person who had been driving a tank in battle for a very long time. She told me that it was time to get out of that tank, that I had been in it far too long. It was time to get out and start taking care of myself and living life again. Of course, she is right, and that is my plan.

DNA technology is progressing rapidly and soon it may point us to the real killer. At this moment, Damien Echols is having some success in getting permission from the Arkansas courts to retest some evidence with some new DNA technology. At this moment, I may even have a viable suspect. Others may pop up along what's left of my life's journey.

My life's journey includes spending time with my grandchildren, fishing and maybe even hitting a golf ball again. But there's always that chance that I might have to fire up my old tank again. It has its dents and scars just like me, but it will be ready to go when needed, and so will I. Never, never, never give up...

ACKNOWLEDGMENTS

The journey of writing this book really began 30 years ago when I started journaling about the case in its aftermath. It began in earnest in 2012 in the wake of the Alford Plea that ended the case. I was fortunate enough to have the generous assistance of Dr. Haley Fitzgerald who listened to me tell my story in the study of my home while working on her doctoral thesis about the case and provided the initial outline and framework for the book. Her assistance was invaluable. In June 2014, I began collaborating with my co-author, Tom McCarthy. Nine years later, here we are at the finish line.

In those nine years, many people assisted me in reviewing chapters or led me to discover materials that I would have never known about in this ever-evolving tragic story. Others offered advice on the manuscript or proofread the many drafts along the way. Special thanks to my friend and colleague, Dr. Tim Derning who reviewed the chapters regarding Jessie Misskelley's intellectual challenges to make sure that I got his conclusions right. I must also give many thanks to another friend and colleague, John Philipsborn, Esq., who gave me much needed encouragement all along the way.

Many thanks go out to Jason Baldwin who provided invaluable contributions to the book from his unique perspective which also included providing some photos. We've managed to stay in touch all these years and have a special bond. Also, I wish to offer special thanks to Robert "Bob" Richman the director of photography for the *Paradise Lost* documentaries for graciously providing access to his work for many of the photos used in the book. Also, many thanks to Amy Berg and Olivia Fougeirol who gave me, as a curtesy, a photo of me standing in front of what Amy referred to as the "Wall of Truth" during a break in shooting a scene of *West of Memphis*. their generosity and kindness are most appreciated. I would also like to say thank you to Evan Agostini who graciously gave me a couple of photos of Lea and I on the red carpet in New York.

There were many others who made significant contributions to this book. There is always the risk of leaving someone out, but here are some of them: Lea Ann's late daughter April Biggs, Kelly Duda, John Brooks, Joel Brucewitz, Brad Broadaway, Kathryn Nicole Stidham, Jamie Thomas McClelland, Renee Kreienbrink, Erik Wright, and Mike Mihaljevich all of which offered much encouragement and letting me bounce ideas off them, proofreading the manuscript, or preparing it for publishing. Erik Wright was amazing for being generous with his time and expertise as an author.

There are others who may not have made a direct contribution to this book, but with their help and assistance in this case, they made the telling of my story possible and the release of Jessie Misskelley, Jason Baldwin and Damien Echols inevitable. They include Eddie Vedder, Dr. Richard Ofshe, Warren Holmes, Greg Crow, Joe Berlinger, the late Bruce Sinofsky, Mike Bonfiglio, Sheila Nevins, Peter Jackson, Fran Walsh, the late Chris Stidham, the late Ron Lax, Metallica, Natalie Maines, Winona Ryder, Henry Rollins, Johnny Depp, Mara Leveritt, Ken Lanning, John Douglas, Steve Drizen, Laura Nirider, Gail Zimmerman, Erin Moriarty, Michael Gladis, Lonnie Soury, Aphrodite Jones, Dr. Michael Baden, Kathy Bakken, the late Jessie Misskelley, Sr., Jessie Misskelley, Jr., Damien Echols, Grove Pashley, Burk Sauls, Lisa Fancher, Michael Burt, Jeff Rosenzweig, Blake Hendrix, J. Gordon Cooney, Jr., Mike Napier, Sean Flynn, Vicky Krosp, Karen Nobles, Marc Taylor, my mentor W.H. Taylor, James Morgan, Dr. Martin David Hill, Dr. Neal Haskell, Stephen Lemons, Jack Black, Margaret Cho, Alan Leveritt, Justin Sayles, the late Dennis Riordan, Donald Horgan, Scott Ellington and Trey Parker.

I cannot thank my good friend and co-author, Tom McCarthy enough, without whose collaboration this book simply wouldn't have been possible. He is an immensely talented writer and stuck it out with me for nine years to the finish line. He, like me, never, ever gave up.

I also want to thank and express my love for my children. I missed ball games and piano recitals as I worked feverishly on this case. They encouraged me all the way and understood even when they were just children that Dad was working on something very important. I also send out love and thanks to my parents, Troy, and Eva Stidham, who calibrated my moral compass at an early age and convinced me as a child that I could accomplish anything I put my mind to. I still believe it.

Finally, I thank my wife, Lea Ann, who always kept me moving forward and focused on this project. Her way of keeping me moving and focused was refusing to read any draft of the book along the way waiting instead for the publishing of the book. Well, here it is Darling. Over the course of the past nine years, we have faced many obstacles, including the loss of two of our adult children beginning in October of 2021. Each of us are still grieving in our own separate ways, but our love for each other has always prevailed. This book is a testament to that love.

Dan Stidham
October 2023

www.ingramcontent.com/pod-product-compliance
Lightning Source LLC
LaVergne TN
LVHW011943060526
838201LV00061B/4199